Allen Lane The Penguin Press

Eric de Maré · The London Doré Saw

A Victorian Evocation

First published in 1973
Allen Lane The Penguin Press
74 Grosvenor Street, London W1

ISBN 0 7139 0195 0

Phototypeset in Monophoto Ehrhardt by Oliver Burridge and Co. Ltd, Crawley, Sussex
Printed in Great Britain by Butler & Tanner Ltd, Frome, Somerset

Designed by Gerald Cinamon

London is not a poetical place to look at; but surely it is poetical in the very amount and comprehensiveness of its enormous experience of pleasure and pain. . . . It is one of the great giant representatives of mankind, with a huge beating heart.

LEIGH HUNT, *Table Talk* (1851)

Comparisons with the past are absolutely necessary to the true comprehension of all that exists today; without them we cannot penetrate to the heart of things.

CHARLES BOOTH, *Life and Labour of the People of London* (1889)

The Vision of Gustave Doré

It is impossible to put the world in a nutshell . . . we have selected the most striking types, the most completely representative scenes, and the most picturesque features of the greatest city on the face of the globe – given to us to be reduced within the limits of a volume. We have touched the extremes of London life.

BLANCHARD JERROLD, preface to *London: A Pilgrimage* (1872)

In 1872 a famous volume was published by Grant and Company of Turnmill Street. *London: A Pilgrimage* was no handy pocket guide. Its pages measured sixteen inches by twelve and the whole weighed a stone. The text, framed in double red lines, was perfectly printed on thick creamy paper, and each illustration was lovingly protected by a tissue. The work seems to have been issued first in thirteen parts at five shillings each, but by December 1872 the single bound volume was being advertised – alongside Forster's *Life of Dickens*, and Stanley's *How I Found Livingstone* – as a Handsome Christmas Present at £3.50. Today you would be lucky to obtain a mint copy for £50, and it is hard to come by.*

The one hundred and eighty engravings, from drawings by Gustave Doré, were romantic impressions rather than exact records, while the supporting essay by Blanchard Jerrold was in the evocative essayist's rather than the guide-book compiler's tradition. The artist composed his finished drawings as much from memory as from the brilliant, rapid sketches he made on his wanderings with the author through the imperial metropolis. '*J'ai beaucoup de collodion dans ma tête*,' Doré said: to refer to the artist's eye as a photographic apparatus was by then an easy metaphor. Yet wilfully he placed French baskets on the arms of London flower girls, allowed at least fifty horses to run in the Derby, and designed slum chimneystacks, in that scene of railway arches so beloved by social historians, with a waste of brickwork that would scandalise any speculative builder. 'Within the covers of this immense album lay London in light and shadow, as seen by a poet'; and, Jerrold insisted, the pair were pilgrims (a Dante with his Virgil, he could have said) 'not historians, not antiquaries, nor topographers'.

One of London's familiar icons that Doré depicted: the clock tower of Barry's and Pugin's Houses of Parliament.

*So also is the French edition of *London* published by Hachette in 1875 with a text by Louis Enault – an event that greatly offended Jerrold, who wrote the original English text.

Yet the work does contribute to social history. My aim, with Doré's powerful support together with that of other contemporary illustrations, is to recall the development and fabric of London between 1851 and 1889, from the year of the Great Exhibition to that when the London County Council began its benign work. During those four decades occurred the most remarkable changes in the whole long history of this great node of humanity.

What was London like a century ago? How did it look? How and why did it expand so explosively? How did its inhabitants behave, dress, and sometimes manage to enjoy themselves, whether they lived in Bethnal Green or Brompton, whether they were Pooters or Forsytes, bankers or barrow boys, reactionaries or reformers, evangelists or convicts, shopkeepers or prostitutes? These are some of the questions this book tries to answer.

Although it has its architectural approach, the environment as such is only one of its concerns, for it assumes that a city is formed far less by the works of architects, planners and bureaucrats than by history as it rolls through the passing moment: by external events, by current economic pressures, by what people happen to believe, and now and then by the efforts of exceptional individuals who are the product of their period; in short, by a certain cultural and social-economic situation. My motto has been: 'Only connect'.

Doré's drawings are valuable in supporting such a synoptic analysis less in their statements of fact than in their intense impression of the mood of those times. They express so vividly not only the vitality but the full foggy horror of mid-Victorian London – the Hell and the Heaven of the Two Nations, the poor and the rich. In his poet's prose Doré is like Dickens. Jerrold noticed that Doré was forever talking about Dickens and thought he recognized in the novelist 'powers akin to his own'. In their energy and love of drama and caricature the two were alike though Doré, unlike Dickens, was no social reformer. He was first of all an artist, with an eye that responded to the picturesque, the grim and the touching in the life and environment of London's poor, more directly than ever it did to those of the comfortable classes. Since his designs inspired the undertaking of my book, more than this must be said about the great illustrator.

He was born in 1832 under the weird medieval shadows of the cathedral in the border town of Strasbourg. Both parents were of middle-class Alsatian stock, his patronym being an adaptation of the German Dorer. Of all Gallic artists he is indeed the most Teutonic in his love of the grotesque – and sometimes of the cruel.

When he was about nine the family moved to Bourg whither his father, the son of an officer in Napoleon's army killed at Waterloo, had been posted as chief Government Engineer of Bridges and Highways for the Department of the Ain. The influence upon the boy's imagination of the two old towns in which he grew up, and of the countryside around them, is evident in the Gothic silhouettes and gargoyles, and in the landscapes of mountains, gorges and gloomy forests depicted in the work of his maturity. 'These spectacles were my first vivid impressions,' he wrote in later life. 'They were those *éblouissements d'enfant* which determine a taste.' Even his plates of contemporary London were to show Doré's 'power to bury himself in the Middle Ages, and create a new world of his own out of them', as Jerrold was to put it.

He was an infant prodigy. His old nurse Françoise, who attended both his birth and his death, recorded that she rarely saw him without a pencil in his hand after his fourth year. While his doting mother encouraged him, his father, wishing him to follow his own career as an engineer, disapproved of his leanings. His wish to become a professional artist was gratified, however, when he visited Paris with his parents in 1847, and there found the patronage of the celebrated publisher Philippon, who had just launched the *Journal pour Rire*. Doré studied for a time at the Lycée Charlemagne and witnessed the revolution of 1848. He attributed his early ability to draw crowds to the careful observation of Paris streets in that year, said Jerrold. Entirely self-taught as an artist, Doré was supporting himself by his work by the time he was sixteen. By the age of twenty he had achieved an international reputation as an illustrator and was on his way to fortune.

In his illustrations for *Rabelais* (1854) Doré discovered himself. Here the extravagant humour and fantastic, ribald imagination of this *gamin de génie*, as his solemn friend, Théophile Gautier, was to call him, achieved their full flavour. The work made him famous.

The rest of his life, passed chiefly in Paris, was dedicated to work, but was otherwise uneventful. Sometimes he

Portrait of Doré
from Jerrold's *Life*.

would travel abroad, once to Spain to obtain backgrounds for his *Don Quixote*, and frequently to London, where in 1869 he opened his gallery at 35 New Bond Street (where Sotheby's now reigns). This was his time of triumph in England, for 1866 had seen the publication there of his *Paradise Lost*. Less triumphant were his designs for Tennyson's *Idylls of the King*, engraved on steel in 1868-9: Doré's vision was more suited to Milton, to Dante, and to Coleridge. His great illustrations of Dante bracketed the sixties: the *Inferno* came in 1861, the *Purgatorio* and *Paradiso* in 1868 (Paris editions). *The Ancient Mariner* was to come later, in 1876.

His daily life in Paris was controlled and cosseted both by his manservant Jean and by his mother, a shrewd, hook-nosed matriarch, dressed always in black after her husband's death in 1848. Doré had fallen in love at the age of nineteen, proposed and been refused. He never married and that may have been one cause of the melancholia which plagued his last years. At six o'clock every morning he was at work in his huge *atelier* in the rue Bayard, the finest in Paris, where in a corner two eagles fluttered in a gigantic cage. In the morning he would draw on his wood blocks, break for *déjeuner* at the Moulin Rouge, make a round of his engravers' workshops, and then return to the studio to toil until nightfall on one of his huge canvases. Such was his typical day. Once a week he would hold a *soirée* or perhaps visit the Opéra.

On his annual sojourns in London, which began in the 1860s, he led an active social life that, apart from the interminable dinner parties, he enjoyed. He became a lion who was received in all the Best Houses; he was invited even by the Prince and Princess of Wales, and the Queen, who bought one of his paintings, requested his visit to Balmoral. He would return, a richer man, from the hurly-burly of the London Season to resume his regular celibate life in Paris.

Doré became the most popular of Victorian illustrators. Much of his success must be credited to the dedicated and highly skilled craftsmen who engraved his drawings and whom he schooled to a certain unmistakable style: Pisan, Pannemaker, Pierdon, Brevière, Deschamps, Maurand, to mention a few. He kept them all busy. Pisan and Panne-maker were his favourites and both contributed to *London: A Pilgrimage*. Pisan, who made all the engravings for *Don Quixote*, was at his bedside when he died.

It was in 1869 when Doré was staying with him in Jermyn Street that Jerrold broached his scheme for the book on London. Doré grew enthusiastic, and the pair set out to explore the town from East End to West. 'We saw the sun rise over Billingsgate and were betimes at the opening of Covent Garden market,' Jerrold relates.

We spent a morning in Newgate; we attended the boat-race, and went in a *char-à-banc* to the Derby. . . . We spent an after-noon at one of the Primate's gatherings at Lambeth Palace; we entered thieves' public-houses; in short, I led Doré through the shadows and the sunlight of the great world of London. His constant remark was that London was not ugly; that there were grand and solemn scenes by the score in it . . . [he] soon agreed with me that it abounded in delightful nooks and corners; in picturesque scenes and groups and figures; in light and shade of the most delightful character . . .

We went, once, at midnight to London Bridge, and remained there an hour, while he meditated over the two wonderful views – that above, and that below the bridge. His heart was touched by some forlorn creatures huddled together, asleep, on the stone

Outcasts on London Bridge, one of Doré's rapid sketches.

seats. He has reproduced it, again and again, with pencil and with brush. He never appeared to tire of it. . . . He was enchanted with Petticoat Lane by night, the sailors' haunts in Ratcliff Highway, Drury Lane by night, the slums of Westminster, the thieves' quarters round about Whitechapel, and the low lodging-houses. The long back kitchens of these houses had a particular charm for him. The groups of street-folk eating, lounging, drying their clothes at the common fire, sorting their baskets; the heavy toil- and care-worn sleepers in the shadowy dormitories; and the children tumbling about in rags – constituted scenes that never faded from his memory. He noticed, as Dickens would, old toy-makers, making card-board cabs in a corner.

Later the friends went slumming to see the opium-smoker in the room described by Dickens in *Edwin Drood*, and this resulted in one of Doré's most theatrical designs. No doubt the place had become a profitable tourist attraction. The old woman was there, in bed, preparing her drug, while her tame mice ran about the ragged bedclothes.

At Newgate Gaol, Doré stood long in a corner of the yard observing the prisoners exercising in a circle of wretchedness, and this visit produced the drawing that, engraved, was so to fascinate Van Gogh that he copied it in paint. On this occasion Doré would not even make a rough sketch; he was always shy with his sketch-book and would often ask Jerrold to stand in front of him as he drew. Yet he could record such scenes vividly enough afterwards with his mental collodion, and in the evening he would fill a book with his day's observations.

Negotiations for the book's publication were concluded in 1870, and Doré was about to return to London from Paris when the Franco-Prussian War broke out. Soon the capital was under siege. This was a distressing experience for the artist and it was at this time that the *gamin* lost his youthful gusto. After the siege, wrote Jerrold, 'the abounding spirits, the love of athletic tricks, the wild forms of humour, even the practical jokes, the romps with his dogs, seemed to have fallen away from him'. His beloved dogs were eaten by starving Parisians, and the loss of Alsace was another blow, for he would never again set foot in a German Strasbourg. In spite of the sunshine of fame in which he could now bask, Doré was a sad and frustrated man.

Not until the war was over, and further drawings had been made, did *London: A Pilgrimage* appear. Although it was well received, Doré could not shake off his depres-sion. The reason may have been partly physical, for in the Garde Nationale, which he had joined, he suffered the severe bronchitis that was to bother him for the rest of his life. Universally acclaimed as an illustrator, and now a member of the Légion d'Honneur, Doré hungered for recognition by his countrymen as a great painter. While he was idolized in England and the United States as a

The opium-smoker described by Dickens in *Edwin Drood*, Doré's most theatrical London design.

painter, France never accepted him as such, and significantly the main documents on his life are not written in French but in English. It was as a painter that he wished to succeed, and it was chiefly to that end that he had opened his Bond Street gallery. In later years he declared that if he could live his life again he would not illustrate books at all. By then he had become soured to a point of obsessed sensitivity by the unfavourable comments from both the French critics and his fellow artists. 'I am my own enemy,' he told Hippolyte Taine. 'I must efface and kill the illustrator, and be spoken of only as a painter.' He never achieved his ambition. He could not take refuge in the articulation of principles for he was no intellectual; nor could he find moral support from rebellious comrades, since he represented no new school. He began and remained a unique phenomenon. 'They will not accept Doré *peintre*!' he would cry. Perhaps they were right. He was not a painter's painter, for his canvases reveal no sensual delight in the colour and texture of paint as a medium; even his mythical, floating nudes, though rotund enough, do not encourage touch. Yet he worked ceaselessly at enormous battle scenes, landscapes and historical and biblical anecdotes. His major work, 'Christ Leaving the Praetorium', measured twenty feet by thirty feet and took the artist five years to complete. It could best be viewed, said the guide books, at a distance of sixty feet. Such works were well enough received in the Bond Street gallery, where middle-class mums could safely take their children for that edifying entertainment and moral instruction of which the Victorians were fond. The pictures shown there sold well in England and the United States.

In 1881 Doré's mother – his Hebrew Prophetess, as he called her – died. He had never imagined 'so awful a void'. The Moulin Rouge closed. Then his faithful servant and helpmeet, Jean, died too, and in 1883, aged only fifty-one, Doré's heart gave way. He was exhausted. '*Je suis perdu. J'ai trop travaillé.*' In three days he was dead. Nadar arrived at the rue St Dominique with his camera to record the head of his old friend in death, and then they buried Gustave Doré beside his mother in the cemetery of Père-Lachaise.

What was he like? 'In the time of the painter's youth, I found him insupportable,' wrote Edmond de Goncourt. 'Later I found beneath the gross and clumsy exterior an honest fellow.' Jerrold held him in affection and appreciated the generosity of his nature and his mercurial

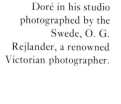

Doré in his studio photographed by the Swede, O. G. Rejlander, a renowned Victorian photographer.

vitality. Small, plump, bright-eyed and dapper, with a choirboy complexion and the look of a spoilt but intelligent child, he could pass in a moment from a wild, gay, clowning mood to one of thoughtful gravity, from irritable vituperation or angry sarcasm to smiling warmth. This contradictory quality is evident in his illustrations, and seems to personify the contrasts and conflicts of his age.

'He danced a perpetual tarantella for the pleasure of his mother,' writes Millicent Rose in her excellent monograph of 1947 on Doré, 'and when she died ran down like a spent top.' There is a naïveté in his work which often charms and it is clear that he never grew up. He never formed a mature relationship with any woman; his Silver Cord was never severed. Thus his whole energy was concentrated on ceaseless work and escape into fantasy. Yet he was no Puritan; he lived well enough, and enjoyed his cigars and champagne, good food, good music, and good company.

The obituary notice in *The Times* judged harshly that 'Doré, though he studied England closely, never quite entered into the spirit of English things, and his illustrations to his friend Blanchard Jerrold's *London* were hardly a success'. As precise factual records of course they were not. Today those illustrations seem to many to be the most successful illustrations Doré ever accomplished. That they represent a foreigner's fresh visions of the metropolis adds to their haunting appeal. His slum scenes in particular have left us graphic memorials of the Victorian urban nightmare as intense as the verbal descriptions of Mayhew and Dickens. The illustrations to *London* have, of course, their faults, not only in their inaccuracies but in their omissions. There are no views of the new middle-class suburbs and none of those homely pictures of daily life which enchanted so many English illustrators of the time. In his theatrical way Doré preferred to stress the contrasts of poverty and wealth – between the fog-bound Inferno of the Seven Dials and the effulgent Paradise of the Ladies' Mile. Even at the two annual festivals of Derby Day and the Boat Race, when all classes were supposedly mingling in democratic jollity, he emphasizes the class separations. He shows us no Purgatory, no middle way, no domestic normality.

Neither he nor Jerrold was able to make close human contacts on their pilgrimage; they were accompanied in some quarters by policemen, and in any quarter Doré's command of English was slight. In contrast, Henry Mayhew, that greatest of social investigators, wandering alone and unprotected down the dangerous back alleys, could make anyone talk freely, whether hawker, beggar, prostitute or thief. Doré and Jerrold were slumming. To the ragged inhabitants of the East End rookeries, declared Jerrold, 'we were as strange and as amusing as Chinamen;

and we were something more and worse. We were spies upon them; men of better luck whom they were bound to envy, and whose mere presence roused the rebel in them. A few of them, loitering about the Whitechapel Road, flung a parting sneer or oath at us, as we hailed a returning cab, and buried ourselves in it, after hours of prospecting in an Alsatia that numbers its inhabitants by the hundred thousand.'

If Doré showed crowds as 'unindividualized and menacing masses' (Millicent Rose), he also showed working Londoners, such as the brewery men, as full of individual dignity as Dickens did. And as for melodramatic scenes, such as the reception of a starving waif at the night shelter, it must be remembered that Doré lived in a damply sentimental period when story-writers and their illustrators would return repeatedly, for instance, to the pathos of the death-bed of a child – of which they knew a good deal more than we do. Dickens, who declared that he would prefer the power to make the world cry rather than laugh, could reduce an entire audience of two thousand souls to

A flower girl – one of the many street characters Doré sketched.

unrestrained sobbing with a reading from *Little Dorrit*. If, as Millicent Rose suggests, 'policy prevented his giving expression to the critical thoughts about the West Enders, which he must surely have had', the set expressions Doré gave to his rich people may be seen as a sort of judgement upon them. Or perhaps he was simply not particularly interested in people as individuals.

How can one now assess Doré as an artist? As a painter, not highly. Indeed, who today knows his paintings at all? Where can they be seen? Certainly nowhere in Bond Street, for his gallery closed more than half a century ago. It continued to flourish for some time after Doré's death as a gallery of Sacred Art that included the work of other artists; this survived right up to 1914, a year in which, ironically, the place was hired by the Italian Futurists. Then the war broke out and the Doré canvases which remained were rolled up and shipped to America. A legend

has it that they went down during the crossing, and that was no great loss.

Yet Doré's illustrations will always appeal, not least those of *London* which display so well his sense of atmosphere expressed in splendid architectonic compositions.

Doré did learn from other artists. The lighting effects of both Rembrandt and Watteau are in his designs, and, most noticeably, the apocalyptic chiaroscuro of John Martin. He had something of the wry vision of that great age of French caricature – less bitter, less deeply human than Daumier. Doré's drawings belong to that romantic tradition which goes right back to Piranesi's etchings of Roman prisons. Yet his own eccentric style emerges in all his illustrations. They have influenced no one. They are perhaps inimitable.

Apart from his grotesqueries, first inspired by Grandville, Doré was above all a romantic, a teller of tales

Detail from 'Found in the Street', showing one of Doré's masterly lighting effects.

(*romans*). His talents were perfectly suited to book illustrations, a fact that in his ambition to achieve fame in more socially impressive media he did not care to admit. To the modern taste he is at his worst when in religious or sentimental mood; at his best he displays a touch of genius. His illustrations will always be enjoyed, not least these powerful evocations of Victorian London in which his talent for theatrical exaggeration found fulfillment.

This triumphal theatricality was noted by Gordon Craig when writing about one of Doré's distinguished admirers:

As producer, Irving absorbed much from the work of this Frenchman of prolific fancy – a very theatrical fancy – not only scenical, but a dramatic fancy. Doré was illustrator, and the producer-actor is an illustrator also. . . . Sometimes he would take a whole design of Doré's and put it on the stage. . . . I, who owe a debt to Doré, know quite well what it was H.I. found so excellent. Décors? Oh dear, no. Drama expressed visually? yes.

Who was Doré's Boswell? (William) Blanchard Jerrold was born in 1826, the son of Douglas Jerrold, who was a close friend of Dickens, writer, actor and playwright, contributor to *Punch* since its inception (his most memorable series there being *Mrs Caudle's Curtain Lectures*) and from 1852 until his death in 1857 editor of *Lloyd's Weekly*. His son succeeded to that editorship at his father's death, an event which inspired Dickens to organize a play and to give one of his earliest public readings, to raise funds for the Jerrold family. One of the elder Jerrold's claims to renown was his inspired invention of the title Crystal Palace for Paxton's Great Exhibition building; it was printed in *Punch* and undoubtedly aided the exhibition's phenomenal success.

Hardly remembered today, the younger Jerrold wrote a number of books and contributed to several magazines. Among his early works was a guide to the 1851 Exhibition; in 1852 he compiled a guide to the British Museum and the following year travelled through Norway and Sweden as a Commissioner of the Crystal Palace. After 1855 he lived much in Paris, working there as a correspondent. He wrote a few plays and achieved distinction as a gastronome. His chief works are *The Life of Napoleon III*, a four-volume apology for the Second Empire, *The Life of George Cruikshank*, and *The History of Industrial Exhibitions*. He was still working on his biography of Doré in 1884 when he died, only a year after his friend, which may account for the chaotic structure of that work.

Jerrold was unlike Doré. For one thing, he was a liberal who cared about the interests of the under-privileged, seeing them as more than picturesque objects. If he did not possess either the vivid personality or the genius of his friend, he left behind him the impression of a versatile, civilized and likeable man. He knew many of the famous people of his day, including Dickens and Napoleon III. Since he lived through most of Victoria's reign, it is a pity he did not leave a diary; it might have formed a valuable social document.

Doré's *London* designs are given pride of place in this book, but they are complemented by contemporary engravings from other sources, mostly the *Illustrated London News* and the *Graphic*. The Victorian period in which Doré and Jerrold lived has been called the Railway Age. It could as well be dubbed the Boxwood Age, for its hallmark is as much the wood engraving as the pennon of steam. The wide distribution made possible by the railways, the rapidity of the steam press (first used in Britain by *The Times* in 1814), the increase in a literate public to whom reading was as important a recreation as television is to us, produced an enormous output of books and periodicals. When these were illustrated, as so many were, the wood block was the only available means by which pictures could be printed together with type. Hence its importance to the period. This was a factor which stimulated a whole generation of brilliant black-and-white artists. They have left us historical records of the greatest value which are more revealing than contemporary photographs can ever hope to be.

Unlike most forms of graphic expression, boxwood engraving is firmly articulated in time. It was born with Thomas Bewick and died in the nineties when the photomechanical process arrived, just in time to make the best of Beardsley's brilliant eccentricities.

Vincent Van Gogh had a high regard for many of the boxwood illustrators. At one time he even considered working for the *Graphic*. In 1881 he began buying back volumes of this magazine and of the *Illustrated London News*, from which he cut favoured pictures to mount with loving care on dark grey paper. He especially favoured the early volumes of the *Graphic*, those which appeared about the time Jerrold and Doré were making their London pilgrimage. 'There are things among them,' he wrote to his brother, 'which are superb. . . . They are great artists, these Englishmen.' Van Gogh was always on the side of the underdog, and no doubt it was partly the social realism of these illustrations that appealed to him. His approach was surprisingly literary, for he wrote in another letter, 'For me the English black-and-white artists are to art what Dickens is to literature.'

Some of the examples reproduced here were favoured by Van Gogh and, together with Doré's engravings, may be appreciated as skilful works of art and craft in their own right. Their main purpose, however, is to support this text in reconstructing the remarkable, and often horrifying, realities of the London that existed only a century ago.

A November Fog
(*Graphic*, 1872).

Mid-Victorian London: Formative Forces

The decline of England, my dear Geoffrey, dates from the day we abandoned coal fuel. No, I'm not talking about distressed areas, but about distressed souls, my dear. We used to live in a fog, the splendid, luminous, tawny fogs of our early childhood. . . . We designed a city which was meant to be seen in a fog. We had a foggy habit of life, and a rich, obscure, choking literature. The great catch in the throat of English lyric poetry is just *fog*, my dear, on the vocal chords. And out of that fog we could rule the world; we were a voice of Sinai smiling through the clouds. . . . *Then* some busybody invents electricity or oil fuel or whatever it is they use nowadays. The fog lifts, the world sees us as we are, and worse still, we see ourselves as we are.

Ambrose Silk in EVELYN WAUGH's *Put Out More Flags* (1942)

The quantity and scale of new constructions that appeared in the four decades between 1850 and 1890 in London were unprecedented: not only tens of thousands of speculative houses and hundreds of churches but numbers of massive, solid public buildings bearing lavish hand-wrought decoration, huge railway termini with their attendant arched approaches, goods yards, grand hotels, the noble river embankments with their solid granite walling, a vast new sewage system to serve the entire metropolis, nine new road bridges plus five for railways across the river, a tunnel below it, acres of new docks, the world's first underground railway, wide new thoroughfares carved through the rookeries, model tenements and great blocks of flats, Bedford Park as the first garden suburb, huge exhibition halls like the Crystal Palace, the Agricultural Hall at Islington, and Alexandra Palace (built, destroyed and at once built again), the giant oval of the Albert Hall and the many museums and cultural institutions south of it, numerous new office buildings in the City core, new emporia in the West End, central markets like Billingsgate, Leadenhall and Smithfield, music halls and theatres, great monumental workhouses and hospitals. The list is startling. All this was achieved in a single generation with only a few of the powerful technicals aids and materials we possess today.

What caused this vigorous expansion? What formed the character of the city that Doré depicted so vividly halfway through our chosen period? The increasing momentum of the Industrial Revolution does not in itself explain the phenomenon. Without the faith in *laissez-faire* linked to the Puritan revival whose origins lay back in the Reformation, the enormous accomplishments of mid-Victorian England, not least London's explosive growth, could not have been accomplished. The faith released tremendous energy – at an appalling price.

On the other hand without the limited but widening controls exercised by government authority, both local and national, such individualism would have brought either universal plague or violent upheaval. Minds like those of Jeremy Bentham and James Mill saw the need for balance. Undoubtedly the optimistic social philosophy of Bentham and his group – of those secular evangelists called Utilitarians, Felicitarians or Philosophical Radicals – deeply affected Victorian England. 'They came down into the world,' writes G. M. Young in his brilliant, if somewhat recondite, *Portrait of an Age*, 'where medieval prejudice, Tudor Law, Stuart economics, and Hanoverian patronage still luxuriated in wild confusion, and by the straight and narrow paths they cut we are walking still. . . . It would be hard to find any corner of our public life

A lavish detail of the roof of a lesser staircase, designed by Matthew Digby Wyatt, within Scott's Foreign and India Office – the architectural symbol of expanding Empire. The grand staircase is on page 96.

St Paul's seen from the brewery of Barclay and Perkins (Doré).

in the expanding, disordered, provisional London that Doré drew.

By typically British means, through concession and compromise, the three Estates – landed aristocracy, industrial middle class, and artisans and labourers – gradually adjusted themselves. Thus were the revolutions which shook the rest of Europe avoided here and slow progress made towards the greater, if by no means the greatest, happiness of the greatest number. Yet the Victorians did not achieve a democracy and never fooled themselves, as we do, that they had; right up to the eighties 'democracy' was almost a dirty word, almost a synonym for 'revolution', to those in authority. Before the Reform Act of 1867 (officially named the Representation of the People Act and the most important political step of the century, nervously called at the time a 'leap in the dark'), no working-class man could possibly become a Member of Parliament. In spite of the Reform Acts of 1832, 1867 and 1884, membership of the House of Commons remained essentially upper-class, at least until the eighties, and in the Cabinet until the close of the century. Doré's drawings imply it.

During the century exports rose ten times, imports over twenty times, the monetary balance being filled by the invisible exports of shipping, banking, insurance and returns on foreign investments. The production of coal, the very base of the sooty economy, rose more than twenty times, and of pig iron more than thirty times. Total industrial production increased about fourteen times, and although population during the century more than trebled, production per head quadrupled as a result of mechanization and the ruthless division of labour. The number of registered joint-stock companies rose from 947 in 1844 to 9,344 in 1885. Public expenditure, local and national, increased fifteen times during the century, and that in a period of comparative peace.

By the end of the seventies Britain could boast thirty-eight per cent of world trade in manufactures. Of every thousand tons of shipping passing through the Suez Canal, seven hundred were British. The country was indeed prosperous, but – typical of the century's contradictions – a third of the population lived in the direst poverty, not least in London, node of Empire, government, law, banking, trade, and culture, that possessed the largest port on the face of the globe. British supremacy finally came under threat as other countries, particularly Germany and the United States, began to increase their industrial strength, and to beat the British at their own game. Partly as a result of this, a depression, following several years of boom, befell in 1874 and lasted with ups and downs until the end of the century. Yet by 1897, the Jubilee year that celebrated the sixty years of the Queen's

where the spirit of Bentham is not working today.' On Bentham's bookshelves no doubt Thomas Paine's *The Rights of Man*, which by 1802 had already sold some half a million copies, could have been found.

An important example of the impact of imaginative ideas like Bentham's can have upon able individuals, and thus can radically change a whole environment, lies in the physical and organizational development of London initiated by the dedicated efforts of a single individual, a man who did more for his fellows than almost any other official has ever done and received in return far more abuse than gratitude: Edwin Chadwick. In his labours to improve the hygiene of the miasmic metropolis, he represents the primal bureaucratic archetype and may be nominated without exaggeration as the unofficial founder of the Welfare State. Through Chadwick's initiative, the Benthamite process in administrative reform of Survey before Plan – of inquiry, report, legislation, execution, inspection, and again report – became in time part of our working constitution. The interventionist State was thus conceived even before the ideal of individualistic capitalism without social controls had reached its maturity. It saved *laissez-faire* from itself, and made life just possible

Machinery with Doric
decoration
exhibited at the Inter-
national Exhibition
at South Kensington in
1862 – blast-engines
made by the Lilleshall
Company of
Shiffnal, Shropshire
(*Illustrated London
News*, 1862).

reign during which the Empire, largely by military force or threat, had increased its land area by nine times, Britain controlled a quarter of the land surface of the globe containing nearly four hundred million people; some ten per cent of the country's population owned ninety-two per cent of its total wealth. The situation even by the end of the century was not remotely democratic in any real, economic sense.

Just about the time Doré was making his London sketches lay the Great Divide of the nineteenth century. The day of the self-made man, typified by such as Cubitt and Paxton, who relied on hard work, self-help, religious conviction, and the thrift that accumulates capital, were coming to an end. The days of religious scepticism, increasing taxation, limited liability companies growing ever larger and more monopolistic and under the remote control of financiers, were beginning. A new class of mercantile middle-men, together with salaried managers, trade-union leaders and government inspectors, was coming between the operative masses and their bosses – those early factory owners who had actively run their own works and maintained direct personal contact with their men. The class structure was becoming ever more complex. In terms of London's architecture, the Divide is visible between the High Victorian works of Scott, mainly Gothic, and the new secular Queen Anne style of the Aesthetic Movement exemplified by the works of architects like Norman Shaw.

Throughout Victoria's reign the slums that Doré sketched were a depressing and ubiquitous feature of the London scene. Yet incomes of the working class did grow and its hours of work decrease. National income per head of the population quadrupled during the century and by 1871 the average working man was about ten per cent better off in real terms than he had been in 1851, for the increase favoured the middle and upper levels and to some degree the skilled artisans. The number of domestic servants increased faster than the population, from 1,300,000 in 1851 to 2,000,000 in 1881 – an indication of the growing prosperity of some classes – but by the end of the century forty per cent of the working class in London was still below the poverty line, that is too poor even to maintain bodily health. Not until the twentieth century was there a major rise in the wages of the unskilled. The inevitable results of so much poverty were the disease, crime and prostitution rampant in Doré's London. Three quarters of all crimes were then offences against property without violence.

Hordes of country people flocked into the expanding towns where steam power had concentrated the factories – enormous numbers to the metropolis, where nothing in the way of housing or social services was organized to receive them. Every man was expected to fend for himself in the belief, based on faith rather than experience, that God helps those who help themselves. A tremendous social upheaval had suddenly occurred. Within less than a century the old, quiet world of agriculture had been transformed into the humming, puffing new world of industry. Urban expansion came far too rapidly, so that for the vast majority of Londoners life was as tough and as uncertain as that in a mining camp.

The present-day subjugation of the mass of the population to the daily grind of production is precisely what the Industrial Revolution with its wonderful new artifacts could eliminate. The possibility of leisure has been rapidly increasing since men, women, and children grovelled, half-naked, in the mines for fourteen hours a day. On this issue Capitalism and Communism, as opposite sides of a coin, have become anachronistically confused, for both creeds are rooted deeply in that Puritan revival which created the nineteenth century. Hammers and sickles, hand looms, picks and shovels wielded by human muscles are no longer important tools of production; modern technology and cybernetics have seen to that. Yet picks

and shovels certainly were important only a century ago, as the railway navvies were closely aware. For the mass of the people in Doré's day, therefore, the Gospel of Toil made more direct sense than it does today.

The old aristocracy, reared to the idea that leisure and pleasure were their natural rights, rarely felt under the compulsion, either of Puritan guilt or of want, to work in any sphere, any more than they felt impelled to repress their appetites. To the rising middle class, on the other hand, toil, thrift, continence and money gathering, sanctified by a repressive religious outlook, formed the means of both material and social progress. The working classes, although always preached at, on the whole had no religious convictions, and work was simply a means of survival in the carious urban jungle, an alternative to starvation or the workhouse. 'What is St Paul's?' Mayhew asked a costermonger, and received the reply: 'A church, sir, so I've heard. I never was in a church.'

The opiate of the people, in the towns at least, was neither work nor religion: it was gin. Of summary convictions in England and Wales in 1871, nearly one third were on charges for being drunk and disorderly. In the feculent warrens of the poor depicted by Doré the existence of an all-powerful God who was also merciful could hardly be credited even by the most gullible. As G. M. Young comments: 'The imagination can hardly

Waiting for the Excursion Train (*I.L.N.*, 1880). Leisure was extended during the century by longer week-ends and the Bank Holidays Act of 1871. As the engraving shows, advertising had begun its expansion towards being the country's biggest industry.

apprehend the horror in which thousands of families a hundred years ago were born, dragged out their ghastly lives and died; the drinking water brown with faecal particles, the corpses kept unburied for a fortnight in a festering London August; mortified limbs quivering with maggots; courts where not a weed would grow, and sleeping dens afloat with sewage.'

In London, as Doré's engravings make clear, the West End knew little of the East End, and despite violent contrasts within the West End itself, such large-scale segregation had never existed before and was one of the most inhuman effects of the Industrial Revolution. Significantly, mortality was twice as high in the East End as the West.

The London the mid-Victorians built can only be understood as the product of the Puritan ethic. Work to the Victorian middle class was a spiritual purge, a passport to heaven, and it was not intended to give pleasure. The twin goals of respectability and salvation demanded full concentration on money-grabbing toil. The arts were thus regarded by many as at best a frivolous waste of money-making time and at worst as sensual lures of the Devil. Private enterprise and the Protestant ethic were

indeed the head and tail of Victorianism, and these were the true progenitors of the London of Doré. The importance of the Nonconformist Revival, particularly in its Evangelical guise, can hardly be over-stressed. It was visible not only in church–chapel segregation, but in the immense number of religious buildings of all denominations erected during the reign.

Into the midst of the complex of religious sects fell in 1859 a cerebral bomb manufactured by a gentle, unassuming man with a tall brow who spent a large part of his day reclining in contemplation on a sofa. Nothing had occurred to disturb complacent convention to such a degree since Copernicus had revealed that the earth was not the centre of God's universe. (Doré makes his caricaturist's comment by giving monkey-faces to his visitors to the Zoo.)

The decline of faith, with its resulting despair, ennui, and *Angst*, that occurred during the last decades of the nineteenth century – at least among those who dared to think and to whom respectability was not an end in itself – was largely due to Darwin's *On the Origin of Species*. Many now began to fear that, with God on his death-bed, morality itself was in hazard and that men would begin to live on

Left, Wentworth Street, Whitechapel (Doré).

Right, 'Mammon's Rents!! House-jobber*: "Now, then, my Man; week's hup. Can't 'ave a 'ome without payin' for it, yer know!" (See *The Bitter Cry of Outcast London*.)' (A drawing by Tenniel in *Punch*, 1883.)

their moral capital. The fear was groundless, for atheism and agnosticism tied a knot at the end of the long rope of Puritan dissent. To the sceptic, reared in an Evangelical atmosphere but suffering painful doubts, intense activity for practical purposes became an antidote to distressing speculation, a relief from anxiety, a kind of therapy for the boredom and depression of a life that had otherwise lost its meaning. Even to the unbeliever the virtue of unremitting toil thus remained an article of faith and so it remains.

So strong was the belief in *laissez-faire* and self-help during the earlier decades of Victoria's reign that after the slump of the late fifties *The Times* could write on the subject of the East End of London: 'It is always the first to suffer; for it is the creature of prosperity. The whole of that region is covered with huge docks, shipyards and manufactories and wilderness of small houses. . . . Now their brief spring is over. There is no one to blame for this; it is the result of nature's simplest laws.' Against such doctrinaire rigidity, protests increased. By 1880 the Cobden Prize Essay at Oxford could openly state: 'We have had too much *laissez-faire*. . . . The truth of Free Trade is clouded over by the *laissez-faire* fallacy. . . . We need a great deal more paternal government – that bug-

'London's Nightmare', another cartoon by Tenniel in *Punch* (1866). 'Bumbledom – the conflicting jurisdictions of folks who ought to have no jurisdiction at all, and who job, blunder, squabble, and utterly misgovern the metropolis of the world . . .' (The drawing is a caricature of Fuseli's painting 'The Nightmare' of 1781.)

bear of the old economists.' The new society of today was already on its way.

Although much was left to be done by the following century, the Victorians did in time achieve a good deal of social legislation and organization which had a wide influence on the changing fabric of London. They were brought about partly by the trade union movement and by working-class agitation, and partly by a kind of palace revolution in which a minority of the more sensitive and articulate members of the middle class was moved to protest passionately against the prevailing poverty and social injustice that Doré depicted so vividly – directly by Utilitarians like Chadwick and Evangelical reformers like Lord Shaftesbury, and indirectly by the writings of humanitarians like Ruskin, Arnold, Morris, Kingsley and such Christian Socialists, and, later, by the Fabians. Some were inspired by religious fervour, others by the humanism of the agnostic; all were inspired by a common feeling of social guilt. Here the Puritan ethic achieved its most constructive effects.

Ruskin, for one, gave up his aesthetic crusading in despair at the end of the fifties in order to concentrate the rest of his life, until his final breakdown, raging against the hideous poverty that lay behind the complacent middle-class prosperity (although of course it was his family's share in this prosperity that enabled him to act as he did). In his first letter of *Fors Clavigera* he explained: 'I have no particular pleasure in doing good, but I simply cannot paint, nor read, nor look at minerals nor do anything else that I like, and the very light of the morning sky, when there is any – which is seldom nowadays near London – has become hateful to me, because of this misery that I know of, and see signs of when I know it not, which no imagination can interpret too bitterly.' Ruskin did not only rant; he also gave monetary and moral support to Octavia Hill in her direct and personal enterprises to improve slum dwellings.

Ruskin's *Unto This Last*, which Lord Clark has called 'one of the great prophetic books of the nineteenth century', encouraged progress away from the ideology of mercantile individualism towards firmer communal controls and protective legislation – from *laissez-faire* to welfare. The struggle of the nineteenth-century reformers was long and hard and, bonded joylessly though we still may be by the Gospel of Toil, we are its beneficiaries.

Doré's vision of London symbolized the mid-Victorian psychic crisis. The metropolis, no longer a group of organic communities of comprehensible size, had become a huge, expanding, amorphous, uncontrolled growth of toil and commerce, black with soot and filled with rootless, indigent multitudes – not a Home but a sprawling yet overcrowded Doss House.

'Ludgate Hill – a Block in the Street' (Doré). Traffic congestion is clearly not a phenomenon confined to the twentieth century.

The River

This, surely, is one of the mighty spectacles of our planet. . . . A forest of masts and rigging grows out of the river: ships coming, going, waiting in groups, in long files, then in one continuous mass, at moorings, in among the chimneys of houses and the cranes of warehouses – a vast apparatus of unceasing, regular and gigantic labour. . . . The gleam of brown river water, the diffusion of light trapped in vapour, the white and rosy luminosity playing over all these colossal objects, spread a kind of grace over the monstrous city – like the smile on the face of some dark and bristling Cyclops.

HIPPOLYTE TAINE, *Notes sur l'Angleterre* (1860–70)

On the Embankment below Hungerford Bridge stands the modest monument to one of London's great men – Sir Joseph Bazalgette. He not only created the river embankments but also the tremendous main drainage system that conquered King Cholera and on which London still depends.

Doré stresses the river. His best designs depict it – the shipping, the caverns and canyons of the dock streets and warehouses, Billingsgate, the Albert Embankment, the bridges, the Boat Race. Wisely, he and Jerrold began their pilgrimage by river approach, first by the London boat from Boulogne, lingering at Greenwich, and then exploring the docks. 'We agreed,' writes Jerrold, 'that London had nothing more picturesque nor striking to show than the phases of her river, and her boundless docks. And hereabouts we tarried week after week, never wearying of the rich variety of form, and colour, and incident.'

The Thames made London. No other city in Europe has shown such dependence on its river, a dependence that began when the Romans built a crossing here at a point nearest the river's mouth where two dry, hard gravelly patches faced each other and made bridge-building possible. The medieval stone bridge, built in the twelfth century, became, with its projecting houses, a wonder of the world, a point not ignored by Doré, who provides an imaginative if inaccurate reconstruction of it. Right up to 1750 when a bridge was built at Westminster, London depended on this single crossing.

Now let us leap the centuries and look at Wyld's New Plan of London for 1851. Eight bridges span the river. The farthest downstream is John Rennie's classic, balustraded New London Bridge opened in 1831 to replace the tired old medieval structure. Then upstream in turn come Southwark Bridge, also by Rennie and opened in 1819, the largest cast-iron bridge of its day; Robert Mylne's noble Blackfriars Bridge of 1769; Waterloo by

Rennie, originally called the Strand Bridge and opened in 1817; Hungerford Bridge (opened 1845) with its square Italianate towers, built to lead to Hungerford market (on the site of Charing Cross Station) by Isambard Kingdom Brunel, engineer to the Great Western Railway, whose Clifton Suspension Bridge was finally completed with the iron chains saved when Hungerford Bridge was demolished in 1863; then Westminster, tottering relic of the beautiful high-arching stone structure completed in 1750 by the Swiss engineer, Labelye, and immortalized by Canaletto and Samuel Scott; Vauxhall running into Kennington Lane by Vauxhall Gardens, designed by James Walker, opened in 1816 as the first iron bridge to cross the Thames; and at Battersea, still the old wooden structure of 1771, recorded in Whistler's 'Nocturne' at the Tate Gallery. Out in the countryside to the west at Putney, a similar bridge of timber crossed the river, while still further upstream at Hammersmith stood a charming suspension bridge of 1827, similar to the one that still exists at Marlow and designed by the same architect, William Tierney Clark.

Thus in 1851 every bridge except Brunel's was of Georgian origin and not one railway yet crossed the river. Now look at Cassell's great map of 1868, at nine inches to the mile: within barely seventeen years, by the time Doré and Jerrold were exploring the metropolis, an extraordinary change had occurred. London, Southwark, Waterloo, Battersea and Vauxhall Bridges were still there, and so were old Putney and Hammersmith, but J. Cubitt's Blackfriars, in Venetian Gothic with squat pillars of red granite, was building, and Labelye's grace-

Penny steamers leaving Westminster Stairs
below the Houses of Parliament (Doré).

possessed character; only Blackfriars, Albert and West-minster remain with us to show it.

Three more bridges were to come later from the Metro-politan Board of Works under Joseph Bazalgette, its chief engineer: the new suspension bridge of 1887 at Hammer-smith, the plain granite affair at Putney of 1884, and the replacement at Battersea of the picturesque but rotting timber structure of the eighteenth century that Whistler painted. The last great Victorian crossing was to be Tower Bridge by Sir Horace Jones, architect to the City of London, and John Wolfe Barry, opened in 1894.

All these bridges indicate how fast London grew in the second half of the century, particularly south of the river, and how urgent a solution to the traffic problem had become. A number of important riverside buildings appeared between 1851 and 1868 to accommodate the snorting 'iron horses', notably the great arching cavern of Cannon Street Station and the less impressive Charing Cross Station, both with grand hotels (by E. M. Barry) attached and both the property of the South-Eastern Railway. By 1868 the London, Chatham and Dover Railway had also crossed the river to Blackfriars Station and had continued its line north to Farringdon Street, crossing Ludgate Hill on a decorated iron viaduct of 1865 which affected the view up to St Paul's and produced much heated controversy at the time.

Another crossing had existed since 1843, in the form of Sir Marc Isambard Brunel's double underwater tunnel between Wapping and Rotherhithe, the first of its kind in the world and a heroic feat of pioneer engineering. The intention was to form carriage ramps at each end but these were never built and so the tunnel remained for some time a little-used footway. The Great Bore, as it was called, was more of a curiosity than convenience and proved to be a costly white elephant. Nathaniel Hawthorne visited it in 1855 and found it to be:

an arched corridor, of apparently interminable length, gloomily lighted with jets of gas at regular intervals. . . . All along the extent of this corridor, in little alcoves, there are stalls or shops, kept principally by women, who, as you approach, are seen through the dusk, offering for sale views of the tunnel, with a little magnifying glass, in cases of Derbyshire spar; also cheap jewellery and multifarious trumpery; also cakes, candy, ginger-beer, and such small refreshment. . . . So far as any present use is concerned, the Tunnel is an entire failure.

In 1868 it was converted to railway use and so it has remained.

The second Thames tunnel was begun in 1869 to run between Tower Hill and Tooley Street, the engineer being P. W. Barlow, designer of the Lambeth suspension bridge, who was helped here by J. G. Greathead. The elder Brunel's tunnel had taken nineteen years of calami-

ful arches at Westminster had vanished and been replaced by a Gothic balustraded affair of iron, completed in 1862 (called the world's widest bridge then) to the design of Thomas Page, with some initial attention by Charles Barry before his death in 1860. A new but modest suspension bridge by P. W. Barlow had been erected at Lambeth in 1862 to take the place of the horse-ferry that had plied there perhaps since Roman times (hence Horseferry Road); and an impressive and ornate new suspension bridge had appeared in 1858 at Chelsea, with toll houses at each end, again to the design of Thomas Page. Farther west the Albert Bridge, by R. M. Ordish, a curious but attractive half-breed of suspension and cantilever, was about to be built. As a result of the second railway boom of the late fifties and sixties no less than five railway lines now also crossed the river – at Cannon Street, Blackfriars, Charing Cross (replacing Hungerford), Chelsea (where the Brighton and the London, Chatham and Dover Railways ran into the new Victoria terminus), and, to the west, at Battersea (the West London Junction Railway). The only one of these of any visual merit was that at Battersea; the others were grim iron affairs which added little to the river scene and prove that what is functional may not always be beautiful. Much trouble had been taken with the road bridges, however, and they at least

Right,
'Inside the Docks' (Doré).

Above, the Thames Subway between Tower Hill and Tooley Street, the second tunnel built under the river and prototype of the tube railways (*Graphic*, 1870). *Below*, the entrance to the elder Brunel's heroic feat of 'putting a pipe into old Thames's mouth', the first river tunnel that ran between Wapping and Rotherhithe (from *Old and New London*, 1874).

tous effort to complete and had cost a number of lives, but Barlow's structure, although only seven feet in diameter as compared with Brunel's twins each about twice that, was completed in a year without a single mishap. About a quarter of a mile long and lying twenty-two feet below the river bed, the tunnel was built of cast-iron rings, eighteen inches wide, bolted together on their flanges, a far quicker and more effective material than Brunel's brickwork, for here a progress of five feet each day made behind a shield was possible. This was historically an important structure as the early prototype of all London's later underground railway tunnels. At first the tunnel took a small-gauge railway, carrying twelve passengers, worked by a steel wire from stationary engines turning drums at each end, the fare being one penny. The train remained but a few years and the subway was then used only by foot-passengers who were charged a halfpenny. When the Tower Bridge was completed in 1894, it became a convenient case in which to carry hydraulic water mains across the river.

What remained from the past on the river banks in 1851? Of monumental buildings there were, of course, Wren's Hospital for army pensioners at Chelsea still with its grounds running to the water's edge, and far downstream the Greenwich Hospital for old sailors, which became in 1873 the Royal Naval College. On the south of the Strand Adelphi Terrace still stood – the elegant housing speculation of the Adam brothers set above arched catacombs. At Westminster Barry's Houses of Parliament were nearing completion, although Big Ben was not yet in his tower. Where the Tate Gallery now stands, the huge grim star-shaped fortress of Millbank Penitentiary had existed since 1821. Sir William Chambers's Somerset House, London's first great non-commercial office block, though begun in 1776, was not yet finished at its western end. Beside London Bridge on the north stood a prim but pleasant little building, which is still with us: the Greek Revival Fishmonger's Hall built in 1833 by Henry Roberts, the only Hall of all the City Companies to hold a riverside position. Its link with Victorian London lies in Roberts's chief assistant during its building being George Gilbert Scott, who was to become the most prolific of Victorian architects. Stranded medieval relics remaining near the river included the Tower, which William the Conqueror had erected just outside the City Wall more to threaten than to defend the citizens, Southwark Cathedral near the southern approach to London Bridge, and, up-river, nearer to the shore than now, Westminster Abbey.

West of the Tower stood the grey stone building of the Customs House which replaced Wren's building in 1817. The designer was David Laing, who built a central hall there with three domes, but he was not experienced and in 1825 the hall subsided owing to decay in the piling. Robert Smirke demolished the whole of the centre part and rebuilt it as we can now see it, with some alterations effected by the bombs of the Second World War.

The old dock of Queenhithe, indenting the bank just west of London Bridge, remained in 1851 from Roman times, and, indeed, is still there today, but recent and important innovations were a number of enclosed docks built since the start of the century. At the close of the eighteenth century shipping conditions at the port were appalling. By then the East India Company alone was sailing to London a greater number of vessels than had arrived at the port each year a hundred years before. The congestion was becoming insupportable for the ships were still moored in mid-stream and unloaded into open lighters which then carried the cargoes to the legal quays along the banks. Two months could go by before ships could turn round and sail away. Supervision was lax and the goods would lie about untended for days, even weeks, in the open. Pilfering and smuggling were highly organized. Colquhoun and Harriott's River Police had some effect but not enough, and the solution came in the form of new enclosed docks entered by locks so that vessels could float on an even keel in deep water unaffected by the rise and fall of the tides, right up against the quays where cargoes could be at once unloaded and stored in the surrounding warehouses. Behind their huge walls both

Siberian mammoth tusks on the Ivory Floor of the London Docks (*I.L.N.*, 1873). Seventeen tons of mammoth ivory were sold by auction in July 1873 at £60 to £70 per ton.

docks and warehouses could be easily protected from pilferers.

In the manner of the times, all these new docks were built for profit by private companies, the first being the West India Docks of 1802 on the Isle of Dogs with convenient entrances on both east and west. The same year the London Docks were begun at Wapping, the engineer being Daniel Alexander who also constructed the gaols at Dartmoor and Maidstone. His warehouses were magnificent in their bold and simple way, for Alexander was a poet of structure. In 1804 Ralph Dodd's Surrey Docks were begun south of the river, together with the Grand Surrey Canal that was to run to the Wey navigation, but in the event did not extend further than the three miles to Camberwell. The fourth enclosed dock was begun in 1805 at Blackwall for the East India Company, the engineer being the great John Rennie. Finally Thomas Telford's St Katherine Docks, with their three basins and warehouses of iron columns and yellow brickwork, were opened in 1828 just east of the Tower. (Doré illustrates these twice.)

In 1855 the Royal Victoria Dock was opened east of Bow Creek as the first large enterprise to be built to the east of the River Lea in rural Essex; to this was added the Royal Albert with three miles of quay in 1880 and then, in 1921, the King George V Dock was built to form the inter-communicating Royal Group – at 246 acres the largest area of impounded dockwater in the world. Something of the original grandeur of these nineteenth-century dock buildings can still be grasped from their remains.

With the ever-growing competition, dock companies began in time to amalgamate, and to cut costs to the bone. Organization again became chaotic, the inter-dock competitive warfare became ruinous, and strikes of the underpaid dockers became ever more frequent, ending in the successful Tanner Strike of 1889, for sixpence an hour. It was led by John (Thames-is-liquid-'istory) Burns, who was to be the first Labour M.P. to reach Cabinet rank. Burns also saw the need for dock reform and agitated for the amalgamation of all dock companies into one municipal enterprise, a need which was eventually met when the Port of London Authority was formed in 1909.

The docks of today still possess their maritime fascination but much of their romance and beauty vanished with the passing of the tall ships. Right up to the close of the century sailing vessels could still be seen there in considerable numbers. As late as 1896 about forty per cent of ships entering the Port were still moved by sails, although by then steam accounted for eighty-three per cent of the total tonnage. In 1874 nearly two thousand ships in the docks were sailers as against nearly nine hundred steamers, although many ships were by now combining steam with sail. The famous clipper *Cutty Sark*, now dry-berthed at Greenwich as a monument, was all sail, though not launched until 1869. As late as the seventies Richard Jeffries could report on the docks: 'Masts to the right, masts to the left, masts in front, masts yonder above the warehouses; masts in among the streets as steeples appear amid the roofs; masts across the river hung with drooping half-furled sails; masts afar down thin and attenuated, mere dark straight lines in the distance. They await in stillness the rising of the tide.'

Around these docks grew up the poor districts of the East End, a drunken rowdy jungle where life was always hard and, in times of trade depression when the docks were slack, quite desperate. Slumming parties, well protected by police officers, would explore the squalor, at first with sociological and philanthropic intent, but eventually as a morbid form of entertainment. Jerrold and Doré went because they had a job to do and there Doré could satisfy his sense of theatre, evident, for example, in his scene of the dockers' brawl called 'Night Scene' and his macabre 'Opium Smoking'.

In spite of the East End squalor, the scenes around the docks were thrilling, for everywhere, in warehouse building as well as on quayside and on water, was revealed that honest, robust beauty of form in the nautical tradition which seafaring everywhere produces. Moreover, as Jeffries wrote: 'Masts are always dreamy to look at. They speak a romance of the sea; of unknown lands; of distant forests aglow with tropical colours and abounding with strange forms of life.' Henry Mayhew has left us a vivid picture of the London Docks:

As you enter . . . the sight of the forest of masts in the distance, and the tall chimneys vomiting clouds of black smoke, and the many-coloured flags flying in the air, have a most peculiar effect; while the sheds with the monster wheels arching through the roofs look like the paddle-boxes of huge steamers. Along the quay you see now men with their faces blue with indigo, and now gaugers with their long brass-tipped rule dripping with spirit from the cask they have been probing. Then will come a group of flaxen-haired sailors, chattering German; and next a black sailor, with a cotton handkerchief twisted turban-like round his head. Presently a blue-smocked butcher, with fresh meat and a bunch of cabbages in the tray on his shoulder; and shortly afterwards a mate, with green paroquets in a cage. Here you will see sitting on a bench a sorrowful-looking woman, with new bright cooking tins at her feet, telling you she is an emigrant preparing for her voyage. As you pass along this quay the air is pungent with tobacco; on that, it overpowers you with the fumes of rum; then you are nearly sickened by the stench of hides and huge bins of horns; and shortly afterwards the atmosphere is fragrant with coffee and spice. . . . Here you sniff the fumes of the wine, and there the peculiar fungus smell of dry rot; there the jumble of sounds as you pass along the dock blends in anything but sweet concord. The sailors are singing boisterous nigger songs from the Yankee ship just entering; the cooper is

Overleaf, 'The Thames' – a London riverside idyll depicted in an engraving in the *Graphic*, 1873, from a painting by J. J. Tissot.

'The Docks – Night Scene'
(Doré).

hammering at the casks on the quay; the chains of the cranes, loosed of their weight, rattle as they fly up again; the ropes splash in the water; some captain shouts his orders through his hands; a goat bleats from some ship in the basin; and empty casks roll along the stones with a heavy, drum-like sound.

Some of the dock labourers were permanently employed at a steady wage, but the majority were casual, and from them the employers demanded no recommendations or training. So, Mayhew informs us, 'we find men of every calling labouring at the docks. There are decayed and bankrupt master butchers, master bakers, publicans, grocers, old soldiers, old sailors, Polish refugees, broken-down gentlemen, discharged lawyers' clerks, suspended Government clerks, almsmen, pensioners, servants, thieves – indeed, everyone who wants a loaf and is willing to work for it'. The work, paid at fourpence an hour, was sporadic, dependent insecurely not only on the state of trade but on the fortuitous arrival of the laden ships, that brought the riches of the world, in the words of Doré's friend Théophile Gautier, 'to tip them into the bottomless gulf of misery and luxury which is London'.

In Doré's 'Night Scene' a full moon shines above a distant thicket of masts and rigging. In the foreground a violent mob struggles around a hovel through the door-way of which a light is streaming. It is Friday night in Bermondsey. Doré was probably unaware of what was going on, but Mayhew would have known. The dockers were paid their wages in the public houses owned by the employers in the system of trucking which Disraeli had depicted and deplored in *Sybil* in the terrible tommy-shop scene – a system on which a Royal Commission was to report in 1872. The men were kept waiting for their pay until midnight or later, so that, in boredom, they might drink away a large part of their earnings in advance. The worried wives would besiege the taverns in a desperate effort to save what they could of their men's pay, and violence often resulted.

Upstream at Westminster Doré made a drawing of a pack of penny steamers breathing heavily below the Clock Tower of the Gothic Houses of Parliament as the passengers went aboard. Since London was born, the river had served not only for shipping but as a broad High

The Grand Saloon of
I. K. Brunel's
Great Eastern steamship,
launched from
Millwall in 1858 (*I.L.N.*,
1859).

Street, the city's main line of communication along which everyone could move from one landing stage to another; only since late Victorian times did the Thames cease to serve in this way, partly on account of the spread of the metropolis, and partly because land transport became quicker and easier, especially after the underground railways and tramways were developed.

In Doré's time, while the small skiffs of the watermen had disappeared, the river was still busy with passenger traffic. As early as the 1830s passenger steamers had been plying along the river, up to Richmond and Twickenham and down to Greenwich and Woolwich. By the fifties steam traffic, both long-distance and local, was considerable. As Alfred Bennett recalls in his reminiscences, *London and Londoners in the Eighteen-Fifties and Sixties*:

A look over the western parapet of London Bridge at any hour of the day revealed at least eight or ten steamers in the offing: morning and evening as City people were reaching or leaving their work the number would be increased to twenty or more. . . . The above-bridge boats – all the Thames passenger vessels were of the paddle-wheel type – belonged respectively to the Citizen

Steamboat Company, the Iron Boat Company and the West-minster Steamboat Company. . . . The fare by all these was one penny between London Bridge and Lambeth or Vauxhall. . . . The traffic by them was tremendous.

Just below London Bridge lay Billingsgate Fish Market, and Doré makes a good deal of this. Since Roman times this had been an important docking place; indeed, in medieval times it had been London's most important harbour, eventually wresting the marketing of fish from Queenhithe, which lay just above London Bridge. In 1699 Billingsgate had become by Act of Parliament a free wharf for fish and here sea food straight from the boats was sold from stalls around the harbour. It has been a fish market ever since, but when Doré and Jerrold heard 'the deafening vociferation, where the fish auctions were going on in the steamy open shops of the salesmen', the new market building with its iron and glass roofs we can see today had not yet been built. Designed by Horace Jones, the City Architect, it was opened in 1877. In Doré's day the fish came by river, but now it comes less naturally by road and rail.

That paddle-steamer traffic was tremendous in the fifties is surprising considering the frightful stench the river exuded, particularly when the paddle wheels churned up the soup. The Thames had become a huge open sewer for the entire metropolis.

The Census of 1841 had shown that over 270,000 houses stood in the metropolis, most of which had one or more cesspits beneath them. In poor districts these would often overflow through the floor-boards into the rooms above. A result was that the Metropolitan Commissioners of Sewers, formed in 1847, decreed that, in their unsuccessful attempt to curb the recurring epidemics of cholera, all cesspits should be abolished. So the excrement of three million Londoners began to run into the Thames down such buried tributaries as the Fleet River; most of these 369 sewers of all shapes and sizes emptied themselves either into the river or on to the foreshore only at low tide and as the tide rose the outlets became closed and the sewage was dammed back and became stagnant.

That cholera was a faecal microbe carried by water was not then understood and so the sewers were allowed to form a culture bed for its propagation. At one point the sewage was flushed into the river opposite a main intake of London's water supply. It is not surprising, therefore, that the outbreak of cholera in 1854 affected one in every 151 of the population and carried some twenty thousand people to a ghastly death. Protests became loud and general and that in *The Lancet* for July 1855 is typical:

The waters of the Thames are swollen with the feculence of the myriads of living beings that dwell upon the banks, and with the waste of every manufacture that is too foul for utilization. Wheresoever we go, whatsoever we eat or drink within the circle of London we find tainted with the Thames. . . . The water is already so turbid that the lower part of a bit of card, sinking edgeways, is invisible before the upper part has become immersed. The abominations, the corruptions we pour into the Thames are not, as some falsely say, carried away into the sea. The sea rejects the loathsome tribute, and heaves it back again with every flow. Here, in the heart of the doomed city, it accumulates and destroys.

That same year of 1855 saw the formation of the new administrative body for London, the Metropolitan Board

43

of Works, and hopes arose of some mitigation of the dangerous nuisance. But three years later in the hot, dry summer of 1858 came the Great Stink, an event that took on the aspect of a national calamity and vied with the Indian Mutiny and the completion of the Atlantic cable as a conversational topic. In June *The Times* expostulated:

What a pity it is that the thermometer fell ten degrees yesterday. Parliament was all but compelled to legislate upon the great London nuisance by force of sheer stench. The intense heat had driven our legislators from those portions of their buildings which overlook the river. A few members, indeed, bent on investigating the subject to its very depths, ventured into the library, but they were instantly driven to retreat, each man with a handkerchief to his nose. We are heartily glad of it. It is right that our legislators should be made to feel in health and comfort the consequence of their own disregard of the public welfare.

There was talk of transferring the Law Courts, then still at Westminster, to Oxford or St Albans, and the windows of the Houses of Parliament were draped with curtains soaked in chloride of lime. A Mr Mangles stated in the House of Commons that when he was a young man Thames salmon were celebrated and he had been informed that cartloads of fish had recently been taken out of the Thames which had died in consequence of the state of the river. Clearly the pollution of rivers is no new occurrence. That month also *The Builder*, always a lively agitator against official apathy, reported: 'Last Sunday a waterman who was in the habit of working on the Thames, near the Tower, died of Asiatic cholera, and the jury, after a careful examination returned a verdict "that the deceased died from the effect of Asiatic cholera brought on by inhaling the noxious vapour of the Thames".' The rich soup was growing thicker year by year for the sea refused to accept the sewage which regurgitated back and forth through London at each turn of the tide. Thus eight miles of London's river was in a permanent state of putrid and ever-increasing fermentation as ninety million gallons of sewage was discharged into it each day, a compound not only of human and animal wastes but of effluents from bone-boilers, soap boilers, chemical works, gasworks and breweries. Eventually all came to realize that here was a problem that could be solved only by a public service organized on a municipal scale.

Not until 1883 was the organism causing Asiatic cholera isolated by Robert Koch. Edwin Chadwick as Secretary of the Poor Law Commission, however, had already proved by the statistics of his *Sanitary Report* of 1842 that most of the mortality and sickness in towns was preventable and was caused by poor living conditions; his Sanitary Maps showed that the black crosses of death crowded most thickly in the poorest districts where ventilation, water supply and drainage were most inadequate and where overcrowding was at its worst.

London drainage was chaotic. Sewers everywhere were unco-ordinated, unconnected and unmapped. Many were built as huge brick caverns, with flat bottoms and sides, on insufficient gradients so that their filth collected and had to be scooped out at intervals by buckets and deposited for collection in noisome heaps by the roadside. Dung, night soil and rotting refuse were marketable as manure and would lie about the metropolis in laystalls for weeks waiting for collection, and as the town rapidly grew and the distance of the centres from the surrounding countryside and market gardens increased, this method of disposal by small scavenging contractors began to break down and the secretions of filth in basements and backyards increased steadily. Nor was the cleaning of road surfaces related to sewers; the connection was, indeed, forbidden by some local authorities. Large sewers discharged into small sewers, some sewers were at a higher level than the cesspools they were expected to relieve, while many had irregular gradients with hollows. Some sewers were even laid seemingly in the belief that liquids flow uphill. Rivers, open or buried, became stagnant pools of filth and in Lambeth, Bermondsey, and Rotherhithe miles of ditches served as open sewers.

Henry Mayhew in his *London Characters* (1874) gives a pungent first-hand account of a visit he paid to Jacob's Island, a patch of ground in Bermondsey insulated by a common sewer which he called the Capital of Cholera:

The blanched cheeks of the people that now came out to stare at us were white as vegetables grown in the dark. . . . As we now passed along the reeking banks of the sewer, the sun shone upon a narrow slip of water. In the bright light it appeared the colour of a strong green tea . . . and yet we were assured this was the only water the wretched inhabitants had to drink. As we gazed in horror at this pool, we saw drains and sewers emptying their filthy contents into it, we heard bucket after bucket of filth splash into it, and the limbs of the vagrant boys bathing in it seemed, by pure force of contrast, white as Parian marble. And yet, as we stood gazing in horror at the fluvial sewer, we saw a child from one of the galleries opposite lower a tin can with rope, to fill a large bucket that stood beside her. In each of the rude and rotten balconies, indeed, that hung over the stream, the self-same bucket was to be seen in which the inhabitants were wont to put the mucky liquid to stand, so that they might, after it had been left to settle for a day or two, skim the fluid from the solid particles of filth and pollution, which constituted the sediment. In this wretched place we were taken to a house where an infant lay dead of the cholera. We asked if they *really did* drink the water? The answer was, 'They were obliged to drink the ditch unless they could beg or thieve a pailful of the real Thames.'

Shortage of clean water was a serious sanitary problem. As Chadwick showed, the sudden expansion of population had produced an immense amount of cheap speculative housing with the result that the poor were being exploited everywhere in their hovels by the 'ignorance, cupidity, or negligence of landlords'. London sprawled,

'The Silent Highway-Man' – *Punch*'s protest of 1858 against the pollution of the Thames.

'Limehouse Dock'
(Doré), showing steam-
powered cranes.

without planning or control. Chadwick sighed for the great design Sir Christopher Wren had prepared after the Great Fire, which, he believed, would, if it had been carried out, have reduced the death rate of all succeeding generations by a third. In the matter of water supplies, Chadwick had advocated the replacement of the nine private companies by a single municipal one which would provide plenty of clean, filtered water for everyone, but so powerful was the support of private enterprise, even in matters of public concern, that London had to wait until 1903 for its Metropolitan Water Board.

All drainage and road construction, Chadwick insisted, should, for the sake of efficiency and economy, be brought together as a single public service. The revelations of the *Sanitary Report* of 1842, for which Chadwick was mainly responsible, had come as a shock, and more copies of it were sold by the Stationery Office than of any previous Government publication. In spite of this public interest and the universal fear of the return of King Cholera, to say nothing of typhoid, typhus, dysentery, and other prevalent diseases, by 1858 nothing really useful had been done and the sanitary situation was worse than ever.

Chadwick's General Board of Health had been closed down in 1854 and a new Public Health Board had been appointed. The indefatigable Chadwick was sacked, though mollified by a comfortable pension of £1,000 a year which he was able to enjoy until he died, aged ninety,

in 1890. He was, of course, tactless and overbearing but met opposition chiefly because his sensible calls for social and municipal enterprise and co-ordination ran counter to the spirit of the age even in matters like drainage, water supply, interment, and communications on which the health and convenience of all depended. As *The Times* put it when Chadwick's régime ended, 'we prefer to take our chance of cholera and the rest, than be bullied into health'.

To his single discredit Chadwick had supported the scheme for flushing all sewers into the Thames, but as he pointed out, whatever was to be done, a proper, general, large-scale survey of London's levels must first be prepared. This was the origin of the Ordnance Survey, begun in 1848; on its valuable maps Bazalgette was able to prepare his main drainage scheme for London.

One of Chadwick's concerns, and a worthy one, was to save London's sewage for manure. The idea of moving filth to tilth was not a new one, for 'Mad' John Martin, painter and planner, who has been called the Buckminster Fuller of the Steam Age, had in 1832 produced a scheme to save manure by draining London's sewers into large reservoirs from which the sewage could be distributed by canal in covered boats to agricultural districts. These main sewers would also serve as foundations of arcaded quays along the banks. It was a highly imaginative pro-posal, on the same principle as that of the main outfall sewers and embankments which Bazalgette was to design and which serve London still.

In 1858 a Bill for the purification of the Thames was at last passed and the next year Joseph Bazalgette (1819–91), at the Metropolitan Board of Works, began his gigantic works for providing the whole metropolis, both north and south of the river, with a properly planned main drainage system. London owes a great deal to Bazalgette, and perhaps because so much of his drainage scheme is unromantic, unaesthetic and underground, he, like 'Drain Brain' Chadwick, has never received the recognition he deserves, even if he was knighted after the achievement of the Embankments. He has his modest monument on the Embankment wall just by Charing Cross railway bridge. The son of a commander in the Royal Navy of French extraction, he set up as a consulting engineer as a young man but joined the staff of the Metropolitan Commission of Sewers in 1847, a body which had been formed to amalgamate the eight separate local bodies nominally responsible for London's drainage. This period of confusion was resolved by the formation of the Metropolitan

Board of Works in 1854, to which Bazalgette was appointed Chief Engineer. He began at once to prepare a major scheme, but there were many delays until Disraeli passed a short act in 1858 giving the Board full control of the proposed works, secure in the knowledge that they had the recommendation of such eminent Commissioners as Robert Stephenson and Sir William Cubitt. The Prince of Wales declared the system open in 1865, though the whole vast enterprise was not fully completed until 1875. It was acclaimed as a most competent, skilful and valuable work and its effect on the health of Londoners was immediate and dramatic. The cholera epidemics were over.

The sketch map here shows how the scheme works. The main sewers – high, middle and low on both sides of the river – converge on outfall sewers running to reservoirs some twenty-six miles below London Bridge. Through these both sewage and surface water is discharged except during excessive rain storms when the waters can be flooded into the Thames. The high- and middle-level sewers discharge by gravitation, while the low-level sewers are aided by pumps placed at strategic points. On

Sketch map of Joseph Bazalgette's scheme for the main intercepting sewers prepared for the Metropolitan Board of Works and begun in 1859.

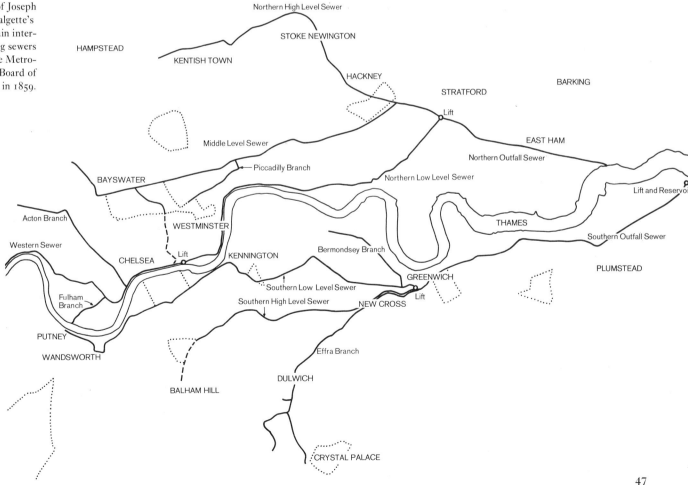

the north the three lines unite at Abbey Mills where the contents of the low level are pumped up to the upper level and the aggregate stream then flows through the northern outfall sewer, which is above ground and is carried in a concrete embankment across the marshes to a reservoir just west of Barking Creek. On the south the three intercepting lines unite at a lift at Deptford, where the contents of the low level are pumped to the upper level and from there the southern outfall sewer runs east through Woolwich to a lift and reservoir at Crossness. At Pimlico a lift was required to raise the flow from the low western sewer and Fulham branch up to the level of the northern low-level sewer; the pump house, like a French *château* with an ornate chimney, can still be seen just by the railway bridge that runs trains into Victoria Station.

At first the sewage from north and south was discharged at Barking and Crossness respectively straight into the river and there conditions were soon as bad as they had been in central London. A Royal Commission appointed in 1886 denounced the outfalls 'as a disgrace to the metropolis and to civilization' and revealed that in 1884 'the sewage water from the outfalls manifestly reached London Bridge', while at Woolwich 'the river for its whole width was black, putrid sewage – looking as if

unmixed and unalloyed. The stench was intolerable.' In 1887, therefore, the decision was taken to precipitate the sewage chemically, allowing only the effluent to flow into the river, the sludge being removed by ships to the Black Deeps beyond the Nore where it could be discharged into the sea. In spite of such adaptations London still relies to a great extent on Bazalgette's original system.

In a paper read to the Institution of Civil Engineers in 1865 Bazalgette described the whole system in a factual statement. The general form of the intercepting sewers, he informed his audience, was circular stock brickwork, but minor branches were egg-shaped to obtain a greater scouring power at the bottom and sufficient width above for storm water as well as to provide human access. Altogether 1,300 miles of sewers now existed in London, he declared, 82 miles being main intercepting sewers. In their building, 318 million bricks and 880,000 cubic yards of concrete had been used, while three and a half million cubic yards of earth had been excavated. It was a thorough job, carried out with despatch and efficiency in spite of strikes and a shortage of bricks.

Important structures in these works are the pumping stations at Abbey Mills, Chelsea and Crossness. All deserve preservation as fine examples of Victorian engineering. Although at the time of writing the tall campanile at Crossness has gone, the magnificent beam engine still survives, forming a single entity with its house, a highly ornamented design with much decorative ironwork, described by *The Builder* at the time the Prince of Wales opened it, in 1865, as being 'Medieval with Byzantine and Norman features'.

Bazalgette's other colossal works were the Albert, Victoria and Chelsea Embankments, built between 1868 and 1874. A length of the northern low-level sewer was incorporated – together with a subway for gas and water mains and a tunnel for a section of the new Metropolitan District Underground Railway – into the construction of the Victoria Embankment. Like the new sewers the Embankments were truly stupendous Victorian works, with the immense amount of muck-shifting and street-laying involved, their brick and concrete constructions, and their facings and parapets of solid blocks of dressed granite. (Doré has only one fairly small drawing of the Albert Embankment on the south, for when he was making his pilgrimage only the Albert was complete.)

If Chelsea lost its old picturesque riverside and Somerset House now no longer dipped its broad terrace straight down into the river as it was designed to do, the Embankments brought a number of gains. The shabby, shambling warehouses and wharves and the gas works lying west of Blackfriars, where the riverside coal trade had declined with the coming of the railways, were demolished and replaced by gardens and a broad new thoroughfare. The unsightly, useless, stinking foreshores of mud disappeared and the widely varying widths of the river were made more uniform; Londoners could see more of their river, while at Charing Cross and Cheyne Walk new strips of tree-filled parks, open to the public, were created, and the Temple Gardens were enlarged. In their total of three and a half miles, the Embankments reclaimed no less than thirty-two acres of mud. Although Victoria Embankment was not carried as far as London Bridge on account of the high cost of land there and the business of the wharves, a wide new roadway did extend the Embankment thoroughfare as far as the Mansion House in the form of Queen Victoria Street, which was opened in 1871.

With their battered walls, thick parapets, occasional landing steps and stages, all of grey granite, with their rhythmical rows of plane trees lining broad avenues, their dolphin-decorated lamps of cast iron, lion-headed mooring rings, and general character of bold and solid indestructibility, the Embankments are the most enduring monuments of Victorian energy and practical enterprise that London offers. Like the new sewers, the Embankments were an old idea, often proposed but long delayed. The first authentic information concerning embankment

Opposite, Bazalgette's drainage system under construction – the tunnels near Old Ford, Bow (*I.L.N.*, 1859). *Near right*, the Penstock Chamber at Old Ford (a gate to regulate flow where the Northern High-Level, Middle-Level and Hackney Brook Sewers meet); *far right*, the invert for the Southern High-Level Sewer (*I.L.N.*, 1861).

Top left, Victoria Embankment under construction, looking east from Somerset House (*I.L.N.*, 1864). *Below left*, the proposals for Victoria Embankment showing, 1, the Subway for services; 2, the Low-Level Sewer; 3, the Metropolitan Railway; 4, the Pneumatic Railway (*I.L.N.*, 1867). *Right*, progress on the Victoria Embankment; cutting off below water-level with a steam-driven saw the piles of the cofferdam within which the granite-faced river wall was constructed (*I.L.N.*, 1866).

of the Thames goes back, in fact, to the year 1367 in the reign of Edward II. After the Great Fire of 1666 Wren prepared a design for an embankment between Temple Gardens and the Tower. In the 1830s Sir Frederick Trench produced a tremendous scheme and then John Martin, as we have seen, proposed one in connection with intercepting sewers. Now their visions had become realities. London was at last properly drained and its river in large part properly embanked. Even that Chelsea resident Carlyle was impressed.

Let us end this river picture with a decorative touch: a fine Chinese junk which could be seen and visited on the Thames for some years during the middle of the nineteenth century. It arrived by way of the Cape in 1848 and lay for a time off Blackwall, where Dickens inspected it: 'If there be any one thing in the world that this extra-ordinary craft is not at all like,' he wrote, 'that thing is a ship of any kind. So narrow, so long, so grotesque, so low in the middle, so high at each end, like a china pen-tray; with no rigging, with nowhere to go aloft; with mats for sails, great warped cigars for masts, dragons and sea-monsters disporting themselves from stem to stern, and on the stern a gigantic cock of impossible aspect.' In the *annus mirabilis* of 1851, this floating folly was established on a mud bank at the end of Essex Street and was open twice daily with a variety of strange entertainments including conjuring tricks and a grand assault of arms *à la Chinoise*. It produced a fair income for the Chinese crew, who had, according to Dickens, 'not a profile amongst them', and were dressed 'in gauze pinafores and plaited hair, wearing stiff clogs a quarter of a foot thick in the sole, and lying at night in little scented boxes'.

Overleaf, the Oxford and Cambridge Boat Race at Hammersmith Bridge (*I.L.N.*, 1872). This is the old suspension bridge of 1827 by W. T. Clark. The Boat Race was an even more popular event a century ago than it is today.

Rail & Road

Blue carts and yellow omnibuses, varnished carriages and brown vans, green omnibuses and red cabs, pale loads of yellow straw, rusty-red iron clanking in paintless carts, high white woolpacks, grey horses, bay horses, black teams; sunlight sparkling on brass harness, gleaming from carriage panels; jingle, jingle, jingle! And intermixed and intertangled, ceaseless changing jingle, too, of colour; flecks of colour champed, as it were, like bits in the horses' teeth, frothed and strewn about, and a surface always of dark-dressed people winding like the curves on fast-flowing water. This is the vortex and the whirlpool, the centre of human life today on the earth.

RICHARD JEFFRIES, *The Story of My Heart* (1883)

In 1851 outer London was composed of separate villages set around their greens. Then a short drive from the centre would convey one into the depths of the country. London may already have become Cobbett's Great Wen, but it was not yet Dickens's Great Oven, nor yet that Monstrous Amalgam of Microcosms of the Victorian journalist, George Augustus Sala. The main roads out of the metropolis along which the mail coaches had careered for a brief period had become built up like the arms of an octopus, but between them lay copse, field and farmhouse.

The railways had taken over the mails in 1841 and soon after that few stage coaches were running. Until the motor-car arrived, that is for over sixty years, the main roads of England were comparatively empty except for local traffic, or, near London, the occasional fine equipage of a coaching club. The heydays of coaching, which have left such a beloved legacy to the popular imagination with their coaching inns, long brass horns and Pickwickian associations, had extended only for some fifteen years.

In the year of the Great Exhibition – 'that singularly happy year', as Macaulay called it, 'of peace, plenty, good feeling, innocent pleasure, and national glory' – the first railway boom of the forties was over and the second boom of the sixties had yet to come; as we have noticed, no lines yet crossed the river. Brunel's broad-gauge Great Western ended at Paddington where the new terminus of iron roofing and the huge Frenchified railway hotel, the first of its kind in London, were under construction, while Lewis Cubitt's King's Cross Station, plain, functional and dignified with two train sheds, one for arrivals, the other for departures, articulated at the end by a pair of

great stock brick arches divided by a clock tower, was nearly finished. At the Chalk Farm depot, where Robert Stephenson's Round House served the engines, the London and Birmingham line emerged from a long tunnel and branched down to Euston Station, half a mile to the west of King's Cross, where Philip Hardwick's Doric Gateway (so ruthlessly murdered in 1962) and the noble hall concealed a ramshackle collection of sheds.

London's first railway line was, just, pre-Victorian. Completed in 1836, only six years after the Liverpool and Manchester Railway, it ran for four miles from Southwark, south of London Bridge, on 878 brick arches all the way to Greenwich. The Croydon Railway, opened in 1839, and to which it was linked, ended at the Bricklayer's Arms Station in the Old Kent Road. One of the most powerful lines south of the river, by the fifties, was the London, Brighton and South Coast Railway under the chairmanship of Samuel Laing, who was also chairman of the company that acquired and re-erected the Crystal Palace at Sydenham, a convenience that resulted in a special excursion line of the L.B.S.C. being opened in 1854 on which return tickets included the admission fee. (A second approach to the High Level Station at this important centre, called the Railway to a Turnstile, was built four years later from Battersea.)

At Nine Elms the new Southampton Railway had its terminus. From there the line ran south-west across a mill pond, past a few houses of Battersea New Town and across the open marsh south of Battersea Fields. In 1858 Battersea Park was opened there, after the whole damp surface had been raised by dumping great quantities of earth

An iron arch of one of the great railway termini of the Railway Age – Paddington Station at the end of Brunel's Great Western Broad-Guage Railway, completed in the early fifties.

'Over London by Rail' –
Doré's most
famous London scene.

excavated from the Victoria Docks and carried up river. North of the river to the east the Blackwall to Fenchurch Street Line, also on arches but running on an endless rope powered by stationary steam engines, had been completed in 1840; it was linked with the Eastern Counties Railway ending at Shoreditch, having joined with the Northern and Eastern at Stratford in the Hackney Marshes – the open, sodden land west of a village called Hudson New Town. To the north-west, the North London Railway ran from Chalk Farm, where a few houses were appearing along Adelaide Road, thence through Islington, round the east side of Victoria Park and down to the West India Docks, where it joined up with the Blackwall Railway.

So, as early as 1851, London possessed on its outskirts a good deal of railway communication, but the main impact of the railways on the fabric of London came in the sixties, when the companies stretched their lines right to the periphery of the centre where they ended in a number of great termini, four of them by crossing the river. To the sixties belong the first stations at Victoria, Charing Cross, Cannon Street, St Pancras, Broad Street, Blackfriars, Holborn Viaduct, and the earliest part of Waterloo.

The new railways, like the canals before them, were all built by separate private speculative enterprises with little co-ordination. Civic amenities and public convenience were purely incidental; profit was the overriding object. Their effect on the London scene was overwhelming, particularly in the poorer districts where land was cheap, and on this Doré's famous engraving 'Over London by Rail' provides a powerful comment. The railways were, indeed, the main progenitors of Victorian cities and they arrived with the force of an earthquake. A good description appears in John Kellet's *The Impact of Railways on Victorian Cities* (1969). 'In London,' he says, 'something of the order of eight hundred acres of central land was taken for railway uses in the course of the nineteenth century; an area sufficient for a fair sized town in itself.'

The railways, in fact, made the logistics of gargantuan city growth possible. They did so, just as the motor-car

56

The banquet held in a large room, specially erected for the occasion and adjoining Farringdon Street Station, to inaugurate the opening of the Metropolitan Railway (*I.L.N.*, 1863). The guests had made a preliminary trial run in open carriages from Paddington. The railway was opened to the public on 10 January, when 30,000 passengers used the line during the day.

does today in its own manner, by wrecking civilized urbanity. More viaducts were added in the sixties along the approaches to the termini, striding above the slums at roof level (as the new motorways do now) and so walling in and pinning down whole areas by their inter-sections, triangular junctions, and link lines, which formed wide and sterile wastelands like the Battersea and New Cross tangles still to be seen south of the river. Sometimes these viaducts were needed to maintain a level of approach, but mostly they were built in order to avoid the closure of streets and the building of level crossings. Attempts were made, as on the early Blackwall line, to convert the resulting arcades into houses, even in one case into a school for infants, but their usual end was to serve as workshops, stores, or casual overnight shelters for human derelicts. The railway arch is the very symbol of Victorian urban squalor.

Although the railway companies, once they had ob-tained their parliamentary sanctions, possessed the privi-lege of compulsory purchase, some control of their

grasping activities had to be exercised or London would have been completely cut to pieces. This limited control was exercised by Select Committees and an occasional Royal Commission; at least it prevented railway en-croachment right into the heart of London and so helped to form that oval, some four miles wide and one and a half miles deep, into which main-line railways and their termini do not intrude. The worst encroachment was to Victoria Station, for this completely divided Belgravia from Pimlico; but at least the parks and squares of Central London were saved. A traffic problem was thus created: because the main lines did not meet in the centre but ran north and south as from a watershed, the inter-station traffic, then – as it still is today – was considerable, so that street congestion in the central oval was thereby aggrav-ated. It was this problem which the new underground Metropolitan and District Railways, built in the sixties, attempted to mitigate.

The worst effects of the railways was on the housing of the poor. The land acquired by the railway companies in their ruthless competition with each other caused the demolition of hundreds of houses, already overcrowded, and the cramming of those rendered homeless, without aid or compensation of any sort, into the surrounding slums that remained. The complicated process of slum-growth was accelerated in areas hemmed in by the new viaducts: only some industries and the poorest housing could survive therein amidst the din and the dirt.

Packing the Poor was especially bad around the area of King's Cross, St Pancras and Euston with their maze of branch lines and depots. The wretched inhabitants of entire working-class districts such as Somers Town were reduced by railway clearances, in the words of Lord Shaftesbury, delivered in Parliament in 1861, to the state of 'people in a besieged town, running to and fro, and not knowing where to turn'. It has been estimated that of all who lost their homes through railway displacement during the second half of the nineteenth century probably some seventy per cent were dislodged in the two decades after 1859.

'The poor are displaced,' wrote *The Times* in 1861,

but they are not removed. They are shovelled out of one side of the parish, only to render more over-crowded the stifling apartments in another part. . . . But the dock and wharf labourer, the porter and costermonger cannot remove. You may pull down their wretched homes; they must find others, and make their new dwellings more crowded and wretched than their old ones. The tailor, the shoemaker and other workmen are in much the same position. It is mockery to speak of the suburbs to them.

Two years later the *Illustrated London News* declared: 'They enter upon a new and terrible competition, which is for the most part finally settled by fresh discoveries in the art of huddling the largest number of human beings into the smallest possible spaces.' Added to the desperate search for alternative accommodation at increasing rent was the sad breaking of old community ties.

The railway promoters preferred to run their new lines through poor districts because the inhabitants there had almost no effective or legal means of protest; if on weekly tenancies they had none at all. As early as 1851 *The Builder*, a magazine of far wider interests than construction, and, like *Punch*, often on the side of the oppressed, was lamenting the destruction by the modern Attila:

> Who builds? Who builds? Alas, ye poor!
> If London day by day 'improves',
> Where shall ye find a friendly door
> When every day a home removes?

A reporter on *The Working Man* in 1866 made inquiries about the effects of railway developments: 'Where are they all gone, sir? Why, some's gone down Whitechapel way; some's gone to the Dials; some's gone to Kentish Town; and some's gone to the Workus.' A railway com-

pany might give a displaced family a guinea compensation now and then, but never another home. A few attempts, largely ineffectual, were made to provide those displaced by clearances with alternative accommodation. In 1853 the Shaftesbury Standing Order, for example, required the preparation of a Demolition Statement on the number of working men likely to be evicted by each urban railway scheme, but until the London County Council came into being rational and humane rehousing was negligible. An Evicted Tenants Association was formed but could achieve very little. Then in the seventies, when most of the damage had been done, a number of Acts were passed to try to deal with displacement, but for a further decade these were all successfully evaded.

Working people were unable to move to decent surroundings even if they wanted to do so, for they had to live near their work and that was often on the railways. In the mid-sixties, for example, 680,000 workers in central London depended on casual labour and were engaged by the hour or the day; to them local domicile was essential. In the forties Charles Pearson, solicitor to the Corporation of London, pointed out in his evidence to a Royal Commission: 'A poor man is chained to the spot; he has not the leisure to walk, and he has not the money to ride.' Nearly fifty years later Charles Booth declared in his survey: 'It is only the man whose position is assured who can treat railway or tram fares as a regular item of his daily budget.' A slum was all too often the nearest local source for local casual labour. Covent Garden required the slum dwellers of Drury Lane, the docks were manned from the East End, the tailoring trade lived in Soho, and so on.

So the working man could not live, like a member of the middle class, out in the fresh air and roominess of the suburbs. His situation grew worse as the century advanced. Even cheap speculative building without adequate planning controls in unventilated back-to-back and tunnel-back terrace housing was limited in extent, for available land was scarce in central districts and its price was high. New roads cut through the rookeries were welcomed by the authorities as a form of slum clearance which not only improved communications and brought better ventilation but helped to shovel out the destitute and so reduce local poor relief. Where the homeless were to go was no one's business, and so the overcrowding already produced by railway clearances became even worse.

Eventually cheap workmen's fares helped the situation to some extent for it made expansion outside the central and eastern slums possible. A brochure of 1865, *The Metropolitan Railway*, reveals that special workmen's trains were being run morning and evening on the new Metropolitan and District Railways at fares of one penny.

Above, a railway arch, squalid emblem of Victorian London, here being used to relieve the distress of the unemployed of East London through the action of the Bethnal Green Employment and Relief Association formed by Miss Burdett-Coutts; men are breaking granite for road works at nine shillings a week (*I.L.N.*, 1868). *Below*, the Metropolitan Railway at King's Cross completed in 1863 (*Builder*).

The terminus of the South-Eastern Railway, Cannon Street (*I.L.N.*, 1866).

This came as a boon to many who could now travel to the suburbs where better accommodation at lower rent could be found. One labourer

assured us that he saved at least two shillings a week by them, in the matter of rent only. He lived at Notting Hill and would have to walk six miles to and from his work every day if it were not for the convenience of the railway. He had two rooms now, almost in the open country, for the same price as he would have to pay for one in some close court in the heart of London, besides what he saved in medicine for his wife and family. A plasterer, who had to go all the way to Dockland to his work, said that it was impossible to reckon up how much workmen gained by what is called the Workmen's Trains, especially if you took into account the saving in shoe-leather, the gain in health and strength, and the advantage it was for men to go to work fresh and unfatigued by a long walk at the commencement of the day. The plasterer, too, was great on the *moral* effects (it is astonishing how working men delight in the morality of a question), and urged, with some force, that the best thing in connection with such institutions was that it enabled operatives to have different sleeping-rooms for themselves and their young children.

The works of the big railway enterprises produced hideous and dire effects, but they were regarded generally with a good deal of pride, even of awe. To their credit, the railway companies, in spite of their greed and myopic lack of social concern, did create some magnificent and daring structures, particularly in their terminal stations – the cathedrals of the Victorian Age. The most splendid of all was that of the Midland Railway at St Pancras with its famous hotel attached. That station and hotel (the latter completed in 1873) may be discussed as the archetypes not only of Victorian railway architecture and engineering but of Victorian structure in general.

The train shed is a masterpiece of daring function. Its engineer was William Henry Barlow (1812–1902), associating with R. M. Ordish who was then the leading man on cast-iron structure and was to design not only the Albert Bridge but the iron dome of the Albert Hall. Their aim at St Pancras was to avoid all columns which might cause catastrophic accidents, and so they built one enormous arch of iron framework, filled with glass, and having a pointed crown. It spanned no less than 243 feet, rose up one hundred feet, and was seven hundred feet long. An additional advantage of the clear space was that the railway lines through the arch could be rearranged as convenience demanded at any time. Below the platforms a lower floor was built, mainly for Burton beer storage, and here columns and girders were used, the module, or unit of measurement, being the length of a beer barrel. Hydraulic lifts ran between the platforms and the store. The train shed is an outstanding work which happily, and for the moment, survives.

Connected to the shed on the south, the fabulous hotel, the work of that clergyman's son, George Gilbert Scott (1811–78), pointed its Wagnerian pinnacles to the sky in a way which must have appealed to Doré. In fact Doré's frontispiece to *London* depicts the distant skyline of the great city which young Dick Whittington (no cat in sight) is approaching, and it looks remarkably like that of St Pancras Station Hotel; Doré was, in fact, in London at the time the hotel was nearing completion. Scott's building is merely stuck on to the train shed without any visual relationship or graduation. To the Victorians this did not seem in the least odd and the complex may thus be seen as a symbol of that Victorian schizophrenia which could so completely and artificially divorce engineering and architecture. To the Victorians the train shed was a functional, if impressive, structure without any great aesthetic merit; the hotel, on the other hand, was Architecture – that is, a piece of eclecticism created by a member of a learned profession who understood his period details, and who was, above all, a purveyor of style and ornament applied to solid load-bearing walls in which holes for doors and windows are cut.

Dick Whittington on his journey to London – the frontispiece of Doré's *London*. Compare the distant silhouette with St Pancras Station Hotel on page 196.

Scott was the leading architect of his time with a huge practice, a pushing character of monumental self-esteem, not over-sensitive to the niceties of professional etiquette. He cannot be regarded as one of the great architects but he was competent and the most important and prolific one of his generation, who has left his forceful mark not only on London but all over the country. (His office in the end produced about one thousand buildings and restorations, nearly half of them churches.) In the Battle of the Styles he was a passionate Goth and an admirer of Pugin. His competition design for the Foreign Office was Gothic, but eventually, through the insistence of Lord Palmerston, he swallowed his principles and, after much strange manoeuvering since the commission was a large and profitable one, he designed the Italian palazzo building which, though now under threat of demolition, still stands. (Palmerston was certainly right because a Gothic design in the Whitehall district would have been visually out of key with its neighbours.)

The St Pancras Hotel commission was also won in competition – one limited to eleven selected architects – and typically Scott gave his design two extra storeys not included in the conditions. Although it is difficult to judge the extent to which a design can be attributed to a chief architect or to his gifted assistants in a practice of the size built up by Scott, St Pancras was undoubtedly his personal creation wherein he was able to give full rein to that enthusiasm for the Gothic which he had been compelled to repress at the Foreign Office. It is a curious kind of Gothic; in Sir Nikolaus Pevsner's description it is 'High-Victorian-Franco-Early-English'.

As Jack Simmons reveals in his excellent monograph, *St Pancras Station*, the construction was a huge and costly enterprise involving formidable problems. For one thing intricate tunnelling connections had to be made with the new Metropolitan Underground Railway, and while construction was under way in 1866 cholera was raging in the area. The same year a financial crisis occurred in the City when the discounting house of Overend & Gurney failed, and Bank Rate rose to ten per cent. Midland Railway shareholders repeatedly demanded that the costly hotel scheme be abandoned. The site was also a difficult one, occupied by a canal, a gas works, an old church with a crowded graveyard, and a confusion of dilapidated dwellings, while through the whole ran the Fleet River as a large underground sewer.

As usual the slum dwellers were evicted without compensation or offers of alternative accommodation. The skeletons from the graveyards received better treatment, for they were found new accommodation under the supervision of the Bishop of London and the Medical Officer for Health for the Parish of St Pancras. (Arthur Bloom-

Overleaf, the train shed of St Pancras Station by Barlow and Ordish with its splendid single span of 243 feet (*Building News*, 1869).

field, then a rising young architect, was appointed to supervise the nauseating proceedings of removing the piled and rotting coffins, and the young assistant he sent to keep an eye on them was none other than the future poet and novelist Thomas Hardy.)

But the building was finally accomplished, in Scott's own complacent opinion, as 'possibly too good for the purpose it is to serve'. What are we to make of the hotel today? Much controversy has been aroused by the threat of its demolition but although an object of derision forty years ago, general opinion has now decided firmly on preservation. The hotel, with the station, is a perfect combined example of its period and should be preserved, whatever the financial and mercantile pressures, on that count alone, in all its self-confident grandeur of scale. (On the sixth floor the central corridor of the hotel is twelve feet wide.) The train shed even impressed the pompous Mr Bultitude in *Vice-Versa*, for it gave him 'an altogether novel sensation of utter insignificance upon that immense brown plain of platform and under the huge span of the arches whose girders were lost in wreaths of mingled fog and smoke'.

From its inception, St Pancras Hotel has been both derided and lauded. The *Quarterly Review* of 1872 called it 'a monument of confectionery covered inside and out with ornament . . . and there is polished marble enough to furnish a cathedral. The very parapet of the cab road is panelled and perforated, at a cost that would have supplied foot-warmers to all trains for years to come'. It proposed that to be consistent the Midland Railway should dress its porters 'as javelin men, their guards as beefeaters, and their station-masters don the picturesque attire of Garter-King-at-Arms'. The anonymous critic, presumed by Scott to be a former articled pupil of his with whom he had fallen out, found the King's Cross terminus of the Great Northern close by to be, by contrast, 'simple, characteristic and true'. Yet in its obituary notice of Scott in 1878 *The Times* declared St Pancras to be 'the most beautiful terminus in London, remarkable alike in its convenience and its inspiring effect'.

Today one of the more sensitive London guidebooks (David Piper's) praises this 'great Gothic phantasmagoria . . . high as a cliff crowned with pinnacles like a castle in a Grimm's fairy-story', for its value to the London skyline, 'even more so as the rigour of concrete and glass envelops more and more of London'. Who would now disagree with him? 'There is no other building in London anywhere else that embodies more precisely the achievement of mid-Victorian Britain', Professor Simmons concludes soundly in his book. 'To remove it would be to impoverish not merely a street but a whole quarter of London.'

The main streets of central London and the City became ever more densely crowded as the years passed and by the sixties this density reached crisis proportions, particularly in and around the City itself at commuting hours. Doré was aware of this and devoted three of his drawings in *London* to traffic jams, notably the one called 'A City Thoroughfare' which shows hansom cabs, drays, horse buses, a coal cart, a waggon-load of firemen and milling pedestrians in an immovable tangle which a harassed policeman is trying, without visible hope of success, to untie.

Most people walked to and from their work, at least until the cheap workmen's fares became general on the railways, for a bus fare from a suburb like Islington to the City could cost sixpence ($2\frac{1}{2}$p) and for an unskilled labourer earning an average wage of one pound a week travelling by bus was prohibitive. Thus twice a day all the main arteries into the metropolis were thronged with pedestrians, particularly on the toll-free bridges. Even in the early years of Victoria's reign one hundred thousand pedestrians crossed London Bridge each day, and this traffic increased rapidly during the fifties, when not only pedestrians but seventeen hundred vehicles crossed the bridge at rush hours. Henry Mayhew recorded that in the sixties in the London streets one could 'walk over the roofs of vans and buses as readily as over the united up-raised shields of the Roman soldiers outside the walls of some beleaguered city'. In the early decades of the reign many people rode through the streets on horseback, but by the eighties equestrians were rarely seen.

For wealthier folk the four-wheeled hackney carriage, commonly called the crawler or growler, which seated four people, was available, but for speed one hired a hansom cab which seated only two. The hansom, romantically termed the gondola of London but officially known as the patent safety cab, was a modification of the cabriolet. It was invented by Joseph Aloysius Hansom (1803–82), a Yorkshireman and an ardent Roman Catholic, who became an architect and founded *The Builder* magazine in 1842. He accomplished little architectural work in London apart from the spire of the Catholic church at Brook Green, Hammersmith, but for Birmingham he designed the Town Hall, and there are buildings by him at Leicester and Manchester. He patented his cab invention in 1836 and later sold his rights to a company for £10,000 which, apparently, he never received. The design of the cab was revised from time to time but in principle it ran on two large wheels, the driver being perched up behind and the passengers being seated in a snug cabin below with a clear, open view in front of them over the horse's back, and their knees enclosed behind a pair of doors; in this way weights were evenly distributed on the

'A City Thoroughfare' (Doré).

A block in Park Lane. The driving of livestock through the streets increased traffic congestion in Victorian London
until in 1867 this was prohibited by statute between the hours of 10 a.m. and 7 p.m. (*I.L.N.*, 1864).

axle and did not bear down on the horse. Passengers could communicate with the driver through a trap door in the roof, as Doré shows in one of his small sketches. The cab was speedy and safe, affording a pleasant journey with a jingling style and dash, so it was highly popular and lasted well into the twentieth century. Having been born in 1910, the author can himself recall an authentic whiff of Victorian London: the rich ammonia smell in the courtyard of East Putney Station where hansom cabs were lined in a row on the cobbles waiting to clatter city gents home to their suburban nooks at twilight. A few, however, even ran in the West End between the wars for the pleasure of gay young couples. Its ever-growing popularity in Victorian London can be gauged by some statistics: of licensed carriages plying in London in 1871, 4,523 were four-wheelers and 3,295 were hansoms, but by 1896 only 3,449 were four-wheelers, whereas 7,585 were hansoms, even though their charges were higher.

Growlers were often dilapidated affairs driven by surly coachmen in top hats and layers of capes, but the hansom cab drivers were often dandily dressed with jaunty billycock hats and smart check coats enriched with buttonhole flowers – men proud of their vehicles who kept the brasswork shining and the coats of their horses gleaming. Hired carriages and their horses were usually housed in the poorer districts of the inner suburbs, and there in the stables a goat would often be seen, for it was believed to offer some kind of mysterious prophylactic against glanders, a highly contagious disease among horses.

Towards the end of Victoria's reign private hansoms were sometimes favoured by men-about-town and by doctors, but the usual types of private vehicles for the carriage folk were broughams, landaus and victorias. (The electric brougham did not appear in the London streets until 1897.) Adding immensely to the traffic, too, were vans running between the railway termini (generators of more traffic than any other buildings), as well as the country waggons converging daily on Covent Garden Market with fruit and vegetables and returning with horse manure collected from the stable yards. Since no foreign meat was imported, at least until the eighties, because no means of preserving it yet existed, droves of sheep, cattle and pigs would clatter along the streets at all hours of the day to the meat markets of Smithfield and Islington, an invasion mostly concentrated into two days of the week. Cattle trains reduced this nuisance only to a limited extent,

Above, 'Inside a London omnibus', engraved from a painting by W. M. Egley (*I.L.N.*, 1859).

Overleaf, 'London Bridge at Noonday' (*I.L.N.*, 1872).

George Train's street railway at Marble Arch at the end of the Bayswater Line (*I.L.N.*, 1861).

and so in 1867 a statute was passed prohibiting the driving of livestock through London thoroughfares between ten a.m. and seven p.m. In the streets, too, would run coal carts, drays, bakers' barrows, two-wheeled milk trucks, hawkers' barrows, and now and then a wagonnette filled with children on an outing, or a fire-engine in flying career. After 1886 an occasional new safety bicycle, chain driven and with two wheels of equal size, which had replaced the awkward penny-farthings, would roll by.

Brightly coloured horse-buses, first introduced from Paris by Shillibeer in 1829, plied their regular routes throughout the whole of Victoria's reign, both in the centre and to and from the suburbs. The earlier models could accommodate twelve passengers inside and ten more on the roof sitting back to back against a so-called knife-board, the ascent being gained by an iron ladder or by projecting steps; the conductor, known as a cad, stood on a board at the rear and held on by a strap. Straw covered the floor within to keep feet warm in cold weather. By 1855 over eight hundred such buses were running in the London streets. Generally drawn by a pair of horses, they travelled at an average speed of five miles an hour. By 1867 an estimated 41,500,000 passengers a year were carried on horse-buses.

In 1881 an entirely new type of bus appeared, drawn by three horses. Behind the driver's seat a pair of stairs rose to a landing and thence in a single flight to the roof, below which the conductor could stand protected from the rain. About two years later, transverse garden seats were introduced, while a spiral stair replaced the double approach. These new buses became popular because now at last women could enjoy a ride in the fresh air without affronting the proprieties. But the knife-board type still appears in photographs taken around 1900.

Another kind of bus was run by the Metropolitan Railway between terminal stations. Drawn by three horses abreast and, for a time, divided both inside and out into first- and second-class sections, these huge contraptions could carry forty-two people. A great and glorious red umbrella protected the driver and his surrounding passengers from rain and sun.

In 1861 the first horse-drawn tram was introduced along the Bayswater Road for a mile between Marble Arch and Notting Hill Gate, and soon afterwards between Westminster Abbey and Victoria Station. These were due to the enterprise of an ebullient American, George Francis Train, who had been encouraged to come to the metropolis after his success at Birkenhead with his People's Carriage, as he called his tram. Each car, pulled by a pair of horses, could accommodate twenty sitting and twelve standing inside, and some cars carried roof passengers protected by an awning. Train attempted to extend his rails but came up against strong opposition from the Metropolis Road Commissioners who objected to the rigidity of their course and the inconvenience they caused to other traffic. So his ventures in England came to an end, to Train's abiding disgust with the whole darned island and its inhabitants.

Then the Tramways Act was passed in 1870 and a tramway system developed rapidly. In 1875 various new companies had laid down some fifty-four miles of track and between them owned 350 cars and some fifteen hundred horses. Trams, in fact, became an important part of London's traffic and were popular on account of their speed, smooth ride, and commodious accommodation. By 1878 horse-trams were carrying well over fifty-three million passengers a year. (The curious word 'tram' is sometimes traced to Benjamin Outram, founder of the Butterley Ironworks and first engineer to lay down an iron way – and father of General Sir James Outram, hero of the Indian Mutiny – but the *Oxford English Dictionary* gives it a longer lineage in jargons of mining and weaving.)

Trams added further to the congestion of the street. Even the arrival of the underground railways had done far less than had been expected to reduce street traffic, and by the close of the sixties, while the Metropolitan Railway was carrying twenty-five million passengers a year, the London General Omnibus Company was still carrying forty million. Horse-drawn traffic continued to grow throughout the century, for despite the railways and apart from passenger transport by far the major part of retail distribution was carried out by carting within a ten-mile radius of the centre. At the same time the horse-buses and trams gained passengers faster than the railways during the last quarter of the century, helped, no doubt, by the fall in price of fodder brought by cheap imports from the prairies. By 1891 those employed in horse-drawn transport in London were three times the number of those working on the Metropolitan Railway.

All this horse traffic generated a good deal of filth in the streets in wet weather for some six tons of dung are dropped by a single horse in a year. This explains why we hear so often of shoe-blacks and crossing-sweepers in Victorian London. The din in the streets was often nerve-shattering, for wheels as well as hooves were shod with iron and many roads were cobbled with granite setts; hence the common practice of laying down straw across a street to deaden the noise before a house where someone lay ill.

The idea for an underground railway to relieve road congestion at the centre and between the main-line termini was first proposed in 1837 by Charles Pearson, the City Solicitor and a man of vision. As Mayhew records in *The Shops and Companies of London* (1865): 'We knew him

well, and while discussing our joint schemes for the utilisation of convict labour, have often smiled at the earnestness with which he advocated his project for girdling London round with one long drain-like tunnel, and sending people like so many parcels in a pneumatic tube, from one end of the metropolis to the other.' Pearson spent thousands of pounds from his own pocket in propagating the scheme but the public only laughed at the idea of a railroad among the sewers. Yet in the end the idea was realized, the first of its kind in the world. To us it seems mundane; to the Victorians it was a wonder.

The chief engineers were the ambitious, avaricious but brilliant John Fowler (1817-98), and the young Benjamin Baker (1840-1907). Both men were eventually to be knighted after they had accomplished the construction of the Forth Railway Bridge. The first line of the Metropolitan Railway was opened in 1863 with a broad gauge between Farringdon Street and Bishop's Road, Paddington, and it ran below Farringdon Road, King's Cross Road, Marylebone Road and Praed Street, so linking the edge of the City with three termini (St Pancras was not yet built and Marylebone did not appear until the nineties). Here the Great Western Railway ran steam trains every fifteen minutes, the venture becoming at once highly popular despite the smoke and sulphurous stench. It had been built in two and a half years, a remarkable achievement considering the amount of digging involved, the complications of diverting sewers and gas and water mains, and the serious delay caused when the Fleet Ditch sewer burst its side and flooded the workings as far as King's Cross.

Fowler's first plan had been to run trains on compressed air generated at each end of the line. This was a kind of traction which had a number of advantages later achieved by electric trains. Brunel had experimented with the method, which he called 'atmospheric traction', by means of which suction was created in a vacuum tube running between the rails, the exhaust power being supplied by stationary engines situated at intervals along the line. In 1861 the Pneumatic Despatch Company had opened an experimental cast-iron tube a quarter of a mile long near Chelsea Bridge for carrying letters and parcels, and it appeared to work well, conveying the carriages, fringed with rubber flanges fitting fairly tightly against the tube, at twenty-five miles an hour by air suction. Two years later the company built a thirty-inch-gauge line worked on the system for conveying parcels from Euston Station to the North-Western Post Office in Eversholt Street and soon they extended the line to Holborn. It was not in use for long and the tube was eventually applied to another purpose – that of carrying telephone wires. A similar kind of railway passing through a tunnel six hundred

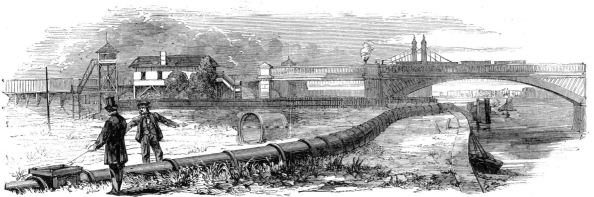

THE PNEUMATIC LETTER AND PARCEL CONVEYANCE : THE DESPATCH-TUBE AT BATTERSEA.

Atmospheric railways run by vacuum power: *left, top to bottom*, the letter and parcel conveyance tube at Battersea of the Pneumatic Despatch Company; the disc in the engine house; the mouth of the tube and carriage (*I.L.N.*, 1861). *Right*, the carriage with its suction fringe that ran through a tunnel between the high- and low-level stations in the Sydenham Crystal Palace grounds (*I.L.N.*, 1864).

SECTION OF DISC IN THE ENGINE-HOUSE.

THE MOUTH OF THE TUBE, AND CARRIAGE.

yards long and conveying passengers in an ordinary railway carriage was erected in the Crystal Palace grounds in 1864 to link the low- and high-level stations. In the end, in spite of all the experiments, the pneumatic railway never really took; air leakage seems to have been the problem, one cause of this being the rats, who improved their diet by chewing away the leather valving.

The idea of using atmospheric traction on the Metropolitan was therefore abandoned and the old steam propulsion was applied. To reduce the smoke nuisance in the tunnels a cut-and-cover system was constructed, the spoil being conveyed to the Chelsea football ground at Stamford Bridge to form the terraces there. The ditches and tunnels were wide enough to take both the standard trucks and the broad gauge, seven feet wide, as originally laid on Brunel's Great Western Railway.

The Metropolitan Railway, soon to be rapidly extended, was yet another of the vast construction works the Victorians accomplished in London, and it impressed the public. The original line was opened in January 1863, when Mr Gladstone and other celebrities travelled through the tunnels in open trucks, to end their journey with a great banquet held in Farringdon Street Station. (The scene is depicted on page 57.)

The general public took to this new means of transport at once; nearly ten million people travelled on the line the first year and twelve million the next. Soon the line was extended west to Hammersmith and east to Moorgate Street and Liverpool Street, and in 1876 to Bishopsgate and Aldgate. It also eventually extended a number of spurs – to St John's Wood, for example, and thence right out to Buckinghamshire into what became known as Metroland. In 1880 a line reached Harrow-on-the-Hill. Thus whole new middle-class suburbs came into being.

The Metropolitan District Railway, as opposed to the plain Metropolitan Railway, began building its lines to

fittings and allocation of space. Being illuminated either by gas jets or oil lamps which merely increased the smoky gloom and rendered the darkness visible, a charming improvisation was provided by the passengers themselves in the form of candles burning on the window ledges to give enough light for reading. Curiously, the Metropolitan established a no-smoking rule in all its carriages. Both the Metro and the District were electrified in 1905, and on 22 September of that year the last steam passenger train puffed round the Inner Circle.

The Underground, like the Embankment, was among the dreams that became realities, but in times of great

'Workmen's train, early morning, on the Metropolitan Railway' (Doré).

serve the inhabitants of west London by connecting them to the City, and so they created the Twin Line system. Its first section was opened in 1868 between Kensington High Street and Westminster, and for two years ran with Metropolitan stock. Meanwhile it extended its line below Victoria Embankment to Blackfriars while the Victoria Embankment was under construction. Eventually the two lines of the Metropolitan and the District were joined to form the Inner Circle which came into operation in 1884. By that time the District had extended west to Earl's Court and Hammersmith and was soon to send out further lines, in the open, to Putney and Wimbledon, Richmond, Ealing, and Willesden to the west and to East Ham, Barking and Upminster to the east.

The original passenger coaches of the Metropolitan were divided into three classes, each with its appropriate

enterprise, many great schemes for improving communications remain proposals only. Among them two in particular deserve recall: Sir Joseph Paxton's Grand Girdle Railway and Boulevard, and William Moseley's Crystal Way. Both were among the ideas submitted to the Select Committee on Metropolitan Communications which deliberated in the year 1855.

In his evidence Paxton revealed that more time was then needed to travel from the London and Brighton Station at London Bridge to the Great Western Station at Paddington than from London Bridge to Brighton. He therefore proposed the construction of a covered way ten miles long which would unite all the railways and encircle the centre of the metropolis, crossing the river at Westminster and Southwark and extending a branch from Piccadilly Circus to the south of the river. In form it

The Underground Railway at Blackfriars with *The Times* office and St Paul's in the background (*Graphic*, 1875). The scene must be partly imaginary.

would be a large arcade of glass and iron, 72 feet wide and 108 feet high, flanked by two tiers of railways run on the atmospheric principle on eight tracks, four for express trains, the tracks being separated from the arcade by double walls. The structure would possess the character of the Crystal Palace but would be lined with Stafford-shire tiles that could be easily washed clean. Near the terminal stations the Girdle would be lined with hotels, in the City with offices, and from the City to Regent Street with shops, but when it reached South Kensington it could be lined with residences and where it ran across Kensington Gardens it would form a wide promenade without any buildings, where people could take their exercise under cover in bad weather on foot or horse.

'I should propose,' Paxton declared, 'a side elevation on both sides fronting Hyde Park and also fronting Kensington Gardens which would form what I consider a beautiful object.' On the approaches to the Park, he explained, houses would be built where the wealthy, the elderly and the infirm could live in a kind of glass Riviera, and so 'would not be obliged to go to foreign countries in the winter'. As one who had successfully cultivated the Great Lily at Chatsworth in the special conservatory he built there, Paxton would no doubt have been well able to design properly conditioned ventilation for the arcade. Its whole length was to be open to carts and carriages of every kind for the carrying of coal and merchandise up to nine o'clock in the morning; after nine only horse-buses and passenger carriages would be allowed to use it. When asked if his project would make London as popular to tourists as the boulevards of Paris, Paxton replied: 'The Girdle would be the greatest novelty in the world and the

75

tourist trade would help to pay for it.' (No one raised the question of noise.)

Here was yet another bold conception of a remarkable personality – Member of Parliament, man of affairs to the Duke of Devonshire, designer of the Crystal Palace and of the Great Stove at Chatsworth – whom Queen Victoria had called 'only a gardener's boy'. His Girdle was the kind of bold project that appealed enormously to the Victorians; the Prince Consort gave it his approval and the Chairman of the Select Committee specially recommended it to the House of Commons. It is a pity it was not accomplished for it could have solved many traffic problems and be serving us usefully still.

Unfortunately Paxton only submitted a plan of the Girdle to the Committee and so we do not know how it would have looked, but an approximate idea can be gained by the cross-sectional drawing of the Crystal Way scheme submitted to the Committee by William Moseley which is reproduced here. This was to run in a dead straight line for nearly three miles between the end of Cheapside in the east to Oxford Circus (then called Regent Circus) in the west, with a fork from Queen Street in the Seven Dials district running down south-west to Piccadilly Circus (then also called, confusingly, Regent Circus). The width of the Crystal Way was only thirty feet and its height seventy-eight feet. Two railway lines, not connected with any others, ran below the Way, using

atmospheric power and taking trains which would run without stopping from one end of the Way to the other in five minutes. On the upper level ran a promenade or Superway covered with a glass roof and having shops on either side.

The ingenious point of this design was that the line could cross existing streets without disturbing them, the new railway tracks running below them and the Superway above. Here is an early example of a modern idea in urban design called Vertical Segregation, or the V-Solution.

But what of the realities of London's street-side fabric as it existed, changed, and expanded during those volatile years between 1850 and 1890?

Left, Sir Joseph Paxton. *Below*, Paxton's 'Great Victorian Way or Grand Girdle Railway and Boulevard under Glass'. *Right*, William Moseley's projected 'Crystal Way'. Both projects were presented to the Select Committee on Metropolitan Communications in 1855.

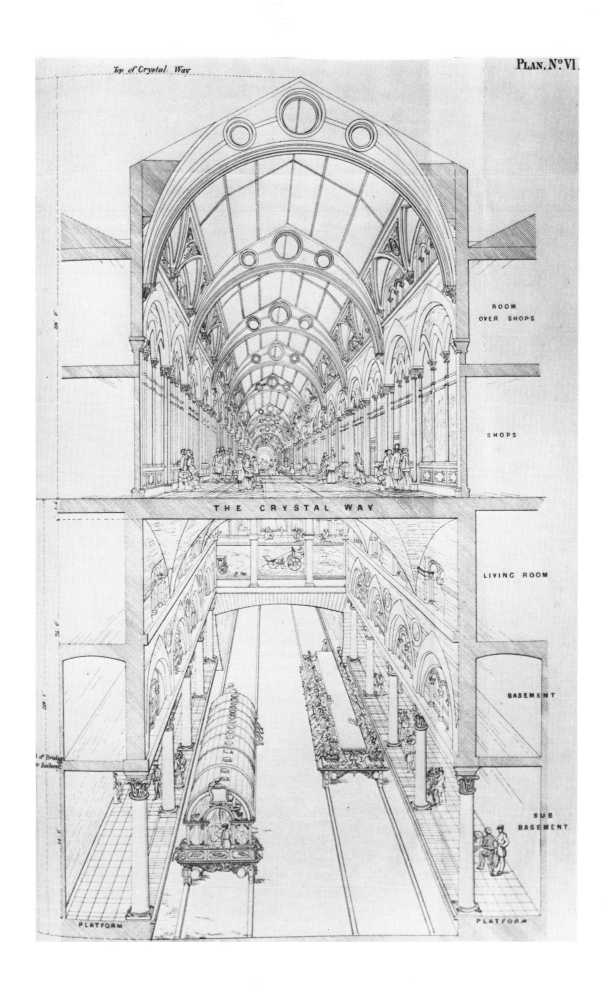

Top of Crystal Way

ROOM
OVER SHOPS

SHOPS

THE CRYSTAL WAY

LIVING ROOM

BASEMENT

SUB
BASEMENT

PLATFORM

PLATFORM

The Changing Scene

Even superficially, how different it is to Paris! The immense town, for ever bustling by night and by day, as vast as an ocean, the screech and howl of machinery, the railways built above the houses (and soon to be built below them), the daring of enterprise, the apparent disorder which in actual fact is the highest form of bourgeois order, the polluted Thames, the coal-saturated air, the magnificent squares and parks, the town's terrifying districts such as Whitechapel with its half-naked, savage and hungry population, the City with its millions and its world-wide trade, the Crystal Palace, the World Exhibition. The Exhibition is indeed amazing. . . . It is a Biblical sight, something to do with Babylon, some prophecy out of the Apocalypse being fulfilled before your very eyes.

F. DOSTOIEVSKY, *Winter Thoughts on Summer Impressions* (1863)

Detail of a familiar London landmark: the giant jewel of the Albert Memorial by Sir George Gilbert Scott completed in 1872, the year Doré's *London* was published.

London buildings, it seems to us now, were still calmly Georgian in character, still unified by the classic idiom, in the year of the first Great Exhibition. (For the Crystal Palace itself, see the chapter on Pleasures.) Though Victoria had been on the throne for fourteen years, the tone was still set by the Metropolitan Improvements of George IV of the twenties.

Battersea, Fulham, Earl's Court, Hammersmith, Kilburn, Hampstead, Highgate, Upper Holloway, Islington, Homerton, Stoke Newington, Hackney, Bow and Bromley, Old Ford, Plumstead, Woolwich, Tooting and Streatham were still rural parishes surrounded by fields and market gardens. Even Kensington retained the character of a self-contained village, Westbourne Grove was a country lane, and free-ranging hens might still end their lives under a carriage wheel as they scuttled across the King's Road, Chelsea.

Out in the suburbs to the west in 1851, beyond the Gravel Pits at Notting Hill Gate, the racing track called the Hippodrome had just ended a brief existence, and where the Grand Stand had stood on the top of the hill on Ladbroke Grove a Gothic Revival church had been built. It served the owners of the new middle-class houses here, which were terraced around gardens in squares and crescents of a debased classic style of stuccoed brick with basement areas and ironwork balconies. Many of these houses were, in fact, still under construction. The whole area is typically early Victorian, not least in its concern

that while houses could still be classic, a church must be medieval; Pugin had spoken. The whole district represents the better sort of Victorian speculation, for it preserved the tradition of the great London land-owners with wide, tree-filled spaces for ventilation, perambulation, and visual pleasure. To the east were added the classic domesticity of the Pembridge Road area and Westbourne Grove beyond it, to the south Holland Park, as final phases of a great urban tradition.

A far more extensive district of speculative housing of the same tradition was still not quite finished in the fifties. It covered land leased from the Duke of Westminster in the districts called Belgravia and Pimlico, and was built by the enterprising contractor Thomas Cubitt (brother of Lewis Cubitt, who designed King's Cross Station). The area stretched almost from the south side of Hyde Park right down to the river, across the marshes of Neat House Gardens to the east of Chelsea Waterworks and the Grosvenor Canal, most of which was soon to be filled in for the building of Victoria Station. Pimlico was less exclusive than Belgravia and lost further caste when Victoria Station and its lines were built and separated the two areas firmly from each other. While Pimlico in this century became somewhat seedy, Belgravia remains today a wealthy area with the splendour of Belgrave Square as its climax on the north, its grander houses designed by George Basevi, a cousin of Disraeli; there today the cars of diplomats cluster thickly. Although they lack the refinement of the Georgian squares and the poetic verve of Nash's works, Cubitt's prosy but solid terrace houses, stuccoed in classical style, form a pleasant link between Georgian and Victorian London; Belgravia and Pimlico, in fact, were among the last of those areas planned round leafy squares, that urban idea developed on the properties of the aristocratic land-owners mostly in the eighteenth century, but originating in the seventeenth century in Covent Garden. 'The great and peculiar beauty of London', Von Raumer called the squares in 1835. They gave to the west of London, and a few other districts like Islington, that semblance of order still to some degree retained in spite of degradations (degradations now taken to the depths of subterranean garages). Belgravia and Pimlico, in fact, were the last major planned development in central London until the new Barbican scheme of Chamberlin, Powell and Bon.

In 1851 Belgravia was not quite complete. The long rectangle of Eaton Square, through the gardens of which the eastern end of King's Road runs, was not ready for full occupation until 1853. (Its name, incidentally, derives from Eaton Hall, Cheshire, the chief country seat of the Grosvenor family, while Belgrave was a village in Leicestershire where the Marquis of Westminster owned much property. The curious word Pimlico is believed to be that of a drink whose composition is no longer known, one which was perhaps served in some garden of refreshment by the riverside there.)

Thomas Cubitt built a good deal on another estate, that of northern Bloomsbury, which belonged to the Duke of Bedford. The area had begun in 1776 with Bedford Square but the whole was not completed until 1860 when Gordon Square was finished. The Duke held two other estates in London: Covent Garden and Fig's Mead. Both Bloomsbury and Fig's Mead were badly affected by the three neighbouring termini of Euston, St Pancras, and King's Cross. Fig's Mead to their north, or Bedford New Town as it came to be called, was particularly badly disrupted. An unusual and late development by the Bedford Estate, and not by Cubitt, it was built, unlike most of its kind, as a model suburb for the lower middle and artisan classes. Development had begun in the 1830s but rapid and sudden changes had to be made in 1834 with the arrival of the London and Birmingham Line. By 1851, 359 houses had been erected and only 49 remained to be completed. Including Ampthill, Harrington and Oakley Squares, it was an admirable conception – and much of it remains today in a somewhat melancholy state of decay.

Through the centre of the West End ran Nash's Via Triumphalis which had been completed in the second decade of the century. By 1851 it had lost its charming arcades on the curves of the Quadrant above Piccadilly Circus (then called Regent Circus). These had been pulled down in 1848 to admit more light into the shops and to discourage street-walkers, who found the covered promenade with its lurking corners a convenience. This, the most monumental work of town planning that London possesses, ran from the Mall and the Duke of York's Column up Regent Street, through the two circuses of Piccadilly and Oxford Street, up Portland Place, already lined with Adam houses, to Park Crescent and Regent's Park, soon to be fringed with its theatrical terraces. The spine, with its peculiarly English mixture of the monumental and the picturesque, combined with the large aristocrats' estates, with their low densities, open spaces and high standards of domestic architecture, helped to give the metropolis some planning form. To these were added in the Victorian years after 1851 Bazalgette's drains and embankments, a number of new broad thoroughfares such as Queen Victoria Street, Holborn Viaduct, Rosebery Avenue, Northumberland Avenue, Shaftesbury Avenue and Charing Cross Road. Central London by the end of Victoria's reign was therefore not completely chaotic.

A penetrating recent comment by Donald Olsen in his *London* is this:

The ordinary Londoner is certain that his is an unplanned city. For many it is a source of pride to reflect on the haphazard nature of London, which seems a concrete symbol of English pragmatism. . . . Depending on one's point of view, London can serve as an object lesson of the deplorable results when planning and foresight are not used, or of the happy result of natural organic adaptation to historical change.

The planning that has in fact taken place is not the kind that immediately impresses itself upon the beholder. . . . Occasional pockets of aesthetic delight burst upon the observer as happy accidents, scattered haphazardly about as if to compensate for the general visual squalor. But good planning can be found by those who know where to look.

Those who accuse London of having no planning at all usually contrast it with Paris. Actually London and Paris are both planned, but their plans differ completely in aim and character. London is a collection of autonomous villages, many of which have been carefully planned within themselves but with little reference to the adjoining villages. Paris is a dense forest that grew up initially with no plan whatsoever, through which a system of magnificent avenues has been cut . . . the main thoroughfares of London, unlike the boulevards in Paris, are almost invariably ugly; to see good architecture and good planning one must go behind them.

Thus the best of central London in Victorian times, as indeed it still is in spite of debasement, was to a considerable extent of Georgian origin and due partly to the Metropolitan Improvements of the 1820s but mainly to the careful local developments of the great leasehold estates such as the Westminster, Portland, Portman, Bedford and Northampton Estates and that of the Foundling

'Bishopsgate Street' (Doré).

Overleaf, looking up-river over the Vauxhall and Chelsea bridges (*I.L.N.*, 1859). 5. South Kensington Museum ('Brompton Boilers'). 13. Cremorne Gardens. 15. Battersea Bridge. 16. Battersea Park. 22. Military School. 23. St Barnabas Church. 26. West-end Railway Station. 27. Lambeth Waterworks. 32. Military Clothing Store. 39. Price's Patent Candle Works. 42. South-Western Railway Station, Nine Elms. 44. Vauxhall Gardens.

Hospital. It was to the advantage of the big land-owners, who usually let their land on ninety-nine-year leases, to see that their developments were orderly and attractive; they were educated men, moreover, and were often personally interested in the visual arts, unlike those who followed them in exploiting land as London exploded. 'No governmental authority, even today,' Olsen writes, 'has anything like the control over architecture, street plans, or zoning that the Bedford, Portland or Portman estate offices had in the nineteenth century.' Why, in that case, he asks, is not London an earthly paradise instead of the lovable mess it is? The answer is that London has had too many little plans and no overall co-ordination, least of all in Victorian times.

The Victorians, with all their confused and romantic ideas on visual design, despised Georgian architecture. They liked to pick on Gower Street (certainly not the best example) as representing the nadir of gloomy boredom and dull uniformity – 'the *ne plus ultra* of ugliness', Ruskin called it. But it was not only the lack of stylistic cohesion that brought chaos to large areas of London as it expanded from its centre and spread across the green interstices between the villages. It was chiefly the result of small-scale and unco-ordinated free enterprise.

The railways did not improve the situation, as we have already seen. Small-scale speculation in housing, sometimes involving only a street or two, added to the chaos. The new middle-class developers wanted quick profits, unlike the big land-owners with their great inherited wealth who could take a longer, saner and more civilized attitude to speculation. This point is borne out by H. J. Dyos's study of Camberwell, comparing the large estate of Dulwich College (Alleyn's College of God's Gift) which became a spacious, upper-class suburb during the Victorian era (and still seems so as 'the Hampstead of the South'), with the small properties to its north, some of which declined from meadowland to slumdom in a single generation as products of overcrowding and the *laissez-faire* philosophy. This is a typical example of how the outlook of an age and the social economy it generates affect the urban environment. As Olsen wisely says:

The whole complex of techniques and practices that go into the town planning of any age will depend on the scale of values then held by the landlord and the householder. A secluded, detached suburban villa would have seemed a less desirable residence before the days of gas lighting and the Metropolitan Police than after. Similarly, a style of architecture which emphasized the uniqueness and individuality of each house would have seemed highly improper to most eighteenth-century town dwellers.

By 1890 London no longer possessed the unity of scale, visual coherence, and comprehensibility it had shown in 1850. During those forty years the population of Greater London had expanded from less than two and a half million to more than five million – double the population of Paris. The housing of the poor in the East End and elsewhere was far worse at the end of that period than it had been at the start. The causes of that are clear: uncontrolled exploitation, not least by railways, low wages, inadequate legislation, and the huge influx into the capital from surrounding counties and from abroad. The new situation was unprecedented, unforeseen, and out of hand. In the early fifties, in spite of the heroic efforts of Chadwick, Lord Ashley (later Lord Shaftesbury), Dr Southwood Smith, and a few of their kind on the General Board of Health, organization in the metropolis was negligible. The only true authority in its own area was that of the ancient Square Mile, the City Corporation. Administering the metropolis was confused by the various Commissioners of Sewers (an anachronism bequeathed, mainly for land drainage, by Henry VIII), to say nothing of its myriad district parish councils. The growth of the sprawl around the old core was watched, as it had often been since Tudor times, with a certain amount of fearful astonishment, its management parcelled out among the several distinct and squabbling courts of Commissioners of Sewers, a number of private gas and private water companies, and the various fire services run by private insurance companies, as well as the many parish vestries with their local rivalries.

Sir Benjamin Hall estimated that in 1855 the metropolis was governed by no less than three hundred different authorities. In that year the Metropolitan Board of Works began work, and, though its powers were limited, this was an important first step towards better organization; at least the new authority could deal in a coherent way with the pressing problem of sewage disposal, bridge building, embanking and road construction, while in 1866 it was able to form the Metropolitan Fire Brigade. Yet in the pervading atmosphere of individualism, self-help, and *ad hoc* adaptation, the idea of greater overall planning, even at local level, was unacceptable. (Although the term 'street planning' was first used in 1851, the term 'town planning' did not enter the dictionary until 1906 – a curious fact since the notion that a city needs some form of guiding intelligence in its planning is as old as town building itself.)

Even the big estates of the aristocracy were not able to avoid deterioration and overcrowding in some of their parts, and on their borders slums proliferated. 'From Belgravia to Bloomsbury – from St Pancras to Bayswater – there is hardly a settlement of leading residences that has not its particular colony of ill-housed poor hanging on to its skirts,' wrote John Hollingshead in *Ragged London* in 1861.

To return to our map of 1868: Earl's Court was still a small village surrounded by market gardens, for the Cromwell Road ended at Gloucester Road and continued from there to the west as a track; Courtfield Gardens was a rustic Lovers' Walk; Stoke Newington, Highbury Vale and Hampstead were still distinct villages, and beyond Swiss Cottage the Finchley Road ran through open country.

Yet formidable changes had occurred since 1851. As already recorded, five new railway bridges now crossed the river and three new road bridges were either in use or under construction. Large railway termini with hotels attached had been completed at Paddington, Victoria, Charing Cross and Cannon Street, while at St Pancras the train shed was up and the hotel was being built. A large part of the Metropolitan Underground Railway had been laid, and the District Railway was progressing. The Crystal Palace had been re-erected with considerable additions at Sydenham, two lines now ran there from the centre, and the grand waterworks in its park had been laid out with huge basins and spouting fountains. Other great new structures included Bunning's Holloway Prison and his Metropolitan Cattle Market at Islington, the South Kensington Museum altered and enlarged, E. M. Barry's Royal Opera House at Covent Garden (the third on the site), Coe and Peck's vast Agricultural Hall at Islington, Horace Jones's meat market at Smithfield, Sydney Smirke's Reading Room rotunda in the courtyard of the British Museum, Scott's Foreign Office, Pennethorne's Gothic Record Office in Chancery Lane and his west end of Somerset House, Bazalgette's main drainage scheme and his Albert Embankment, Heywood's Holborn Viaduct and the Victoria and Millwall Docks.

Barry's Houses of Parliament were now finished, a huge number of new churches had been built and consecrated everywhere, twenty-two acres at South Kensington had been laid out as formal gardens by the Royal Horticultural Society and surrounded by exhibition halls and arcades; the Langham Hotel had opened its doors, several new streets had been formed or were forming, including Victoria Street, Queen Victoria Street, Southwark Street, and Burdett Road, Hackney. Nearing completion or under construction were Bazalgette's Victoria and Chelsea Embankments, Miss Burdett-Coutts's Columbia Market and housing, the Albert Hall and Memorial, the University Building in Burlington Gardens by Sir James Pennethorne (alleged stepson of John Nash, and the government's architect, who here erected one of the best façades of Victorian classicism in London; it now shelters the British Museum's ethnographical collection). The Great International Exhibition of 1862 at the south end of the Horticultural Society's Gardens had come and gone.

These constructions alone represent an astonishing achievement for a mere seventeen years, accomplished as they were in the face of recurring strikes in the building trade and what we should call limited technical means. Moreover they were solid works in traditional materials lavishly ornamented with carvings, much of it hand-wrought, and other decorations.

A good deal was also built in the two decades ending in 1890. The Victoria and Chelsea Embankments were completed; the Metropolitan and District lines consider-ably extended their networks and formed the Inner Circle in 1884, so linking most of the main line termini; the railway boom was over but Liverpool Street and Holborn Viaduct Stations were built, Barlow bored his Tower Tunnel under the river, the Royal Albert Docks were opened, Bazalgette erected the Battersea, Putney, and Hammersmith Bridges and Ordish his eccentric Albert Bridge at Chelsea; Rosebery Avenue, Northumberland Avenue, Shaftesbury Avenue, Charing Cross Road, and Great Eastern Street were formed, while Cromwell Road was extended to the west, Meeson's Alexandra Palace had been built at Muswell Hill, destroyed by fire and immediately built again, Billingsgate Fish Market was rebuilt to the design of Horace Jones, the City Architect. Other new large buildings included Jones's Leadenhall Market, Currey's St Thomas's Hospital opposite the Houses of Parliament, Bedborough's Royal Westminster Aquarium (on the site of Central Hall), East London Museum at Bethnal Green (using the iron framework of the Brompton Boilers from South Kensington), the Albert Exhibition buildings of iron and glass at Battersea Park, Waterhouse's vigorous monsters of the Natural History Museum on the site of the 1862 Exhibition in Cromwell Road, his Prudential Assurance Building in Holborn, his St Paul's School in Hammersmith Road, and his National Liberal Club facing the river across Victoria Embank-ment, Street's Law Courts in the Strand (last of the major Gothic Revival buildings, possessing in its great hall one of the noblest interiors in London), Edis's Constitutional Club in Northumberland Avenue, the reconstruction and additions to Burlington House in Piccadilly, Wyatt's new Knightsbridge Barracks, Edmeston's National Agricul-tural Hall with great iron arch in Addison Road, Robson's People's Palace in the Mile End Road, a number of new middle-class flat blocks (including that crude ten-storey pile, Queen Anne's Mansions, Westminster, now demol-ished), Norman Shaw's Albert Hall Mansions at Kensing-ton, Archer and Green's Whitehall Court adjoining the National Liberal Club (assisting that superb yet fortuitous

skyline to be seen from St James's Park), Gribble's Brompton Oratory and Pearson's splendid St Augustine's Church, Kilburn, as well as a number of large hotels.

To these specific lists must be added not only the immense number of new streets and houses in every district but a bewildering and ubiquitous number of public buildings of an anonymous sort: workhouses, hospitals, prisons, asylums, almshouses, public baths, laundries and schools (including a great many for the London School Board after the Forster Act of 1870 had been passed). The sheer quantity of building in London accomplished within little more than a single generation was indeed formidable.

One entirely new type of building was required by the seething, expanding railway-dominated metropolis of Victorian England when the traditional inns and lodgings of the past were no longer capable of accommodating the hordes of travellers who began to arrive by train from the provinces and from abroad: the grand hotel.

St Pancras, when built, was not only the largest but the most impressive of all international Grand Babylons. The Great Western at Paddington, completed in 1852 and designed by P. C. Hardwick of Euston Arch fame, had set the precedent as a great symmetrical block in vaguely French Renaissance style. Then came the ones at the side of King's Cross and Cannon Street, both by E. M. Barry. (A successful architect and son of Sir Charles, he designed the Opera House, the Floral Market of iron set incongruously beside it, Great Ormond Street Hospital for Sick Children, and the Inner Temple Buildings.) With the obvious exception of St Pancras there was a tendency to adopt a French Renaissance manner in these hotels with their pavilion roofs, a manner extended at Victoria in the mansions of Grosvenor Gardens. Other monsters followed.

One was the Langham, built on a fine site at the south end of Portland Place. It looks a drab pile to us with its blackened yellow brickwork and its war amputation, but in the last four decades of the nineteenth century it was the most glamorous and fashionable hotel in London. Its opening in the summer of 1865 was attended by none less than the Prince of Wales, and that set its chaffy tone. It became an international rendezvous, particularly favoured by army officers and visiting Americans, for it was managed for many years by an ex-Colonel of the Con-federate Army who understood the needs and rituals of such clients. The design, the result of a competition won by John Giles, provided three hundred bedrooms, thirty-six sitting-rooms and among other amenities a swimming pool in the basement, a palm court, and an Ambassadors' Audience Room. Among its rarely observed embellish-ments are some lively simian monsters carved in the

Great Victorian hotels.
Top, the Langham,
Portland Place, now used
by the BBC
(*I.L.N.*, 1865). *Below*, the
dining room of St
Pancras (drawing in the
R.I.B.A. library by
T. G. Jackson who worked
in Scott's office).

external stone trim. Ouida the novelist lived here in a luxurious suite for a while, holding court dressed in white satin, and here she was interviewed by Oscar Wilde.

An important and special contribution to Victorian London lay in the developments lying south of Kensington Gore and the Gardens, and extending down to Cromwell Road. Eighty-seven acres had been acquired by the Commissioners of the Great Exhibition of 1851 partly with the profits of £186,000, and there a museum and cultural centre, a kind of *Forum Artis cum Academicum*, was created. The serious and high-minded Prince Consort was its chief promoter, assisted by his zealous henchman Henry Cole, Secretary to the Government Department of Science and Art, and an accomplished designer

in his own right. The Prince may, indeed, be regarded as the instigator of the museum of art and industry as a type, and he was directly responsible for the developments of the district which he called Our Sanctuary but which scoffers dubbed Albertopolis.

Encouraged by the Prince, Cole began making a collection of works of applied art, following the success of the Great Exhibition. These were first displayed at Marlborough House in 1857 as part of the Library and Museum of Manufactures that had originated as the Government School of Design at Somerset House in 1837 to teach 'ornamental' as distinct from 'fine' art. As the collection grew it was moved in 1857 to a special new building on the south-east corner of the Sanctuary, a somewhat

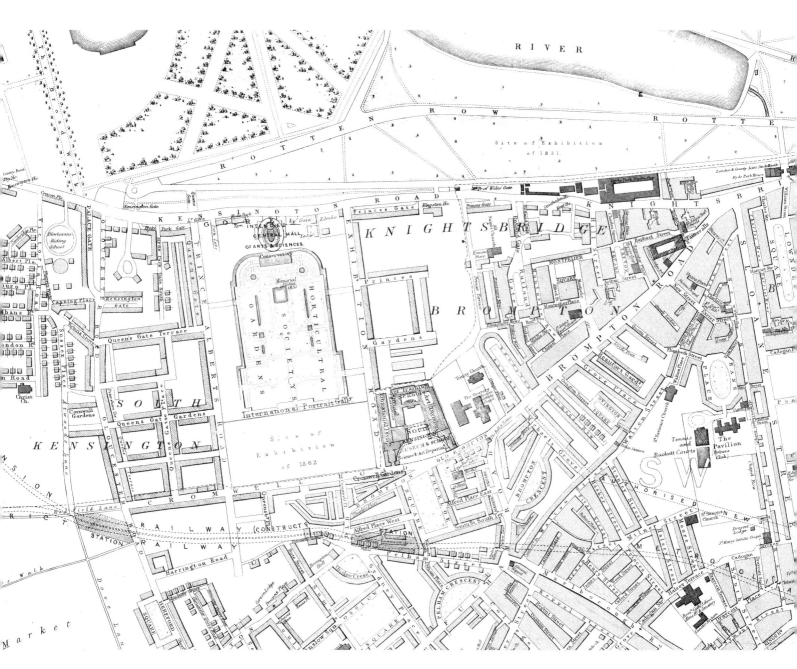

utilitarian affair of iron and glass dubbed by *The Builder* the Brompton Boilers but officially known as the South Kensington Museum. The demountable members of the Boilers having been removed eventually to the East End to form the Bethnal Green branch of the museum, new and more solid structures were erected in its place by stages, to become in 1909 the present Victoria and Albert Museum. Part of the existing building was designed by Francis Fowke, a young captain in the Royal Engineers; he also designed a number of other buildings in the area including the short-lived Exhibition of 1862 and the Albert Hall.

The Royal Horticultural Society's gardens, opened in 1861 on the acres leased from the Commissioners, lay for

surrounding arcades and Crystal Palace-like Winter Garden, under the general direction of Cole, and helped by the architect Godfrey Sykes.

The 1862 Exhibition itself was housed in an enormous new and solid building designed by Captain Fowke to face Cromwell Road (where the Natural History Museum now stands) at the south end of the Horticultural Society's Gardens, his earlier arcading being incorporated in the design. Although it was bigger, the exhibition was far less successful than its predecessor and it made no profit. Both the cotton famine in the north and the sudden death of Prince Albert cast their shadows on the event and the building itself came under much criticism. It contained a good deal of glazing, notably in a pair of enormous glass

Left, part of Cassell's large-scale map of London of about 1867, showing the South Kensington and Knights-bridge districts, including the gardens of the Horticultural Society. *Right*, Fowke's Albert Hall and Conservatory at the top end of the Society's gardens (*Graphic*, 1871).

a while in the centre of the district at the north end of which the Albert Hall was built. Unfortunately for future Londoners, this space was built over in an unplanned fashion with an heterogeneous collection of buildings towards the end of the century, the greatest of these being Colcutt's Imperial Institute. Now much of the area contains the newly built Imperial College of Science and Technology. The gardens, with their parterres, steps, basins, fountains, bandstand and conservatory, were laid out by Nesfield, though Fowke was in charge of the

domes, the largest ever built, with diameters of one hundred and sixty feet, which were joined by a vast nave a thousand feet long. With outer walls of solid brick it was a more conventional and historically far less important building than the Crystal Palace and most of it was demolished after the Exhibition closed. Nevertheless, it had a number of interesting features. Much of it, like the Crystal Palace, was prefabricated to a module, the module being twenty-five feet, one foot larger than that used at the Crystal Palace. The scale was gigantic: 'something

to do with Babylon, some prophecy out of the Apocalypse'. Nearly a million square feet were enclosed and to the construction Fowke brought all his technological knowledge and skill. The roof of the nave, for example, was made of prefabricated timber parts and constructed, and finally decorated, with the aid of a huge travelling scaffold weighing one hundred and forty tons and using steam engines for the hoists.

Two exhibits at the 1862 Exhibition were of some importance in the history of taste, for they strongly influenced the Aesthetic Movement of the seventies and eighties, which in its turn influenced our own century. The first was a large collection of Japanese prints, fans and other objects; the second was the entries of painted furniture, rich embroideries, and other works of handicraft submitted by the firm of Morris, Marshall and Faulkner, to give William Morris's concern its full title.

As *Punch* remarked wryly, the first Exhibition building had been designed by a gardener, and the second by a soldier. Cole relied much on the Royal Engineers, for thus he not only acquired men skilled in construction but he could tap the resources of another government department without extra cost to his own schemes. A sketch by Fowke now at the Victoria and Albert Museum shows a great concert hall as part of the exhibition scheme, not built on account of cost. But such a hall he did before long conceive in the form of the Albert Hall, although he died before it was completed.

The Government bought the site on which the 1862 Exhibition had been held and organized a competition for a new building to house the natural history collection of the British Museum. The judges chose a design with a Latin pseudonym which turned out to be that of Captain Fowke. Unfortunately Fowke died in 1865 at the early age of forty-two. He was a loss for he was a capable designer and his works at South Kensington possess a surprising degree of architectural sensibility. His design for the new museum was in the event not built and the rather forbidding reality we can see today is the work of Alfred Waterhouse, completed in 1881 in a kind of Romanesque style.

Fowke's most famous building, lying on the axis of the Natural History Museum and originally at the northern extremity of the Horticultural Society's gardens, is the Albert Hall, opened by the Queen nearly six years after Fowke died. It was carried to conclusion by another Royal Engineer, Major-General H. G. D. Scott, its details being by Thomas Verity. Its huge oval, like a Roman amphitheatre, seven hundred and thirty-five feet across and capable of seating seven thousand, forms a clean, simple rotunda from which four bold porches project. Around the top of the cylinder, which is composed of hard red

Captain Francis Fowke of the Royal Engineers (*I.L.N.*, 1862).

bricks, runs a decorative frieze of terracotta mosaic executed by women students of the South Kensington Museum school, depicting the triumph of Art, Science and Industry. Inside, around the central arena, rise three tiers of boxes and above them a balcony and a gallery, all roofed by a great unique elliptical dome of glass and iron ribs, the world's largest. In spite of its notorious, now partly tamed, echo, the Hall has served London well for a century.

A number of other buildings were erected on the Commissioners' acres including Fowke's Science Schools (completed by H. G. D. Scott), otherwise called the Huxley Building, which originally included the Royal School of Mines. It was opened in 1872 and its immaculate red brickwork decorated with buff terracotta can still be seen, with its top-storey loggia, in Exhibition Road northwest of the Victoria and Albert Museum. Another Victorian building which remains is the Royal College of Organists, an eccentric one of considerable character on the west of the Albert Hall, the architect being Lieutenant H. H. Cole, R.E. Of the Victorian buildings which began to cover the Horticultural Society's gardens in the eighties Blomfield's undistinguished Royal College of Music remains, and so, barely, does the tall tower remaining from Colcutt's Imperial Institute inspired by the Jubilee of 1887; but Waterhouse's City and Guilds

Overleaf, the Albert Hall of Arts and Sciences, opened by the Queen on 29 March 1871 (*Graphic*, 1871). Tickets could be bought on a lease of 999 years.

The nave of Fowke's International Exhibition of 1862 at South Kensington (*I.L.N.*, 1861).

Sir George Gilbert Scott, R.A. (*Graphic*, 1872),
most prolific of Victorian architects.

Institute in Exhibition Road, certainly among the architect's better creations, vanished in the 1960s. His Natural Museum remains in all its aggressive self-confidence.

Although they now lack any cohesion in architecture or town planning, the South Kensington acres acquired from the profits of the Great Exhibition have in a jumbled way achieved Prince Albert's original aim of creating an umbrella institution to promote education in the application of art and science to industry. Significantly the Science Museum is now separate from the Victoria and Albert Museum of which, as the South Kensington Museum, it once formed a part. Among the many museums and colleges on the site the Royal College of Art, which began as the Government School of Design at Somerset House in 1837, has, in fact, recently fully resumed the purposes that the Prince Consort and Henry Cole so ardently initiated.

Opposite the Albert Hall we must now face the Albert Memorial, the design for which George Gilbert Scott received his knighthood. What are we to make of it today? This 'memorial to our Blameless Prince', as *The Builder* described it, was the result of a competition limited to six selected architects, in which Scott's won first prize. He considered it to be his finest work, and it took nine years to make; begun in 1863, it was not completed until 1872, the year Doré's *London* was published; the huge bronze statue of Albert was, indeed, not in place until four years later.

Set on a high podium of granite steps, which add up in total length to two and a quarter miles, it is in a kind of Gothic style, crocketed, niched, pinnacled and gabled in marbles, granites, bronze and mosaics to a height of one hundred and seventy-five feet, topped by a cross surrounded by angels. Incorporated in the design are over one hundred and seventy-five sculptured figures, the chief one being J. H. Foley's bronze figure, fourteen feet high, of the Prince seated beneath the canopy and holding in his hand the catalogue of the Great Exhibition – a splendidly competent piece of Victorian craftsmanship. Below him is inscribed the single word 'Albert' which, Lytton Strachey observed drily, 'as a means of identification has proved sufficient'.

The monument has often been derided ever since it first came into sight. ('Why don't they put the ornament on top of the cake?' and so on.) The *Quarterly Review*, which had so cruelly attacked Scott's St Pancras Hotel, fell savagely upon the Memorial in 1880, describing a group of its graven worthies as 'a set of weak-limbed, semi-idiotic, and half-naked loungers, wrapped in sheets'. Even the Queen herself never praised it, possibly because she felt her dear, earnest Albert might have had his reservations about such grandiose display. Fussy, pompous, vulgar, exaggerated almost to a point of absurdity the whole magniloquent affair may be, but it has a fine silhouette and it does possess a bold confidence, and a timeless monumentality which we in our own confused and provisional times may well envy. The Memorial is in effect a gigantic piece of polychromatic jewellery, and must be seen as such. As Scott explained, his aim was 'to erect a kind of ciborium . . . on the principle of the ancient shrines. . . . My notion, whether good or bad, was for once to realize this jeweller's architecture in a structure of full size.' Long may it survive, and may Albert soon be gilded again, as he was before 1915.

The Albert Memorial opens the whole complicated subject of Victorian stylism. We are at last far enough away from it to be able to realize more clearly now what the designers were trying to do and how they felt, and thus to see its failings with understanding and its virtues with affection. What is clear is that in its complexity it expressed the Victorian *Zeitgeist* of romantic individualism, of religious evangelicism, of confident *nouveau riche* display, and of getting value for money. Throughout Victoria's reign and well into the twentieth century we see an extraordinary confusion of styles based on historicist revivals. Yet a Victorian building is never a plagiarism, but always and unmistakably Victorian – adventurous, vigorous, confident, often in our eyes in its gathered grime grotesque or depressing, often interesting and sometimes charming, even beautiful by any standards.

In architecture, as in all forms of human expression, we must accept one undeniable fact: we do not, cannot, live by reason alone. Whatever we make we do love, in our hearts, to decorate and embellish.

In large towns like London a spate of new buildings were suddenly required by the expanding population, many of them having entirely new purposes, on an unprecedented scale. Why then did the Victorians not produce their own style which could have satisfied these functions and been, at the same time, coherent in appearance? Why did they not, for instance, develop the established classical idiom of the Georgians which was at least elegant and had served well for a long time? The reasons are involved but probably the main causes were the Industrial Revolution, the Reform Act of 1832, and the sudden growth in power and wealth of the new middle classes who were only half-educated and wished to display their riches in abundant ornamentation and at the same time to express their individualistic attitude to life. The solid, middle-class ranks lacked cultivated taste, most of all in the visual sphere, and this 'barbarism of burgesses' was soon to debase even the taste of the aristocracy. So the Palladian tradition of the educated, leisured gentry foundered. In any case, people were bored with the classical canons, tired of the control of the arts by aristocratic patronage that classicism represented. Moreover, new methods of production and ease of delivery of materials by railway from distant counties – brick, stone, slate, all of varying colours and textures – obviously affected nineteenth-century building and destroyed old local vernaculars.

Romantic revivalism also represented a sentimental flight from the hideous realities that urban industrialism was creating – an escape into an idealized past or into pastoral dreams, a withdrawal into ivory towers and castles in the air. To the Victorians romanticism became, like religion, almost a psychic necessity, a prophylactic against the malaise of industrialization. All the borrowed plumes, the fancy dress, and the facial cosmetics of Victorian architecture can be understood only in the light of this half-conscious effort to escape.

In Victorian England romanticism took its most emphatic form in the Gothic Revival. One of its causes was national pride in that Gothic style was regarded, quite irrationally, as being an essentially English style; another cause was religious revivalism; a third and most potent cause was the fanaticism of a single individual, a frenetic Roman Catholic who died insane: Augustus Northmore Pugin. He was an admirable designer of details as on Barry's Houses of Parliament and in his Gothic court at the Great Exhibition, but he was not an inspired architect. His great influence came through his polemical books such as *Contrasts* (1836), and *True*

Augustus Welby Pugin, fanatic for Christian architecture – portrait by J. R. Herbert (*I.L.N.*, 1852).

Principles of Christian Architecture (1841). Through them he helped to turn the playful, picturesque and secular Gothick of the Georgians into an earnest and universal style for Christians, an article of faith based on sound archaeological knowledge. So Gothicism and morality became entwined. The true Christian, Pugin declaimed, should spurn pagan manners, which were in any case, as he pointed out most reasonably, unsuited to the English climate. His influence was deep: George Gilbert Scott himself declared: 'I was awakened from my slumbers by the thunder of Pugin's writings.'

The most powerful competitor against Gothic in the Battle of the Styles was Renaissance Classic, often of the Italian palazzo type, of which Barry had made the most in his Reform Club. The style tended to grow more elaborate as the years passed, with deep reliefs on the façades and much sculptural enrichment. Scott's Foreign Office building in Portland stone and granite is a major example. Many a building ostensibly Gothic had a classic plan; as Pugin sadly remarked of the Houses of Parliament: 'All Grecian, Sir; Tudor details on a classic body.'

The classic idiom was continued also in much of London's middle-class housing at least well into the sixties as a heavy, debased form of the Georgian tradition, which had not become entirely degenerate when Cubitt was building Belgravia. At least such terraces give that coherence to a street which was not often a major concern of the period. Typical are the stucco terraces of South

Kensington with their endless rows of heavy Doric porticos and black area railings, where still in T. S. Eliot's day, 'breakfast plates rattled in basement kitchens' and one was 'aware of the damp souls of housemaids sprouting despondently at area gates'.

The real weakness of Victorian architecture lies less in its romantic escapism and in its detailing, which was often superb, but in its planning, particularly of large buildings. Another weakness was its failure to express structure. So the Victorians misconstrued, in their obsession with ornament, the real beauty of medieval building – both control of internal spatial relationships and the clear expression of stone engineering. (Its functions were, of course, comparatively simple.)

The most authentic architecture of the Victorians, which we have now come to appreciate fully since the revolution of the 1930s, is that of their functional ferro-vitreous structures, even if these did often apply historical forms to their surface decorations. London examples can be cited: Bunning's fine Coal Exchange (facing Billingsgate but now demolished), Decimus Burton's Palm House at Kew, the great train sheds at Paddington and St Pancras, Fowke's demolished Winter Garden behind the Albert Hall, E. M. Barry's Floral Hall beside the Covent Garden opera house (less interesting since a fire in the 1950s), Owen Jones's project for the Alexandra Palace, the Reading Room of the British Museum, the great roofs of the Agricultural Halls at Islington and Addison Road, the oval dome of the Albert Hall and, of course, the Crystal Palaces of 1851 and 1854. These were truly modern structures owing nothing to the past.

Two more examples of iron and glass construction can be noticed, one a reality, the other a fantastic project. The reality was a kind of miniature Crystal Palace which stood for some years on the corner of Oxford Street and Great Portland Street. Erected in 1858 to the design of Owen Jones, who had been responsible for the brilliant colour decorations of the original Crystal Palace, this was an iron-framed affair filled with coloured glass and consisting of a great nave with aisles – an elegant bazaar for the sale of fancy goods.

The other example, the project, would have been a true folly – a great Gothic fane adapted to cast-iron. It was a commodious winter garden designed by the architect Bedborough and proposed to the Queen in 1877 by a Mr Wills of the Royal Exotic Nursery, Onslow Crescent, who, presumably, had a vested interest in the scheme. Its purpose was to enclose the Albert Memorial under glass in order to conserve it from 'the vitiated atmosphere of London and to protect the admiring thousands from the weather . . . the centre division to cover the whole of the Memorial and the other four to be devoted to the growth

of plants, trees, etc., representing the four quarters of the globe'. So *The Builder* described it. Perhaps it is as well that no one took the idea very seriously.

Whether one likes this folly or not, Sir John Betjeman is right in his declaration that the Victorian architecture of England made two notable contributions to the architecture of the world. One was this development of cast-iron and glass construction. From it has come the method, using a steel or reinforced concrete framework filled in with lightweight panelling of glass or other synthetic sheeting, which forms so distinct a feature of our century and stands in such strong contrast, often with fascinating, if unpremeditated, visual effects, with the solid, ornamented walling pierced with openings which characterized not only the general run of Victorian architecture but that of all preceding ages, at least in Europe.

The other contribution was the small detached house in the vernacular designed for artistic middle-class people of moderate incomes. A sudden change of style that began in the seventies applied mainly to middle-class homes; it was a new national style compiled mostly from English and Dutch domestic vernacular building of the seventeenth and early eighteenth centuries. The Gothic Revival had run its course. Now the middle classes were becoming better educated and more leisured and they were seeking greater refinement in visual design of every kind. In this situation arose the Aesthetic Movement. An ultimate product of the Romanticism that followed the Napoleonic Wars when artists, musicians, and writers, having lost their patrons, turned to *nostalgie de la boue* and the acceptance of a single moral law: Art for Art's Sake, the movement was important. It has had its lasting effects, particularly in the domestic field, and only recently has it received the attention it warrants.

Many of the houses in the new style survive with their fine red brickwork, sash windows, decorated and curving gables, jutting oriels, terracotta ornaments, white-painted balconies and woodwork trim. Gay, fresh and charming, the style came as a relief both from the moral earnestness of the Goth and the massive philistinism of the Pagan, for its aim was to please rather than to improve. Breaking all the rules, it was greeted as an effete and bastard affectation by the architectural establishment. In fact it was a social as well as a visual revolt of the younger middle class – a pennant of youth in yet another battle in the endless war of the generation gap.

Not only was art 'in the air' of the seventies and eighties, science was exciting: *Punch* cartooned the new life with electric lights and telephones as often as it caricatured the Aesthetic Movement. The word 'aesthetic', from the Greek meaning 'perception', then became almost a synonym for fashionable, and from pertaining generally

Project for a Gothic ferro-
vitreous winter
garden to enclose the
Albert Memorial
(*Builder*, 1877).

to the appreciation and criticism of the beautiful, it came
to mean 'in accord with the principles of good taste'.
There were various mouthpieces such as the *Magazine
of Art*, the *Art Journal* and *The Architect*, as well as
illustrated books such as C. L. Eastlake's *Hints on
Household Taste* (1867). Yet it was not an organized
movement so much as a wide-ranging reformist cult that
in domestic architecture led to many a London suburban
street of 'aesthetic' and sub-'aesthetic' houses, and
eventually to the decadence of the by-pass villa.

In architecture its chief representatives were Edward
Godwin, W. Eden Nesfield, J. J. Stevenson, Philip
Webb, E. R. Robson of the London School Board build-
ings and, above all, Norman Shaw; in the decorative arts
Godwin, William de Morgan and, at the top, William
Morris; in painting the Pre-Raphaelites and Whistler.
We see now that many of the products of the Art Move-
ment, particularly in furniture and designs for fabrics
and wallpaper, did possess a beauty that is unfading. It
was the creator of the pleasure-giving Arts and Crafts
Movement, causing the formation of societies like the
Arts and Crafts Exhibition Society and the Home Arts
and Industries Association dedicated to spreading 'knowledge of Art Handwork among the people'.

The whole Aesthetic Movement naturally became the
butt of the satirists, for what began as a sound and healthy
reaction ran in some forms to preciosity and the affectation of a pale and phthisic melancholy, with its tendency,
in James Laver's phrase, 'to look at lilies in lieu of
luncheon'. Mainly through the drawings of George du

Maurier, *Punch* struck many an unkind blow against the
Intense, the Artistic, the Cimabue Browns of Passionate
Brompton, and all such Apostles of Cultshaw. 'To the
average Briton,' writes William Gaunt in his brilliant
and entertaining analysis *The Aesthetic Adventure*, 'it was
all vaguely effeminate and unhealthy.'

Gilbert and Sullivan's *Patience* was immensely popular
in 1881 at D'Oyly Carte's new Savoy Theatre. It was
witty, gay and cruel, but it gave the philistines another
victory, and that was a pity. W. S. Gilbert and his wife
'Kitten' lived themselves in a new house specially designed
for them in an aesthetic manner at 39 Harrington Gardens,
South Kensington, but presumably it contained within
no peacock patterns. It was lavishly decorated, nevertheless, with panelling, stained glass and tapestries, and contained a wealth of novel conveniences – telephone, electric
lighting, central heating and four bathrooms.

As Scott represented the High Victorian in architecture,
so Norman Shaw represented the later period of the
Aesthetic Movement. He built a few churches, some city
offices, the new headquarters of Scotland Yard and, towards the end of his life, the Piccadilly Hotel and the
Gaiety Theatre, but most of his work was domestic and
his influence in that field was immense, not only in
England but on the Continent and in America. The style
he favoured and popularized he himself called Renaissance, major examples being Old Swan House (1875),
its neighbour Cheyne House (1867) on the Chelsea
Embankment and No. 170 Queen's Gate. It was a style
particularly favoured by artists for their studio houses.

98

Other examples of Shaw's houses can be seen in Kensington, Hampstead, and in the suburb of Bedford Park to the west. The origin of the Queen Anne vernacular revival has been attributed to the polemics of a layman - the Reverend J. L. Petit - delivered in a lecture in 1861, and its prototype seems to be a little square lodge of 1867 still to be seen on the edge of Kew Gardens - a highly personal design with a central chimney in a kind of Anglo–Dutch manner by W. E. Nesfield, Shaw's early partner.

Shaw's work has elegance with its red hand-made brickwork, large oriel windows, white painted trim and, generally, informal, picturesque composition; it is only now receiving the appreciation it deserves. One of Shaw's larger houses is the Royal Geographical Society's building in Kensington Gore, originally built in 1874 as a private mansion called Lowther Lodge. It has a pleasant country-house look with a generous forecourt, a large red-brick complex of gables decorated with terracotta ornaments, square bays, wide leaded casement windows, roof dormers, tall fluted chimneys, and white balconies.

Between Lowther Lodge and the Albert Hall rises the cliff of Shaw's Albert Hall Mansions, one of London's earliest blocks of middle-class flats. Such blocks were made feasible by the development of the hydraulic lift. Here the Mansions destroy the scale of both Lodge and Hall, revealing that lack of consideration for the total scene which even the later Victorians, like ourselves today, so often displayed.

London can show a good collection of Aesthetic Movement architecture to the west of Sloane Street in a style which has been dubbed by Osbert Lancaster Pont Street Dutch. It is characterized by ogee gables, red brick embellished with pink terracotta bas-reliefs of cranes flying and sunflowers bursting. Other common elements of the Anglo-Dutch style are the cove-cornice, the projecting bay, large windows with leaded lights, the occasional bull's-eye window, and a fairly frequent resort to tile hanging. It was all new in the seventies and eighties, and a great improvement in its coherence, simplicity and refinement on what had gone before in domestic design.

Edward W. Godwin (1833–86) (not to be confused with George Godwin, who was an undistinguished architect, but was highly influential from 1844 to 1883 as editor of *The Builder*, notably in sanitary and housing reforms) was among the best exponents of the Aesthetic Movement, both in architecture and decoration. His Art Furniture is original, simple and graceful, as one can see in the examples in the Victoria and Albert Museum; if displayed today at Heal's they could give the impression that Scandinavian designers had found their second wind. His houses are delightful. His large works include the town halls at Northampton and Congleton and Bromore Castle in Ire-

land, but his speciality was the London studio house, a few smaller examples of which survive as in Tite Street, Chelsea. The White House he built for his friend Whistler, who after his law case could not afford to live in it, has unfortunately been demolished. Godwin numbered not only Whistler among his friends, but also Oscar Wilde and the architect William Burges. In 1868 Godwin achieved the distinction of elopement with Ellen Terry.

The New Jerusalem of the aesthetics was Bedford Park Estate which was developed at Chiswick, conveniently near the new Turnham Green railway station, as the first garden suburb. With its detached Queen Anne-ish houses lying in their own private gardens it set a pattern for middle-class suburban dwellings for many decades. Its creator was a speculator with aesthetic leanings called Jonathan Carr (1845–1915), who bought a hundred acres of field and orchard here, close enough to the city for commuting but away from the fogs and traffic. Between 1875 and 1880 he built, for professional types and people of taste, this ideal town with quiet fronded roads, both straight and curving, in such a way as to preserve as many existing trees as possible. The whole estate comprised in the end some three hundred and fifty red-brick houses of varying designs letting at £45 to £100 a year, and also such communal amenities as a village store, an inn, a clubhouse and a church, the latter being a rare Victorian piece in its departure from the conventional Gothic. Edward Godwin designed the first few houses but in 1877 Norman Shaw became the chief architect and to him and his assistants most of the suburb must be credited. A ballad in the *St James's Gazette* celebrated the scheme:

> 'Tis there a village I'll erect
> With Norman Shaw's assistance,
> Where men may lead a chaste correct
> Aesthetical existence.

Mrs Humphrey Ward in *The Marriage of William Ashe* described the aesthetic taste represented in the house of Lady Tranmore, and no doubt many interiors at Bedford Park received much the same treatment, for here 'was reflected the rising worship of Morris and Burne-Jones. Her walls were covered with the well-known pomegranate or jessamine or sunflower patterns; her hangings were of a mystic greenish blue; her pictures were drawn either from the Italian primitives or their modern followers.'

It is pleasant to recall that even in the visual confusion of Victorian times quite a few people did earnestly care about the way things around them looked and could appreciate then, as we still do today, the applied decorations of one of the greatest designers not only of his age but of any age - the 'boor, and son of a boor' as he once described himself, William Morris.

The People

I beg any educated person to consider what are the conditions in which alone animal life can thrive; to learn by personal inspection, how far those conditions are realized for the masses of our population; and to form for himself a conscientious judgement as to the need for great, if even almost revolutionary, reforms. Let any such person devote an hour to visiting some very poor neighbourhood in the metropolis.... Let him breathe its air, taste its water, eat its bread. Let him think of human life struggling there for years. Let him fancy what it would be to himself to live there, in that beastly degradation of stink, fed with such bread, drinking such water.... Let him enter some house there at hazard, and, heeding where he treads, follow the guidance of his outraged nose, to the yard (if there be one) or the cellar. Let him talk to the inmates; let him hear what is thought of the bone-boiler next door, or the slaughter house behind; what of the sewer grating before the door; what of the Irish basket-makers upstairs – twelve in a room, who came in after the hopping, and got fever; what of the artisan's dead body, stretched on his widow's one bed, beside her living children.

DR (later SIR) JOHN SIMON, *City of London Medical Reports* (1854)

Doré goes to town in his dramatic depictions of the appalling conditions in which masses of people lived in Victorian London. They find full documentary support in a pile of contemporary writing not only by novelists like Dickens, Kingsley, Mrs Gaskell and George Gissing, who might be suspected of exaggeration, but in factual Blue Books and other official reports, of which Chadwick's *Sanitary Conditions of the Labouring Population* was the first of importance.

We find evidence of a most human and poignant kind in Henry Mayhew's famous *London Labour and the London Poor*, which contained in his own prefacing words 'a cyclopaedia of the industry, the want, and the vice, of the great Metropolis – the first attempt to publish the history of the people, from the lips of the people themselves'. If no other records existed, this great sociological work of honest reportage would alone provide a vivid enough account of how the poor lived in London little more than a century ago – particularly the 'submerged tenth' and the underworld, the casual labourers, crossing sweepers, street vendors and entertainers, beggars, vagrants, mud-larks, petty criminals and prostitutes determined to survive in a hopeless hell of degradation, dirt, hunger, disease and cruelty (including a good deal of child murder), the realities of which imagination cannot exaggerate and which, in spite of the pockets of poverty persisting in our own times of social welfare, now seem inconceivable. Infants and weaklings died like flies in the festering ghettoes and in the worst areas half the children died before they were five years old. There is no doubt about it: life for the vast majority in Victorian London was as unenviable as Doré's drawings suggest. Most of the working class lived in squalid, ailing poverty: a spell of unemployment could lead to utter destitution.

Mayhew's aim was not merely to report but 'to cause those who are in "high places", and those of whom much is expected to bestir themselves to improve the condition of a class of people whose misery, ignorance and vice, amidst all the immense wealth and great knowledge of "the first city in the world", is, to say the very least, a national disgrace to us'.

Above the poorest scavengers whom Mayhew describes and interviews were the 'respectable working classes', endeavouring to retain some pride, people not sunk in

Mirror of splendidly engraved glass in a Victorian gin-palace, one of many that still survive in London. The opiate of the people was not religion: it was gin.

hopeless squalor. They could maintain their families at a low standard on £1 a week or less (say £15 at today's purchasing power), but they did so under the continual threat of sickness or unemployment which could send them rapidly either to the bottom of the abyss or to the dreaded workhouse. Semi-skilled workers or trained mechanics or artisans could earn twice as much and live in moderate comfort in a tolerable, if restricted, way while a City clerk could earn as much as £3 a week and so regard himself as a cut above any member of the 'great unwashed'. Yet junior clerks, shop-assistants and teachers often earned less than the skilled artisan, and Doré's brewers' men at least do not look undernourished. Working-class standards fell between 1851 and 1865 but thereafter they began to improve slightly; by 1870 they were ten per cent higher than they had been in 1850. In the seventies and after, a few pence could sometimes be spared from the weekly wage for an occasional outing or an evening at a music hall; working hours too were slightly reduced and the Bank Holiday Act of 1871 came to provide a welcome relief for urban populations by allowing an occasional day off. The fifty-hour week arrived eventually when Saturday afternoons became free as well as Sundays – a feature of English life continentals found remarkable enough to dub *la semaine Anglaise*.

Throughout Victoria's reign London's main problem was housing, and it grew worse as the century advanced. In 1860 a correspondent in *The Times* stated: 'In one of the largest parishes in London, two-thirds of the whole population are believed to be lodged, with their families, in single rooms; and, from limited personal observation, I am induced to think that at least one million in London alone are in this degrading position.' The sheer magnitude of the twin problems of poverty and housing in the dense and exploding metropolis baffled even the most ardent and conscientious reformers, while the majority of the comfortable middle classes, engrossed in their own pursuits, either had no knowledge of the disturbing situation or turned their backs upon it with a shrug of comforting, if irresponsible, dismissal.

Horrible descriptions of overcrowding and lack of even simple domestic comforts were published from the forties through the rest of the century and after. *The People of the Abyss*, for example, relates Jack London's experiences in 1902 as a young reporter fresh from the States:

Nowhere in the streets of London may one escape the sight of abject poverty, while five minutes' walk from almost any point will bring one to a slum; but the East End region my hansom was now penetrating was one unending slum. The streets were filled with a new and different race of people, short of stature, and of wretched beer-sodden appearance. We rode along through miles of bricks and squalor. . . . Here and there lurched a drunken man or woman, and the air was obscene with sounds of jangling and

squabbling. At a market, tottery old men and women were searching in the garbage thrown into the mud for rotten potatoes, beans and vegetables, while little children clustered like flies around a festering mass of fruit, thrusting their arms to the shoulders into the liquid corruption, and drawing forth morsels but partially decayed, which they devoured on the spot. . . . Not only was one room deemed sufficient for a poor man and his family, but I learned that many families, occupying single rooms, had so much space to spare as to be able to take in a lodger or two. When such rooms can be rented for from three to six shillings per week, it is a fair conclusion that a lodger with references should obtain floor space for, say, from eightpence to a shilling. . . . I learned that there were no bath tubs in the thousands of houses I had seen. . . . 'A part of a room to let'. This notice was posted a short while ago in a window not five minutes walk from St James's Hall. . . . Beds are let on the three-relay system – that is, three tenants to a bed, each occupying it eight hours, so that it never grows cold.

Thousands of Londoners were homeless and slept where they could under the arches of bridges or railways or on park benches. Sleeping out was no sinecure, for those who 'carried the banner', that is walked the streets all night, were harried by the police and sleep might not be possible until the park-gates opened at dawn. Green Park opened at 4.15 a.m., Jack London records, and many would enter at that time to enjoy at least some undisturbed repose. At Spitalfields, London saw them in the garden beside the great church:

On the benches on either side sat a mass of miserable and distorted humanity, the sight of which would have impelled Doré to more diabolical flights of fancy than he ever succeeded in achieving. It was a welter of rags and filth, of all manner of indecency, leering monstrosities and bestial faces. A chill, raw wind was blowing, and these creatures, huddled there in their rags, sleeping for the most part, or trying to sleep. . . . It was this sleeping that puzzled me. . . . It was not till afterwards I learned. *It is a law of the powers that be that the homeless shall not sleep at night.*

Jack London mentions Arthur Morrison's novel *A Child of the Jago*, first published in 1896. This work, too, reveals the extent of the misery existing in London's poor districts even at the close of the century. It is a tale told without sentimentality in the realistic manner of Zola. Morrison, who also wrote the lesser-known *Tales of Mean Streets*, knew by personal experience what he described for he was born in Poplar, the son of an engine fitter, and he wrote without condescension or exaggeration. The Jago was an area in Shoreditch, now covered by an L.C.C. housing estate, which he knew well for he had been employed there himself by a charitable body. The district and the harsh life of its criminal population are vividly drawn. Here is a typical, raucous, daily scene:

Down the middle of Old Jago Street came Sally Green: red faced, stripped to the waist, dancing, hoarse and triumphant. Nail-scores wide as a finger striped her back, her face, and her

'Under the Arches' (Doré).

throat, and she had a black eye; but in one great hand she dangled a long bunch of clotted hair, as she whooped defiance to the Jago. It was a trophy newly rent from the scalp of Norah Walsh, champion of the Rann womenkind, who had crawled away to hide her blighted head, and be restored with gin. None answered Sally's challenge, and, staying but to fling a brickbat at Pip Walsh's window, she carried her dance and her trophy into Edge Lane.

The most extensive slums lay in the East End, which tended to expand ever further east and north-east well beyond Whitechapel and Aldgate, a trend encouraged by the cheap fares of the Great Eastern Railway after 1871. Unsavoury Alsatias existed in a number of central areas, particularly around Seven Dials, Drury Lane, the Tothill Street area of Westminster, and the Little Italy of Clerkenwell. In a slum near Holborn reported by Lord Shaftesbury, parents might have to watch in turn through the night to keep at bay the swarms of rats that appeared from the sewers and would otherwise have chewed the children as they slept (a chore still often undertaken in Negro ghettoes of the U.S.A.). There in single rooms, furnished with a few sacks for bedding, large families slept, ate, cooked, fought, fornicated, sometimes carried on a trade and often starved, sickened, and died.

It is hard to discover the precise extent of poverty in Victorian London but it was certainly appalling. Dr Edward Smith, as Medical Officer of Health to the Privy Council, reported in 1863 that typical home workers were able to spend only about 2s. 8d. a week each on food and many of them were 'insufficiently nourished and of feeble health', while Charles Booth's voluminous survey of the eighties and nineties reveals that over thirty per cent of London's population – that is, some 1,800,000 individuals – lived in direst poverty in the year 1889.

More than a million lived far worse than beasts or savages. The spirit of the age tended to blame the individual for his situation rather than society, and to believe that poverty was the wage of sin rather than the result of circumstance – of exploitation, government sloth, and uncontrolled urban growth in a competitive, money-crazed struggle. A result of this huge poverty, existing in a supposedly self-regulating economy, was a devitalized and degenerate population which became sterile by the third generation. The London workman whose grandparents had been born in the metropolis was rare and the ever-increasing population was drawn from the country and from abroad. The workers who required physical stamina such as carriers, railwaymen, dockers and porters

'Dudley Street, Seven Dials' (Doré). 'In the street market of Drury Lane the mark of misery seems to be upon every man, woman and child. Seven Dials is the nearest approach to Drury Lane in the hopelessness of its general aspect' (Jerrold).

were largely of comparatively healthy rural stock, or, at least, the offspring of such stock; most of the London police, for example, were country-born. Third-generation stock became the sallow, skeletal outcasts at the bottom of the abyss. 'There's no such thing as a Londoner,' wrote E. M. Forster in *The Longest Journey*. 'He's only a countryman on the road to sterility.'

Charles Dickens, who has been called 'the conscience and the consciousness of his age', had read Chadwick's report and it turned him into a propagandist for better conditions. Like most people, he too was worried about the drains. Tom-all-Alone's, the habitat of the boy Joe, a crossing sweeper, which is described with a spine-chilling skill in *Bleak House* (1853), was an actual place existing during the years of cholera before sanitation had been improved: the St Giles area, a lawless casbah in the heart of London lying to the east of what is now the Charing Cross Road. It was a picture intended to scare the smug and the privileged into action.

About ten years later, *The Builder* for 14 June 1862 gave a straight report of a labyrinth in Drury Lane:

Every room contains a separate family if not more and is thickly occupied. The inhabitants are of the dangerous classes. Haggard, drunken women, every trace of womanhood blotted out, are in the pathway. . . . Swarms of children trained to begging and others, it may be feared to worse . . . the rooms are small and without ventilation. . . . On average each house of eight rooms contains, including children, 45 persons, and as there are 21 houses, we have here perhaps 945 persons of the worst class pent up to their own destruction and the danger of the public. In one small room I found a man and his wife and six prostitutes who were set forth as their daughters, but cannot be so. . . . In a respectable house not far from the last occupied by steady artisans and others, I found that nine people slept in one of the rooms (12 feet by 14 feet) – a father, mother and seven children. Nor can any authority interfere, even when this occurs in a house let in tenements, so long as it is believed that the persons lodging are members of the same family. The Nuisances Removal Act would seem to give power to remedy such cases, but practically it fails. . . . 700 cubic feet is the smallest space under ordinary arrangements that will afford healthful space to one person. The occupants described above have not one-fifth of this.

Apart from the tenement houses, with their chronic discomforts, inadequate drainage and lack of water supply, ventilation and privacy, where even the backyards were often built over or covered with hovels, there existed in the poor quarters of London many common lodging-houses, the 'poor man's hotels', usually called doss houses. Here a bed for the night could be obtained in a crowded room from which the occupants would be evicted early each morning. It was squalid enough, but some control was exercised over conditions through the Common Lodging-Houses Act of 1851.

The Graphic in 1872 depicted a room in such a doss house in the poor district of St Giles's:

... for threepence and fourpence per night, any one may find a warm fire, cooking appliances, and congenial company. There may be seen the impudent tramp, the ragged crossing-sweeper, the cunning thief, the noisy costermonger, the broken-down tradesman, and the poor, blear-eyed clerk, who has somehow fallen into disgrace and want. ... The women who resort to these hotels of the poor are of various employments, and very diverse in character. They hawk laces, flowers, fruit, old clothes, mats, earthenware, fuses, pins, needles, threads, writing-paper, toasting-forks, brushes, newspapers, and, in fact anything that will find them a shilling a day. ... Some of the houses pay very well. They produce a clear profit of two, three, and four hundred pounds a year, and enable their owners to live in clover.

Under the Poor Laws some parish benefits were paid to the destitute; there was also a certain amount of charity such as soup kitchens run by benevolent bodies, and, as a last resort, there were the Unions or Workhouses organized by Parish Boards of Guardians. The map of 1868 is dotted with these huge symmetrical buildings which vie in size with the new prisons, hotels and railway stations: London at that time possessed thirty-two workhouses. Most people avoided them if they possibly could, for they were like penal institutions. A youth was once asked why he had smashed windows in the Chelsea Workhouse. 'Because, please,' he replied, 'they gives us four pounds of oakum to pick in the house in the day and it scrubs our fingers and we can't do it, and in the prison we only get two pounds and far better vittles.' Hippolyte Taine visited St Luke's Workhouse:

As everyone knows, a workhouse is a sort of asylum with something of a prison about it. Associated with the Poor Law administration, it is one of the distinctive features of English social constitution. It is an English principle that an indigent person who alienates his liberty has the right to be fed. The community meets the cost of this but imprisons the paupers in question and puts them to work. The one I visited had between five and six hundred inmates, old people, abandoned or otherwise, helpless children, and men and women out of work. ... The whole place was adequately clean and wholesome; but I gather that other workhouses are a great deal less pleasant. ... As a rule, when a workman out of a job applies to the municipality for help he is told, 'Give us proof that you are willing to work: go to the workhouse.' Nine times out of ten the men refuse. What is the reason for this repugnance? I am told they will stick to their 'home' and

their liberty at any price and cannot bear to be shut up and become subject to discipline.

To be forced to go to the workhouse was considered to be a stigma, the final admission of defeat, and once a person was within, escape was difficult. There wives were separated from their husbands and children from their parents, and the general treatment was deliberately humiliating

'A portly gentleman ... waxes rich on his rents'
(Drawing by F. Bernard in *How The Poor Live*, 1883).

and discouraging, as, in fact, it still is today in the spike and the casual ward where the down-and-out seeks a night's shelter.

Taine was continually shocked by the alcoholism of the English working classes. 'Drunkenness among the people is terrible. ... The climate encourages this tendency, because a man needs to warm himself up a bit, revive his body and spirits, and to forget for a while the sorrowful and harassed life he has to lead. ... Thirty thousand people are arrested every year in the London streets for being drunk.'

Dostoievsky too was shocked when he spent a week in London in 1862. In a chapter headed 'Baal' in his *Summer Impressions* (1863) he describes a Saturday night in a poor district in London:

It is as if a grand reception were being held for those white Negroes. Crowds throng the open taverns and the streets. ... Everyone is drunk, but drunk joylessly, gloomily and heavily, and everyone is somehow strangely silent. Only curses and bloody brawls occasionally break that suspicious and oppressively sad silence. ... Everyone is in a hurry to drink himself into insensibility. . . . Wives in no way lay behind their husbands and all get drunk together, while children crawl and run about among them.

In Shadwell, Taine thought, 'the lowest quarters of Marseilles, Antwerp, and Paris . . . come nowhere near this'.

Squat houses, wretched streets of brick under red roofs crossing each other in all directions and leading dismally down to the river. Beggars, thieves and prostitutes, especially the latter, swarm in Shadwell Street. The grating music from gin cellars can be heard from the street; sometimes the violinist is a Negro, and through open windows one sees unmade beds and women dancing. Three times in ten minutes I saw crowds collect round doorways, attracted by fights, especially by fights between women. . . . A few of the women show vestiges of former cleanliness, or wear a new dress; but most of them are in dirty, ill-assorted rags. . . . These women gesticulate with extraordinary vehemence; but their most horrible attribute is the voice – thin, shrill, cracked, like that of a sick owl.

Taine does not spare us:

From the moment you emerge from the tunnel, the whole place is alive with 'street-boys', bare-footed, filthy, turning cartwheels for a penny. They swarm on the stairs down to the Thames, more stunted, more livid, more deformed, more repulsive than the street urchins of Paris; the climate, of course, is

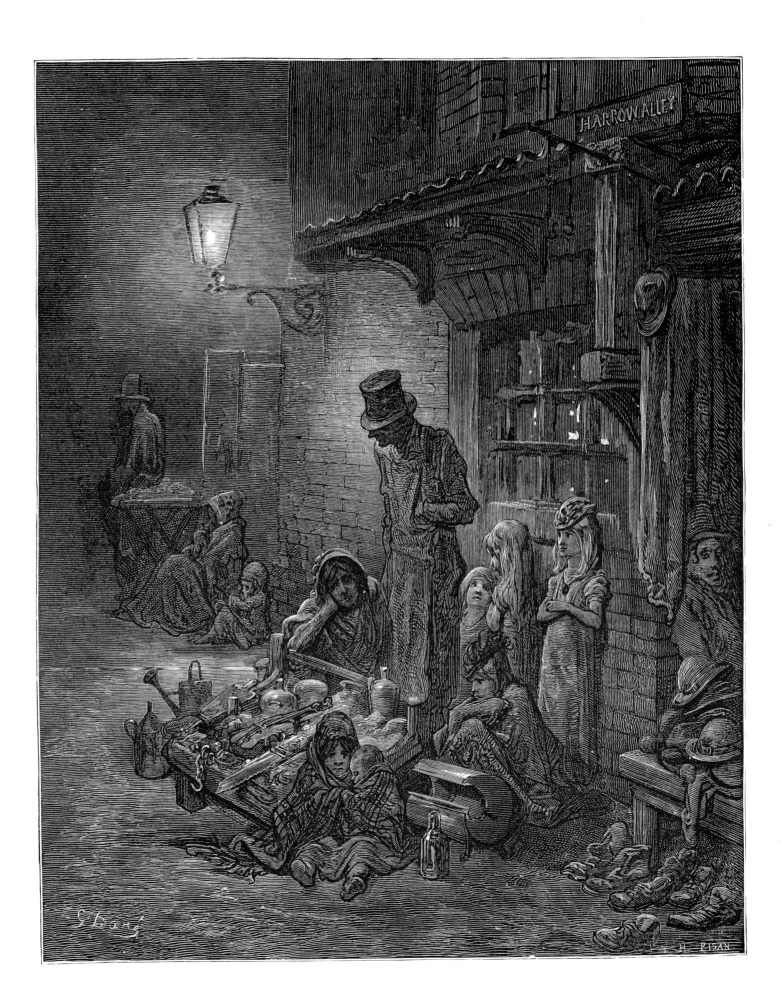

worse, and the gin murderous. Among them, leaning against the festering walls, or crouched inert on the steps, are men in the most astonishing rags: nobody who has not seen them can conceive what a frock-coat or pair of trousers can carry in layers of filth. They doze and day-dream, their faces earthy, livid, marbled with fine red lines. It was in this quarter that families were discovered whose only bed was a heap of soot; they had been sleeping on it for some months. For the human being reduced to these conditions there is only one refuge: drunkenness.

Taine recalls lanes, too, which opened off Oxford Street in the wealthy West End: 'Stifling alleys thick with human effluvia, troops of pale children crouching on filthy staircases.' At London Bridge he sees the street benches 'where all night whole families huddle close, heads hanging, shaking with cold'. In the Haymarket and the Strand at evening,

you cannot walk a hundred yards without knocking into twenty streetwalkers: some of them ask you for a glass of gin; others say, 'It's for my rent, mister.' The impression is not one of debauchery but of abject, miserable poverty. One is sickened and wounded by this deplorable procession in those monumental streets. It seemed as if I were watching a march past of dead women. Here is a festering sore, the real sore on the body of English society.

Was it sarcasm or ignorance which made people speak of taking to the streets as 'going gay'?

Apart from the obvious occupations of building, transport, docking, gas and water servicing, marketing and tending to the comforts of the upper and middle classes – and discounting all the odd and multifarious activities of Mayhew's street folk and the criminal underworld – what were the masses all doing to earn their livings in the Modern Babylon?

London is generally regarded as being above all a port, a business, banking, legal, governmental and servicing centre – mainly a place of distribution, exchange and consumption, a huge market, as it had been at least since the time the Venerable Bede had called it 'the mart of many nations resorting to it by sea and land'. Yet London has always been, not least in the nineteenth century, a centre of considerable industry as well. In Victoria's reign it was the chief manufacturing town in the country, and the most complex, employing in 1861 fifteen per cent of all workers in England and Wales. Yet London had no single, staple industry and much of it was small in scale, the main manufactures being clothing, furniture, stationery, printing, book-binding, coach-building, some ship-building and engineering, brewing, pottery, match-making, candle-making, and precision industry like clock-making and optics. Industry tended to concentrate in the East End, particularly furniture and clothing, because there cheap labour was always available.

Much of London's industry was disseminated in small workshops or distributed as piece-work in homes. Each kind tended to confine itself to specializing localities for convenience of marketing, supply of materials, and as a result of long-established tradition. Spitalfields, for example, where Huguenot refugees had settled in the seventeenth century, was a silk-weaving area and in Victorian times had become impoverished as a result of the competition from the north and from France. Furniture-makers, driven from the City itself by rising rents, could mostly be found on its fringe in Shoreditch and Finsbury, helped there by deliveries of timber via the Regent's Canal; they could also be found around Tottenham Court Road and Euston. As more bridges were built many industries crossed the river to the south, notably printing which had for a long while been established in Fleet Street and around Long Acre. Clerkenwell, being conveniently near Fleet Street, developed colour printing as new processes developed, and there George Baxter worked. In 1861 half the printers in the country were established in London, concentrated also in St Pancras, Islington and Lambeth. The printing trade expanded enormously in Victorian times; it took a leap in 1855 when the Stamp Duty on newspapers was removed and so allowed the growth of the penny press; it took another after the Forster Education Act of 1870 began to increase the literate public.

'The great brewery vats in the Town of Malt and Hops of Barclay, Perkins and Company's Entire, Southwark, associated with Dr Johnson and Mr Thrale' (Doré). 'There's a good deal of "talkee" yet to be done, sir', a sensible drayman said to us, a flower between his lips as he spoke, 'before they teach English workmen that there's sin and wickedness in a pint of honest beer' (Jerrold).

'The Rag Merchant's Home – Coulston Street, Whitechapel' (Doré). 'The old-clothesman's children are rolling about upon his greasy treasure, while he, with his heavy silver spectacles poised upon his hooked nose, takes up each item, and estimates it to a farthing' (Jerrold).

Clerkenwell was among the most important industrial centres in London, and there fine instruments were made, also jewellery, plate, clocks and watches, glass and metal objects – a miniature Brummagem. The highly skilled and traditional craft of coach-making, divided into many specialized departments and generating a number of ancillary occupations, was mostly to be found in Westminster, Marylebone, St Pancras and Long Acre, though vans were made in the dock area. Artisans in this trade were the aristocrats of the working classes and could earn as much as three to five guineas a week.

After 1860 Stratford and Silvertown grew rapidly as a new industrial area where cheap sites, fairly close to the City and the docks, could be found, and here the River Lea was useful in its improved condition. Soap, glue and varnish-making, sugar-refining, match-making and many other industries requiring large-scale factories grew up in these districts, particularly after the Public Health Act of 1875 and the new building regulations imposed by the L.C.C. after 1889 had laid down zoning restrictions against noxious air pollution in domestic areas.

A major industry in the metropolis was clothing and tailoring; London by 1861 was employing nearly a quarter of all clothing workers in England and Wales. The Merchant Tailors had by long tradition worked in the bespoke trade in the City, but in the nineteenth century the West End and Westminster became important centres for high-class tailoring and court dressmaking. Outside the City also, a cluster of tailors which clothed the army was based around Pall Mall.

The production of cheap, ready-made clothing, stimulated by the new sewing-machine and the band-saw, and based on the division of labour, was largely concentrated in Whitechapel and run in the later decades chiefly on the labour of Jewish immigrants who arrived there in their thousands in the eighties. This industry developed into the sub-contracting system known as 'sweating'. Cheap clothes were also made in other parts such as Spitalfields, Stepney and Finsbury. Houndsditch was an early centre of the second-hand-clothes trade. In many trades connected with clothing, toiling in small workshops or outworking in homes was common for there the restrictions imposed by the Factory Acts of the sixties could be avoided. Large capital equipment and factory buildings were not essential to the wholesale manufacture of ready-made garments, as they were, for example, in the manufacture of textiles; thus small sweatshops proliferated, many of them owned by former second-hand-clothes dealers who had turned their energies to the more lucrative business of making new clothes on a wholesale, mass-produced basis.

Four or five times as many women as men worked in all branches of the clothing industry, and they were brutally exploited throughout Victoria's reign. Highly skilled labour could not, of course, be sweated but the tendency was to replace the skilled by the unskilled wherever this was possible. Working conditions were terrible. 'Look into the work-rooms in many parts of the Metropolis and you will find them filled to far over danger point', wrote *The Builder* in 1862. 'In a small room not large enough for three, twenty-five tailors may be seen. In another boys and women strive to get a living in a death-giving atmosphere. Shoe-makers are often as ill placed.'

Women who took in plain sewing at home, mostly of shirts, were called slop workers and these were at the lowest level of the trade. Kingsley in his novel, *Alton Locke*, does not exaggerate the horrible conditions in which slop workers lived and toiled. In 1864, Mrs Gladstone in a letter to *The Times* revealed that needlewomen, after paying for their own cotton, might make no more than ½p a day. Right back in 1843 *Punch*, full of social protest in its early days, had published Thomas Hood's unforgettable *Song of the Shirt* in its Christmas number.

> With fingers weary and worn,
>   With eyelids heavy and red,
> A Woman sat in unwomanly rags,
>   Plying her needle and thread.
>   Stitch! Stitch! Stitch!
>   In poverty, hunger and dirt,
> And still with a voice of dolorous pitch,
> Would that its tone could reach the Rich,
>   She sang this 'Song of the Shirt'.

Hours of work for seamstresses were controlled by the seasonal rushes, and orders were delayed as long as possible in case fashion changed at the last moment. Then girls might work twenty hours a day, but out of season

Left, 'The Haunted Lady, or "The Ghost" in the Looking-glass. *Madame la Modiste*: "We would not have disappointed your Ladyship, at any sacrifice, and the robe is finished *à merveille*."' (*Punch*, 1863). Mary Anne Walkley, seamstress, died that year from overwork in an ill-ventilated room. *Right*, 'Lambeth Gas Works' (Doré).

twelve hours were more normal. 'No slavery is worse than the dressmaker's life in London,' declared a Parliamentary witness in 1843, and that remained true throughout the following decades. A country girl employed in stifling conditions to produce a rush order for general mourning in nine days without proper rest might go blind as a result. Loss of sight and that plague of Victorian England, tuberculosis, were the occupational hazards of the seamstress. Pay was between 5 and 10 new pence a day, plus overtime and meals, and the supply of women, who outnumbered men, was inexhaustible. It is not surprising, therefore, that many desperate dressmakers and milliners took to prostitution; the word milliner, indeed, came almost to serve as a synonym for streetwalker, but often these girls held on to respectability with one arm, augmenting their income by part-time love-making only, when they were known as 'dollymops'.

Sweated labour was extremely varied. Apart from stitching there was the making of match-boxes, fancy boxes, sacks, artificial flowers, brushes, clay pipes, uniform badges, fans, rag dolls, shell ornaments, umbrella bands, necklaces, neckties; there was the pulling of fur from rat, cat and rabbit skins, removing bones from rabbit tails for manure, and, strangest trade of all, mending worm-eaten or broken nutmegs with gum.

Among the severely exploited, also, were thousands of young slaveys – the single servants employed all found at £5 a year by the less affluent lower-middle classes. They often suffered as much from loneliness as from over-work. In White Street, Bethnal Green, beneath an arch of the Great Eastern Railway, a slave market was held on Monday and Tuesday mornings where boys and girls between the ages of seven and seventeen offered themselves for hire as servants. The Rev. Charles Davies describes it in his *Mystic London* (1875):

The young gentlemen, in the intervals of business – and it seemed to be all interval and no business – devoted themselves to games at buttons. Each of the young ladies – I am afraid to say how young – had her cavalier, and applied herself to very pronounced flirtation. . . . The scene was very unlike the genteel West End Servants' Registry. . . . I was informed that a good many small tradesmen do patronize the Market for shop-boys, nurse-girls, or household drudges. . . . 'Want a boy, sir?', 'A girl

Match factory in the East End (*Graphic*, 1871).

for the childer, sir?' said the juveniles, while the offers of the adult ladies were more emphatic and less quotable.

The most horrifying of women's work was the making of fusees or phosphor matches. *Household Words*, which described women's occupations in a series of articles, considered this to be easily the worst labour for women. Hands, face and clothes of a match-worker glowed with phosphorescence in the dark and after a few years many a girl's cheeks and chin would turn green, then black and finally begin to exude a foul-smelling pus, while the jawbone would be slowly eaten away by necrosis. This painful affliction, called 'phossy jaw', compelled the sufferer to eat nothing but soft food and ended in certain and early death.

In the hideous conditions in which the poor of London existed a century and less ago, cheerfulness did sometimes break through and it increased as the century advanced and wages improved a little. 'The whole thing was redeemed by a strange jollity,' reflects Ralph Nevill with an upper-class comment in *The World of Fashion, 1837–1922*,

'which is entirely lacking from the more sanitary dwellings in which the workers live today.' Gin at least was cheap: amidst the mahogany, the friendly fumes, and glittering plate glass of a gin palace you could get drunk for a penny; dead drunk for tuppence – and 'the straw is free'. There were family outings to Hampstead Heath or Epping Forest on Bank Holidays; there was an occasional visit to a Penny Gaff or a music hall and there was the communal liveliness to be enjoyed in the rowdy street markets of New Cut on a Saturday night or Petticoat Lane on a Sunday morning. In such markets the poor did most of their shopping. Here is Mayhew's description of New Cut, Lambeth, from his *London Labour* (1861):

There are hundreds of stalls and every stall has one or two lights; whether it is illuminated by the intense white lamp of the new self-generating gas-lamp, or else brightened by the red smoky flame of the old grease lamp. One man shows off his yellow haddock with a candle stuck in a bundle of firewood, another makes a candlestick of a huge turnip and the tallow gutters over its sides, while the boy shouting 'Eight a Penny, stunning pears!' has rolled his dip in a thick coat of brown paper that flares away with the candle.... These with the sparkling round-glass globes

The London poor at their Christmas marketing in the New Cut (*Graphic*, 1872).

Low lodging house, St Giles's (*Graphic*, 1872). Conditions in such poor people's hotels were controlled to some degree by Shaftesbury's Common Lodging-Houses Act of 1851.

of the tea-dealers' shops and the butchers' gas-lights streaming and fluttering in the wind like flags of flame, pour forth such a flood of light that at a distance the atmosphere immediately above the spot is as lurid as if the street were on fire. . . . Then the tumult of the thousand different cries of the eager dealers all shouting at the tops of their voices at one and the same time, are almost bewildering. 'So-old again,' roars one. 'Chestnuts all 'ot, a penny a score,' bawls another. 'An 'apenny a skin, blacking,' squeaks a boy. 'Buy, buy, buy, buy, bu-u-uy,' cries the butcher. 'Half a quire of paper for a penny,' bellows the street stationer. . . . 'Penny a lot, fine russets,' calls the apple woman. And so the babel goes on. . . . The man with a donkey cart filled with turnips has three lads to shout for him to their utmost with their 'Ho! Ho! Hi-i-i! What d'you think of this here? A penny a bunch – hurrah for free trade!'

By far the most remunerative occupation for working-class women was the free trade in bodies, for this provided the easiest escape from atrocious conditions. It was known as the 'great social evil' against which much righteous propaganda was directed. A West End drab could earn more in a single night than a working man could in a month and, whatever sentimental fiction might make of the type, she was on the whole healthier than most working women because she was better fed and less overworked;

provided she could avoid physical dangers from perverts, syphilis, and over-indulgence in 'blue ruin' (the demotic name for gin), not only comfort but even luxury could be attained. Significantly prostitution increased with commercial slumps in the same proportion as crime against property. Poverty also tended to encourage prostitution in that overcrowding of families in single rooms did not promote physical delicacy and made promiscuity an early and common experience that held no shame, fear, mystery, glamour or guilt for most working-class girls.

As a result of their Puritan beliefs the Victorians were in a neurotic state about sex, a word they tended to equate with sin. (We as their grandchildren, even great-grand-children, are only beginning to recover our balance, and even during this century René Cutforth received the impression about God at his school that 'not much was known about Him, apart from His having created the Universe, except that He was violently opposed to sex in every form'.) It is therefore surprising how much soliciting in the streets was tolerated in Victorian days.

The myth of Victorian purity has prevailed as a result of its middle-class literature whose circulation was con-

A London pub (*Graphic*, 1872).
Some 'slumming' seems to be going on.

trolled to a large extent by Mudie and Smith, both righteous Nonconformists. In fact, most Victorian men clearly enjoyed a vigorous, if often secret and guilt-ridden, sex-life. Dr Wingfield-Stratford has thus summed up the situation: 'Victorian morality reposed upon the belief that if you could not be virtuous, you could at least be respectable. Though the streets of London swarmed with harlots and a male virgin was regarded in the smoking-room as a poor-spirited fellow, the pretence of chastity was to be kept up.' On this issue the Victorians were hypocritical to a point of schizophrenia. Yet even this does not account for the prevalence of infidelity. Cyril Pearl provides one possible reason for promiscuity in an age of large families; 'The Cult of the Double Bed led often to the Cult of the Double Life. While Mamma was presenting Papa with a pair of bouncing twins, Papa might be presenting Mabel with a pair of frisky ponies; the little lovers' villa in St John's Wood became a necessary annexe to the bulging family mansion in Belgravia.' Also the middle-class husbands were very well fed and waited upon; much less effort had to be spent on petty chores and anxieties than today; there was more time, energy, and money for

dalliance. Moreover, guilt itself served as a strong aphrodisiac.

The Rev. T. Garnier, a Marylebone rector, declared in 1858 that England was known as the 'most religious in pretension but in reality the most immoral and licentious nation under the sun'. The worst aspect of this licence, which shocked so many foreign visitors, was child prostitution at a time when the legal age of consent was still only twelve, and when girls of no more than eleven were often employed in the bawdy houses. A Royal Commission reported in 1871 that in three London hospitals during eight years 2,700 cases of venereal disease among girls between eleven and sixteen had been recorded, so the report recommended the raising of the age of consent to fourteen. The London Society for the Protection of Young Females tried in vain to combat the business in children and many other organizations such as the Society for the Suppression of Vice were established to reform sexual morality. The Bible Tract Society issued through the years no less than five hundred million leaflets directed at prostitutes. With typical stupidity such bodies were attacking the symptoms and not the causes: blatant, over-

whelming poverty and the truly immoral exploitation of cheap defenceless labour. Victorians associated childhood with innocence and this also acted as a kind of aphrodisiac for a rife paedophilia.

The prostitute as a type no doubt served the Victorians usefully as a scapegoat for their sexual guilt, just as the witch had done in earlier centuries. 'To some she appeared as a monster,' declared Burgo Partridge in his *History of Orgies*, 'to others as a martyr, to others an angel of mercy. Perhaps the most common view of her was as somebody who, having sucked the poison out of another's system becomes, although a heroine, poisonous and untouchable.' (Doré's, significantly, makes no obvious drawings of London prostitutes.)

The aristocrats of the profession were the demi-mondaines who kept servants, ran their own carriages, hired their boxes at the Opera, rode beside duchesses in the Row and lived in high style on an income of fifty pounds a week or more. In this world lived the notorious, fascinating Catherine (Skittles) Walters, doyenne of the Pretty Horse Breakers, who daily drove their own equipages in Rotten Row. Skitsie numbered among her friends the Prince of Wales and Gladstone (Old Glad Eye) who in the cultivation of his abiding hobby tried to reclaim her. Sir Edwin Landseer painted her portrait for his picture, *The Taming of the Shrew*, which shocked Society one summer at a Royal Academy Exhibition. She dressed her small body with taste and her pony turn-out was so exquisite a sight in the West End streets that it often held up the traffic. She became a legend, books were written about her, and she died in 1920 at the age of eighty-one, clasped

firmly to the motherly breast of the Holy Roman Church.

The number of her kind were limited: their state, wrote Mayhew, 'is the nearest approximation to marriage and finds many defenders and supporters'. Taine records:

Some of these women drive their own horses admirably – but put them all together and they do not compose a demi-monde in serious rivalry to 'society'. Here the gulf which separates virtue from debauchery is deep and sheer; there is no ladder from one to the other, as in France. Their religion has the same quality; paradise on one side, hell on the other and no intermediate stage, no purgatory. What remains then is nothing but an expression of lust, simple and coarse.

The mass of 'fallen sisters' were streetwalkers, many with their own premises. In the West End the more favoured ones, 'Cyprians of the better sort', as Mayhew called them, paraded discreetly out of the weather in Burlington Arcade with its chambers conveniently above the shops, but the humbler walks were in the Haymarket area, then known as Hell Corner. Here the streets were lined with gin palaces, oyster bars, brothels and houses of accommodation displaying notices: 'Beds to Let', and they were haunted, as a commentator in Dickens's *Household Words* remarks, by 'sporting gents and painted cheeks and brandy-sparking eyes'. The accepted approach to prospective clients was always 'Are you good-natured, dear?', and a standard rate was a five-shilling piece.

Dostoievsky recorded his impressions gained in that 1862 Exhibition summer:

Anyone who has ever visited London must have been at least once in the Haymarket at night. It is a district in certain streets of which prostitutes swarm by night in their thousands. Streets are lit by jets of gas – something completely unknown in our own country. At every step you come across magnificent public houses, all mirrors and gilt. They serve as meeting places as well as shelters. It is a terrifying experience to find oneself in that crowd. And what an amalgam it is. You will find old women there and beautiful women at the sight of whom you stop in amazement. There are no women in the world as beautiful as the English. The streets can hardly accommodate the dense, seething crowd. . . . All this mass of humanity craves for booty and hurls itself at the first comer with shameless cynicism. Glistening, expensive clothes and semi-rags and sharp differences in age – they are all there. A drunken tramp shuffling along in this terrible crowd is jostled by the rich and titled. You hear curses, quarrels, solicitations, and the quiet, whispered invitation of some still bashful beauty. And how beautiful they are sometimes with their keepsake faces! I remember once I went into a 'Casino'. The music was blaring, people were dancing, a huge crowd was still milling round. The place was magnificently decorated. But gloom never forsakes the English even in the midst of gaiety; even when they dance they look serious, not to say sullen, making hardly any steps and then only as if in execution of some duty. . . . In the Haymarket I noticed mothers who brought their little daughters to make them ply that same trade. Little girls aged about twelve seize you by the arm and beg you to come with them. . . . Jolly scenes, altogether.

Left, 'Coffee Stall – Early Morning' (Doré).

Right, 'The Great Social Evil. Time: Midnight. A sketch not a Hundred Miles from the Haymarket. *Bella*: "Ah! Fanny! How long have you been *gay*?"' (*Punch*, 1857). This sketch by Leech electrified *Punch*'s readers and was published only because the Editor was away ill at the time.

The Other People

The Radical Mr Harcourt once signed a visitors' book in a country house 'Lulu Harcourt, a friend of the People', and the next guest to leave wrote, under the signature 'Wharncliffe', 'a friend of the Other People'. The Other People were the 'right people', and what they did or said was the right thing to do or to say.

BARBARA WORSLEY-GOUGH, *Fashions in London* (1952)

Yes, there is very much to be said for civilization, if one is in a position to enjoy it.

GEORGE GISSING

In the nineteenth century, as Doré clearly reveals, social classes were far more distinctly divided than they are today. There were three broad levels – Matthew Arnold's Barbarians, Philistines and Populace – but between them rose, as now, intermediate steps; a skilled mechanic would consider himself to be far above the casual labourer, the City merchant a superior being to the shopkeeper. The aristocracy was a caste apart living on the *piano nobile* of the social structure, and as we have seen, from its ranks came much of the political leadership. This was Society. It ran the country and led the fashions, as a small exclusive cabal whose members all knew one another, enjoyed the same amusements, had their own code of manners, and remained unimpressed by the Gospel of Toil. Because its families were interrelated it was able to maintain a resilient strength and a firm solidarity during the transitional times of the nineteenth century, in spite of occasional tensions between the old Whig and Tory families.

The aristocracy possessed a built-in capacity for survival and adjusted itself judiciously to changing circumstances. The beginning of the end did not arrive until 1909 with Lloyd George's People's Budget; then five years later the lights went out and a new age began. After that land no longer meant power. It was a luxury and soon its husbandry was to be maintained by government subsidies and by deliberate financial losses that could be set against the swingeing taxes and death duties. Ultimate power came to lie solely in the creation and control of monetary credit and so, for the confused and irrational moment, it remains.

As land-owners the aristocrats were able to benefit from, and adapt themselves to, the Industrial Revolution by exploiting their possessions largely through rent, and so to preserve their old ways of life, and, if to a decreasing extent, their leisure, privilege and patronage. Mere wealth was no passport to Society; although marriage to wealthy merchant bankers had not been discouraged for a century or more, marriage into trade was beneath their dignity – at least until the seventies when the bottom fell out of farming after a series of disastrous harvests and the import of cheap prairie wheat began. Then the stigma against trade weakened, for support was needed by means of marriage to rich industrialists or American heiresses. This brought a revitalization not only of funds but of thinning blue blood. The enormous fortunes of the new industrial lords such as Burton, Hindlip, Armstrong, Masham, Brassey and Hambledon acquired through brewing, armaments, ironworks, railways and retailing could no longer be despised, even if they might be lampooned in *Punch* by Du Maurier's drawings of that bloated upstart, Sir Gorgius Midas.

The opening of social barriers between the aristocracy and the upper strata of the middle classes was assisted by common education in the new Public Schools initiated by Dr Thomas Arnold. It was also assisted to some extent by the tolerant attitude of the sybaritic Prince of Wales and the Marlborough House set. The Prince had been emancipated from the stern matriarchal control by his marriage in 1863. So long as his companions were rich and amusing, or 'fast and chaffy', and their womenfolk were beautiful, he did not care a damn about their lineage; if a hostess desired his presence at a house party, his friends had to be invited too and thus the visiting lists were perforce extended.

Middle-class domestic doorway at 170 Queen's Gate in the Queen Anne style of the Aesthetic Movement. Built in 1887, typically in red brick and white trim, for a wealthy cement manufacturer, this is perhaps Norman Shaw's finest work. It is now the official residence of the Rector of the Imperial College, South Kensington.

A surviving distinction between the two levels was domiciliary. The real homes of the aristocracy remained in the shires; their London dwellings were needed either for the London Season, or by those with political inclinations during the times when Parliament was in session. The new rich and the professional people – the Forsytes of the later decades of the century – tended to live permanently in town in the West End, fairly near their work. Alternatively they might acquire a large house and grounds in one of the new suburbs and refresh themselves with an annual holiday by the sea; in an attempt to imitate the upper crust, the richer ones built great rambling and often castellated mansions in the country, many of which could be easily reached by rail from London – as a country-house not quite the real thing but an admirable imitation, producing a comfortable and often civilized minority culture that survived until the Great Slump of the 1930s, when the servant problem became insurmountable and the long years of the green baize door passed away for ever.

The idea of the English gentleman (to a large extent the creation of Dr Arnold) was accepted by all. He was a new conception invented, as a cynic has remarked, by the aristocracy to keep the middle classes in order. In practice ladies and gentlemen were those who were comparatively wealthy, had received, if men, a public school education, talked with a definite dialect, ran carriages, and, when in London, lived for the most part in the West End. The gentry had long ago left Soho and Covent Garden, districts whose earlier elegance had degenerated into slumdom by the nineteenth century. They had moved west.

Mayfair and Belgravia were the heart of London's fashionable world, while Bohemia favoured the village atmosphere of Chelsea and Hampstead, although a colony of large studio houses for successful painters existed south of Holland Park where Lord Leighton's oriental fantasy survives as a type. Mistresses were kept hidden behind the boskage of the late Georgian suburb of St John's Wood (Sinjon's Wood they called it), as pictured by Holman Hunt's sermon in paint, *The Awakened Conscience*. Merchants might choose Bayswater or Kensington or still, to be nearer the City, the squares of Bloomsbury. The City itself became less and less domestic, for few businessmen now lived above their counting houses, as they had done for centuries. Most commuted daily, if not to and from the West End, then to the suburbs either by horse-bus or railway. In 1851 the

Middle-class domestic ritual: before dinner – the march past of the children under Nanny's firm control before being put to bed (*Graphic*, 1871).

residential population of the City numbered 128,000, but by 1871 it had dropped to 75,000.

Taine comments: 'My English friends confirm my guesses as to the size and number of large fortunes. "Take a cab and drive to Sydenham; you will pass by five miles of houses all indicative of an annual expenditure of £1,500 or more."' It was on Sydenham Hill that Sir Joseph Paxton built himself a grand mansion, surrounded by stables and out-houses, within sight of his reconstructed Crystal Palace. Suburbs like Islington, Holloway and Hackney on the other hand were lower in the social scale, accessible from the centre by horse-bus for sixpence and inhabited largely by better-paid clerks and small businessmen – the respectable Pooters struggling to keep up appearances in a world of subtle snobberies, where 'retired wholesalers' looked down on 'retired retailers', as Mrs Caudle had complained in *Punch* in 1840. The suburbs south of the river were never really smart although fine establishments with tall reception rooms set in wide gardens where greenhouses glittered might be found at Clapham and Streatham.

In *The Rose of Life* the fecund Victorian lady novelist, Miss E. M. Braddon (most famed for *Lady Audley's Secret* which achieved eight editions in three months in 1862), provides an insight into the social snobberies of her times in her descriptions of the family of Mr Dowden, partner in the firm of Dowden and Plowden, retail drapers:

'It's a pity the tide of fashion has ebbed away from Clapham Park,' said Mr Dowden.
'Oh, father, Clapham Park was never fashionable,' Sally murmured.
'What, not when the Gaylords and the Trowmongers, and the Hartlepools all had houses here?' protested her father, naming three well-known firms in Regent Street and Piccadilly. 'Your mother and I used to dine out three or four times a week 'in the season; and some of the finest run-outs in Hyde Park came from Clapham.'

In the West End a number of big houses surrounded by their grounds survived through part or all of the century, still inhabited as private dwellings during the Season by the old patrician families. Lansdowne House, south of Berkeley Square, indeed, stood until the 1930s and the author can recall paying it a visit in his youth when it had reached a melancholy state of dereliction and broken glass just before it was pulled down. Burlington House in Piccadilly was greatly altered and

The Eton and Harrow cricket match at Lord's – a group of spectators (*Graphic*, 1871).

'A Garden Party at
Holland House
during the Season'
(Doré).

its fine curving colonnades and gateway were demolished in the 1860s when the old house was enlarged for the Royal Academy and flanked by new buildings to house six learned societies. Northumberland House at the west end of the Strand – the last of the old Strand palaces which, with their gardens, had graced the riverside for centuries – came down in 1874 to make way for Northumberland Avenue. Gore House where dandy Count D'Orsay and Lady Blessington had held their serio-comic court in the 1840s, and where, to his loss, Alexis Soyer, famous chef of the Reform Club, had run a smart restaurant called 'The Symposium of All Nations' during the year of the Great Exhibition, soon disappeared and on its grounds rose the Albert Hall, Albert Hall Mansions and Lowther Lodge. The map of 1868 shows such palaces as Holland House, to the west, Devonshire House in Piccadilly, Chesterfield House in South Audley Street, Crewe House in Curzon Street, Grosvenor and Londonderry among others in Park Lane, Portland House in Cavendish Square, Spencer, Stafford, Arlington and Bridgewater all overlooking the Green Park, and Apsley House at Hyde Park Corner. The latter, known as Number One, London, the Duke of Wellington had purchased and altered (there installing iron shutters after stones were hurled at his windows in the Reform Riots of 1831). In the salons of these private palaces, filled with treasures collected by the passing generations, lavish ritualistic entertainment conducted during the Season was regarded as a social obligation. Dorchester House in Park Lane, a new creation of the fifties, was the most splendid of all.

In these mansions and in many of the smaller domiciles of fashionable Mayfair and Belgravia, dust sheets covered the furniture in the shuttered rooms during the winter, but from May to July, when the hunting and shooting were over and the corn was growing, the country families came to town with their retinues of servants, the dust sheets were folded up, the silver was unpacked and the hectic Season began: balls four or five nights a week lasting into the small hours, probably preceded by a visit to the Opera, endless formal dinner parties and huge receptions. In between there were garden-parties, shopping expeditions, visits to the Royal Academy or to Christie's to buy a painting or to Tat's to buy a horse, or to the Prince's Club for racquets, tennis, cricket or skating (until Cadogan Square was built on the site); there was the Eton and Harrow match at Lord's, racing at the Derby and at Ascot, the regular Sunday Church Parade, and the daily routine of taking the air in Hyde Park either in a carriage, on horseback or on foot along the old Route de Roi called Rotten Row. Lady Dorothy Nevill recalled that when she first came out, she attended during the Season fifty balls, sixty parties, about thirty dinners and

twenty-five breakfasts. The latter generally occurred *al fresco*, not on waking but in the afternoon.

Doré shows us a number of scenes of this heaven of the London Season as it appeared in the late sixties, and as a hostess's lion he enjoyed it, apart from the long and tedious dinners. These consisted of at least a dozen courses eaten at tables loaded with *épergnes* and showy decorations, and bright with white linen and glittering candelabra. Doré's rich people are stylized and remote, even sad, but he gives several scintillating and dream-like impressions of the Season: a garden party at Holland House (the old Whig stronghold, where Lady Holland held open house each Wednesday), a Company Dinner at the Goldsmith's Hall, a night at the Opera, a garden fête at Chiswick House.

Above all Doré liked to sketch the fashionable world riding in the Park and in *London* he provided no less than six pictures of the scene. 'This,' he remarked, 'is London: this, and the East End.' To that Jerrold added: 'Hyde Park at the height of the Season; Hyde Park on an afternoon when the Four-in-Hand Club is out in full force, is the best picture we can present to the stranger, of the pride and wealth, the blood and bearing, the comeliness, beauty, and metal of Old England.'

'A City Dinner at the
Goldsmiths' Hall' (Doré).

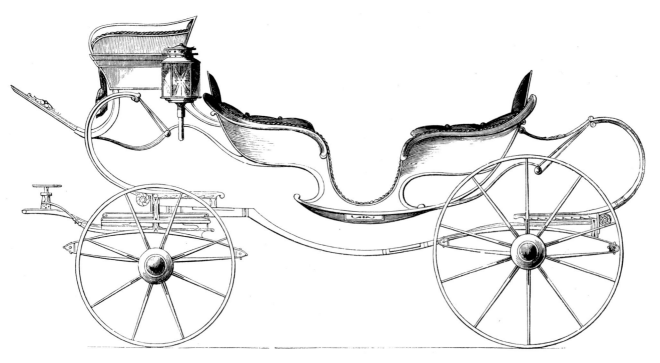

Hyde Park in the brilliance of the Season was well described by a contemporary as 'a large open drawing-room'. Here a magnificent display was presented daily by the noble, the celebrated, the wealthy and the notorious in fine clothing and splendid equipages driven by cockaded coachmen in gorgeous liveries and attended at the rear by a statuesque and carefully matched pair of flunkeys. Here ran smart new victorias with blazing escutcheons, raffish old phaetons, broughams, barouches, gigs, curricles, coburgs, landaus, basternas, buggies, britzkas, berlins, clarences, chariots, gigs, pony chaises and cabriolets (with plum pudding dogs running between their wheels) – masterly constructions of an old English craft that was taken for granted.

Taine took a more prosaic view of Hyde Park than Jerrold:

Round about two in the afternoon the principal road through it becomes a riding-school; there are ten times as many men on horseback, twenty times as many Amazons, as in the Bois de Boulogne, on a big day; tiny little girls and boys not more than eight years old ride their ponies beside their father's horse. I have seen massive and dignified matrons at the trot. This is one of their luxuries; another is their establishment of servants. For example, I have just been visiting a family of three persons: they have seven servants and three horses. The mother and daughter go for a gallop in the park every day, they even pay calls on horseback sometimes. . . . All this exercise seems necessary to their health; girls and ladies ride in the park even when it is raining. Three horses and a carriage cost about £200 a year. One's

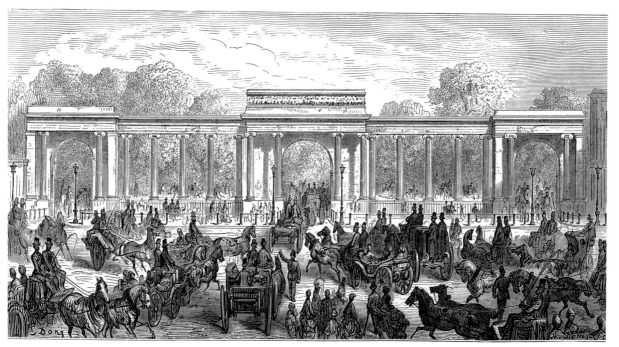

Vehicles for Carriage Folk. *Below left*, the Ionic screen by Decimus Burton at Hyde Park Corner, giving entrance to Rotten Row where the world of fashion took the air daily (Doré). *Top left*, a Sociable painted in rich ultramarine blue; *top right*, a Park Phaeton in the form of a nautilus shell; *centre right*, another Park Phaeton; *below right*, a Piletum with painted cane-work panels (*The Art Journal Catalogue of the Great Exhibition of 1851*).

Overleaf: Rotten Row in the Season (*Graphic*, 1871).

Basil Bradley

conclusion, from this crowd of people on horseback, as from the houses and servants, is that the wealthy class is far more numerous in England than in France. . . . From five o'clock to seven, dress parade. Beauty and adornment are abundant; but there is a want of taste . . . excessively numerous colours each swearing at the others.

By this time, clearly, shrill aniline dyes were superseding the softer vegetable products, two of them, magenta and solferino, being named after the bloody battles of 1859. The Park provided a fashion show, evoking the changing spirit of the age, throughout the Victorian decades – from voluminous skirts and petticoats topped by shawls and poke bonnets, through the fifteen-year reign of the crinoline and snood to the bustle, the Dolly Varden hat, the flowing garments of the aesthetic New Woman, the sealskin jacket, the tight jersey costume and then back to the bustle.

The most important shopping street for clothes and luxuries was Regent Street – 'an avenue of superfluities – a great trunk-road in Vanity Fair,' as George Augustus Sala, the indefatigable journalist, called it in *Twice Round the Clock* (1859). The street would be crowded with fashionable carriages during the Season between two and four o'clock in the afternoon. The grander ladies would remain seated in their carriages if the weather was fine

while the shopkeepers would emerge from their premises to serve them. Indeed, Regent Street, like the Row, was a fashion parade in spite of the visual degradation produced by the demolition in 1848 of Nash's graceful curving colonnades with their Doric columns of cast iron. 'Whatever could have possessed our Commissioner of Woods and Forests to allow those unrivalled arcades to be demolished?' asked Sala:

The stupid tradesmen, whose purblind, shop-till avarice led them to petition for the removal of the columns, gained nothing by the change, for the Quadrant, as a lounge in wet weather, was at once destroyed; it not only afforded a convenient shelter beneath, but it was a capital promenade for the dwellers in the first-floors above. The *entresols* certainly were slightly gloomy; and moustached foreigners, together with some gaily-dressed company still naughtier, could with difficulty be restrained from prowling backwards and forwards between Glasshouse Street and the County Fire Office. But perambulating Regent Street, at all hours of the day and night, as I do now frequently, I see no diminution in the number of moustached or rouged, or naughty faces, whose prototypes were familiar to me, years agone, in the brilliant Quadrant.

Bond Street was the gentlemen's street of high fashion. Oxford Street was less fashionable, though it contained the delightful porticoed Pantheon, which though built by James Wyatt in 1772 as a social centre for balls and

masquerades, had become a bazaar and a picture gallery, remaining so until 1870 when it was converted to a wine store, serving so until demolished in 1937.

A similar emporium was the so-called Crystal Palace, already described, at the corner of Great Portland Street. At the Baker Street Bazaar and at the Pantechnicon in Belgravia (built in 1830 and still standing) could be bought carriages, horse accoutrements and furniture, and at the latter also wines and toys.

In 1875 among the fine shops of Regent Street a novel emporium was opened by Arthur Lazenby Liberty (1842–1917) who, inspired by the Japanese section at the 1862 Exhibition (one result of Commodore Perry's entry into Yokohama Harbour in 1854), had become an ardent reformer of taste. The shop played a big part in the Aesthetic Movement for there could be acquired beautiful and exotic objects of furniture, bric-à-brac and fabrics imported from the Orient. Soon Liberty, who was eventually knighted, began printing his own fabrics based on oriental colours and designs. Morris, Ruskin, Millais, Whistler, Rossetti, Burne-Jones and Oscar Wilde were among his customers and all such as were aware that 'the visible world exists', and were tired of over-ornamented bulbous furniture and heavy upholstery of horsehair and plush, and of the hideously confused interiors of the day

The World of Fashion. *Opposite*, Paris designs (*I.L.N.*, 1866). *Above*, Regent Street in the Season (*I.L.N.*, 1866). *Below*, new entrance by F. P. Cockerell to the gallery of the Society of Painters in Water Colours, Pall Mall East (*I.L.N.*, 1875).

The World of Fashion.
'The Unfitness of
Things. *Impudent Boy*: "
say, Bill! Come
and see the conjuring –
Here's this here gal
a goin' to squeeze herself
into that there
broom!"' (Drawing by
Leech in *Punch*,
c. 1860.) The crinoline
lasted fifteen years;
compare the style of 1881
page 183.

with their strident colours, heavy shrouding curtains and general air of encumbered and suffocating claustrophobia. Liberty's represented a minority revolt against the overcrowded display of the average middle-class home. The puritan has always been particularly afraid of the lures of sight; as Taine noted, 'In the prodigious effort they have made to concentrate their entire attention on man's moral aspect, their optical sensibility has become both distorted and blunted.' But Liberty's showed Taste. Here could be obtained not only cheerful cretonnes and gay, flowery chintzes but softly draping dresses of gentle colours without fuss. Here the tea gown began its long languour.

As the middle classes grew in numbers a new type of shop came into being, the department store which bought in bulk, kept its prices low and demanded cash payment in place of the old yearly credit system on which the small, specialized, skilled shopkeeper had been surviving. In Westbourne Grove, near the new Bishop's Road station of the Underground railway, William Whiteley bought a small draper's shop in 1863 in a district where new residential roads and squares like those at Kensington were being developed for the middle classes. Soon he had built up a large multiple store where he proudly claimed to be able to supply 'anything from a pin to an elephant'.

In 1870 one of Whiteley's department managers named John Barker asked to be taken into partnership, was turned down but was offered instead an increase of salary to £1,000 a year – then quite a large income. Barker refused and proceeded to set up on his own in drapery in High Street, Kensington, where the old, narrow coaching road had just been widened by the Metropolitan Board of Works. Soon he too was running a flourishing department store. Joseph Toms had a small 'Toy and Fancy Repository' in the street and in 1862 he had taken into partnership Charles Derry. They too were soon in a big way of business. The Ponting brothers had arrived from Gloucester and had started a store in this wealthy area in 1863 which also expanded successfully.

Further east in Knightsbridge, close to Belgravia, Benjamin Harvey had founded an establishment in 1813 which he had bequeathed in the late fifties to his daughter, recommending that she take into partnership a Colonel Nichols, and soon another famous store was on its feet. In this way a number of small drapery and haberdashery shops were developed at an opportune moment by enterprising individuals in areas of demand into the famous stores of London whose names have become household words.

Some of these stores began even earlier than the sixties. Fortnum & Mason go back to 1707, Swan & Edgar to 1812, Shoolbreds to 1817, Lilley & Skinner to 1832, Peter Robinson to 1833, Daniel Neal to 1837, Maple's to 1842,

Hair-dos of 1870 (*Graphic*).

and Harrod, grocer of Brompton Road, to 1849. Peter Jones, D. H. Evans, and the Brixton Bon Marché all began in the seventies.

The poorly paid assistants, for a long time only male, did not enjoy a particularly good life. Their days were firmly regimented and disciplined and they worked such long hours that they might not put on their top coats and hats except on Sundays. Mostly they lived in dormitories in attics above, or near, their places of work, and communal meals were provided for them. Such compulsory living-in persisted at least until the end of the century.

Chain stores, too, were a new feature of the last three decades of the century. Thomas Lipton, for example, who had started a small grocery shop in Glasgow in 1872, had seventy branches in London alone by 1890.

In the sixties and seventies arose the middle-class co-operative stores. The Post Office Supply Association was founded in 1864 by a group of clerks in the G.P.O. who clubbed together to buy a chest of tea to save themselves ninepence in the pound. Two years later it changed its name to the Civil Service Supply Association, and opened a shop in the Strand, soon extending its scope from groceries to clothing and household goods. Then in 1871 a small group of army officers combined to buy a few cases of wine at wholesale price and soon it too had formed a trading association. It opened a shop in Victoria Street in 1872 on a part of the site still occupied by the Army and Navy Stores. This was a club as much as a shop where serving officers could meet when in town from Aldershot, Plymouth or Chatham, or when on leave from India or some other distant corner of the Empire. In fact it looked more like a club than a shop for it possessed no display windows along the street.

To the eighties belong the tea shops of the Aerated Bread Company and these were of some social significance in that at last women of respectability had somewhere to eat a meal and meet their friends, for until that time women of virtue could not go unescorted to restaurants; in fact, for a large part of Victoria's reign they did not go to restaurants at all. In the last decades, however, women were becoming more emancipated and beginning to earn their own livings in businesses and professions, and for such the ABC satisfied a growing need. Roger Fulford says in *Votes for Women* that the tea shop was an integral part of the Women's Suffrage Movement: it played its part in the release of the female from her bondage.

Left, 'A Ball at the Mansion House', and, *right*, 'The Limes, Mortlake, on the annual occasion of the Boat Race' (Doré).

Piety and Welfare

English society was poised on a double paradox which its critics, within and without, called hypocrisy. Its practical ideals were at odds with its religious professions, and its religious belief was at issue with its intelligence. . . . It was impossible to maintain for ever the position that Christian responsibility was a duty everywhere except in economic life.

G. M. YOUNG, *Victorian England: Portrait of an Age* (1953)

By the eighties slumming had become fashionable among the well-to-do. The dictionary definition of the word in the sixties had been 'to go into or frequent slums for discreditable purposes; to keep to back streets to avoid observation'. By the eighties it meant 'to visit slums for charitable or philanthropic purpose, or out of curiosity, especially as a fashionable pursuit'. Some of this visiting was morbid; according to *Punch* in one of its more cynical comments, it was the new way to climb the social ladder 'because you meet so many Duchesses in the East End now'. Yet much of the slumming arose from genuine compassion, one good result being the foundation in 1884 of the London Society for the Prevention of Cruelty to Children. Many charitable bodies were formed – to help fallen women, to advocate temperance, to distribute Bibles, to provide free meals for the destitute, and to build new model dwellings for the Industrious Classes. A number of attempts to bring light to the East End degradation were also made by various Settlements, an early one being that formed in 1867 by Edward Denison, a visitor employed by the Society for the Relief of Distress.

The two most famous philanthropists who gave away considerable shares of their private fortunes to the London poor were the American, George Peabody (1795–1869), and the Englishwoman, Angela Burdett-Coutts (1814–1906). She was born in a house in Piccadilly, lived there most of her life and loved her great city. As well as being a benefactor of the poor she was a generous hostess and entertained all the celebrities of her day, including the Prince of Wales, who called her 'after my mother the most remarkable woman in the kingdom'. At the age of twenty-three she had inherited, through the Duchess of St Albans, the huge fortune of nearly two million pounds left by her great-grandfather, Thomas Coutts the banker, and, with her former governess and life-long companion

Miss Meredith (later Mrs Brown), she moved at once to 1 Stratton Street, Piccadilly, where she lived until her death. In 1871 she was raised to the peerage as a Baroness in recognition of her benefactions, and in the following year was granted the Freedom of the City – the first woman to receive either distinction. She numbered among her close friends Charles Dickens, who often served as her almoner and gave her advice on the disposal of her wealth to charity. Among her other intimates were

Baroness Burdett-Coutts, philanthropist (*Graphic*, 1871).

BARONESS BURDETT COUTTS

A Victorian angel in the Greek section of the great cemetery of West Norwood, the south's equivalent of the north's Highgate Cemetery.

The Gothic fantasy of Columbia Market, Bethnal Green, built at the expense of Baroness Burdett-Coutts (*I.L.N.*, 1869).

Sir Henry Irving, the white Rajah Brooke of Sarawak, and the old Duke of Wellington with whom at one time she contemplated marriage. Then at the age of sixty-seven she shocked society by marrying her secretary, a young American of twenty-seven called William Bartlett – a union which, in spite of all the dire warnings, was a happy one. She died at the age of 92 and was buried with honour in Westminster Abbey as the last person to be interred there without being cremated.

Her whole long life and much of her fortune were devoted to philanthropy, and, being an able business-woman, she personally administered many of her own charities, most of which were given to help the poor of East London. She endowed churches and church schools, started sewing schools in Spitalfields where the silk trade was ailing, helped to found the Shoe-black Brigade and the Flower-girls Brigade, placed poor boys in training-ships for the navy and merchant service, supported schemes of emigration to the colonies, and attempted, without notable success, the reclamation of whores by founding, with Dickens, a Rescue Home for Women in Shepherd's Bush. She also relieved distress in Ireland by starting peasant and fishing industries, endowed bishop-rics in Adelaide, Cape Town and British Columbia, helped to found the S.P.C.C., and supported the Ragged

Schools Union. She had become a legendary figure, a kind of fairy godmother, long before she died.

She is best remembered today for having erected Columbia Market in Bethnal Green – a great Gothic folly of yellow brickwork, arcaded, pinnacled and embellished with terracotta ornaments and with such uplifting inscrip-tions as 'Be sober, be vigilant, be pitiful, be courteous'. The Market was like some grand cloth hall of the Middle Ages, and, unfortunately, was demolished some years ago. Built by William Cubitt and designed by Henry Darbi-shire, it was opened in 1869 by Miss Burdett-Coutts herself, received at a grand ceremony by a guard of honour of the Tower Hamlets Volunteers and an august company which included the Prince and Princess of Teck and the Bishop of London. The purpose of the market was to supply a notoriously indigent and overcrowded district with wholesome food at fair prices, for it was known that the poor were often cheated of their farthings by traders. The wholesale dealers who supplied the market were carefully selected for their honesty and good character, the shops on the four storeys were occupied by farmers or their agents so that middlemen could be eliminated and prices reduced, while in the open market square hawkers could display their goods on barrows hired at cheap rates from the market stores. On the east and west wings of the market, flats were erected to provide good lodgings for clerks and artisans. The whole complex covered two acres of ground, and incorporated a large tavern.

The market venture was a failure. For a start the barrow boys preferred the freedom of the streets and that kept the customers away so that the shops did not prosper. The market was then used for a time for the sale of fish, but the Billingsgate dealers opposed this to the extent of buying up all the morning's stock and reselling it at their own place by the river. Eventually the market became disused and empty except for a little trading in potatoes which went on in a desultory way at one end. Doré made a small drawing of this large and typically Victorian pile for his *London*.

A certain amount of organized new housing was built in Victorian London by several wealthy philanthropists and semi-charitable bodies, and much of it survives in the twilight areas of today. Generally referred to by its inhabitants as 'the buildings' and never as home, these utility working-class flats, depressing barracks of grimy stock brick surrounded by sunless deserts of asphalt, have become the slums of today, but when built they were a great improvement on the crowded tenements around them. Some of the earlier examples of the forties are not devoid of architectural merit and they are of social and historical significance as the ancestors of the council flat of the twentieth century.

Lord Shaftesbury was among the reformers who made some attempt to improve the housing conditions of Lon-don's working classes – of those dwelling, to quote him, in 'courts and alleys thronged with a dense and immoral population of every caste and grade of character, but almost every one of them defiled by perpetual habits of intoxication, and living amid riot and blasphemy, noise, tumult and indecency'. These words were spoken at a meeting of the Society for Improving the Conditions of the Labouring Classes, a body formed in 1844. Another moral body, formed the year before, was called the Metro-politan Association for Improving the Dwellings of the Industrious Classes, a joint stock company like the others that followed, which built to provide a return of no more than five per cent, the profit being ploughed back to build more blocks of flats.

The honorary architect to the Society was Henry Roberts, designer of Fishmongers' Hall. One of the first blocks by him was erected in 1849 on a site provided at a nominal ground rent by the Duke of Bedford; it can still be seen in Streatham Street, Bloomsbury. Each flat opens off a gallery and has a living room and two bedrooms, and the whole structure is fire-proof with iron beams, slate floors to the galleries, and roof and all other floors of hollow arched bricks, a system which Roberts patented. The flats, fifty-four in number, were let at 10 to 20 new pence a week and in 1852 yielded 5.75 per cent profit.

Roberts also designed the Model Houses sponsored by the Prince Consort as President of the Society, and shown close to the 1851 Exhibition in Hyde Park. Designed in a Tudor Gothic style, this building can still be seen in Kennington Park today, and is still occupied. Exhibited

Prince Albert's Model Dwellings erected in the grounds of the Knightsbridge Barracks, opposite the Great Exhibition, in 1851 (*I.L.N.*, 1851). The flats were built of hollow bricks to let at 20p a week and to provide a return on invest-ment of 7 per cent.

as a representative unit to which more storeys could be added, it had four flats on two floors, the upper pair being reached by a recessed open staircase. They too were of fireproof construction without any timber, the floors being reinforced with iron tie-rods. The flats had a living room with a fireplace, three bedrooms, a scullery with sink and ventilated larder and a closet off the scullery. A bathroom, of course, would have been an unthinkable luxury at that time.

Other bodies were formed to build model dwellings, such as the Improved Industrial Dwellings Company, begun in 1863 under the chairmanship of Sir Sydney Waterlow, the founder of the famous printing company, Lord Mayor of London, and a considerable benefactor. There was also founded in 1867 the Artisans', Labourers' and General Dwellings Company, which produced among others the Shaftesbury Park Estate north of Lavender Hill in South London. Begun in 1872 it consists of 1,200 terraced brick cottages, each with its garden, set along wide, tree-lined avenues, one block of flats and a group of shops – a pioneer work of its kind. The City Corporation itself built a workers' block in Farringdon Road in 1865 containing 168 flats letting at 22p to 38p a week, the designer being the City Architect, Horace Jones. These Corporation buildings are significant in representing the first example of local authority housing in London and they remained the only example until the end of the century.

The Metropolitan Board of Works, however, had no power to erect buildings. The formation of the London County Council and the passing of the Working Class Act in 1890 changed this situation as the realization at last dawned that the housing problem could not be solved by the profit motive or by sporadic philanthropy but only as a full-scale subsidised public duty. The earliest large development of working-class dwellings were those built by the L.C.C. at the end of the century for some 4,500 people on the site behind the Tate Gallery which had been occupied by the Millbank Penitentiary. They still stand as pleasant, humanly designed dwellings in red brickwork with Georgian windows, and at the time they were built were the best of their kind in the world. The courtyards are somewhat bleak but at least trees were planted in the streets around.

Philanthropic housing efforts had been made by Baroness Burdett-Coutts in Columbia Square around the market site, and also by Octavia and Miranda Hill, grand-daughters of Dr Southwood Smith, the pioneer who worked with Chadwick and Shaftesbury on sanitary reform. The most generous contributor, however, was George Peabody, a self-made American, descended from English yeoman stock, who began life as a grocer's boy and settled in London at the age of forty-three, already a wealthy man, to open a banking business. He entirely financed the American section at the Great Exhibition. Then in 1862 he gave, as a start, £150,000 to help the London poor, recommending that the fund, or part of it,

The American George Peabody, London philanthropist (*I.L.N.*, 1862).

be devoted to constructing improved dwellings; altogether he gave away half a million pounds. His first flats were erected in Commercial Street, Whitechapel, in 1864, the architect being Henry Darbishire, designer of Columbia Market and the flats around it. The Peabody block was four storeys high, the top floor entirely occupied by baths, drying areas for clothes, and covered playgrounds for children. Cooking in the flats was done on small coal ranges and lighting was by candles or rush-lights called 'farthing dips', for gas lighting was a luxury enjoyed only by the upper classes. (Domestic gas lighting did not come into general use until the sixties when pipe joints were improved and explosions reduced, but it was not effectively applied until Welsbach invented the incandescent gas mantle in the eighties.)

By 1875 nearly four thousand people, each family paying an average rent of 20p a week, were living in the comparative luxury of these dreary Peabody Trust estates, which were cut off from their surroundings by tall iron railings containing gates which were locked at night. Many of them are still in use. In a vignette Doré

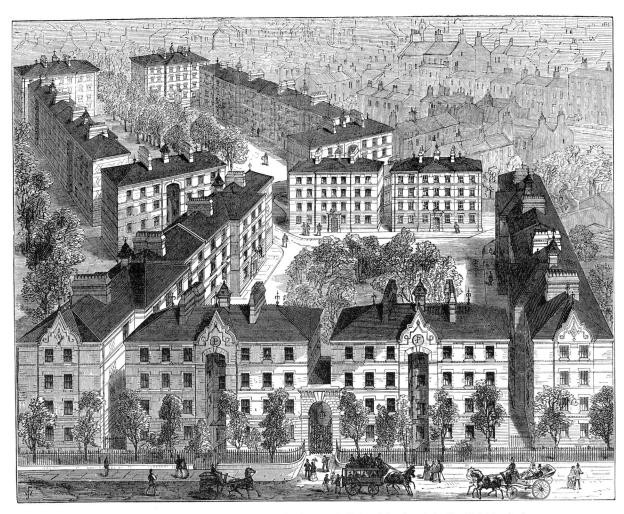

Peabody Square, Blackfriars Road – typical model dwellings for the poor built by philanthropic bodies (*I.L.N.*, 1872).

illustrates the statue of Peabody which remains to this day comfortably seated behind the Royal Exchange. Peabody was, in fact, offered a baronetcy by the Queen, which he declined, but on his death he received the honour of being carried to America for burial in a British warship.

All such worthy efforts only touched the fringe of the huge housing problem of London, and they did so in a manner which would not be acceptable today. In any case, rents of most of these dwellings were fairly high and could be afforded only by those in regular employment or comparatively well-paid mechanics; the very poor remained packed in their warrens. In 1865 the Society of Arts formed a committee which included Lord Shaftesbury, Henry Cole, Edwin Chadwick, J. S. Mill and Sydney Waterlow, to see what could be done about housing London's poor; they reported that only about seven thousand people had so far been re-housed in model dwellings, and that the results of these could not encourage investment. As always, the problem was money.

Another form of charity besides the building of model dwellings was the giving of gifts and bequests to the voluntary hospitals – and giving time, too, in almonry and money-collecting on flag days and on those annual Hospital Saturdays when the wealthy underwent a little gentle penance by rattling collecting boxes in the streets. A new attitude towards health was developing and hospitals were no longer regarded as the dangerous and depressing institutions where the poor went to die, but as highly organized forts against sickness, as places where for once humanity and mutual aid could prevail over competitive aggression.

The famous London hospitals, which were ancient foundations of the medieval Church, required much new building as London grew. St Thomas's, for example, which had originated late in the twelfth century in Borough High Street, Southwark, was rebuilt in a big way in Lambeth opposite the Houses of Parliament between 1868 and 1871. This long string of buildings was designed by Henry Currey on a new hygienic principle with seven four-storey brick pavilions linked by arcades in a kind of Italianate style; supported on a concrete raft, the hospital was erected on a site partly reclaimed from

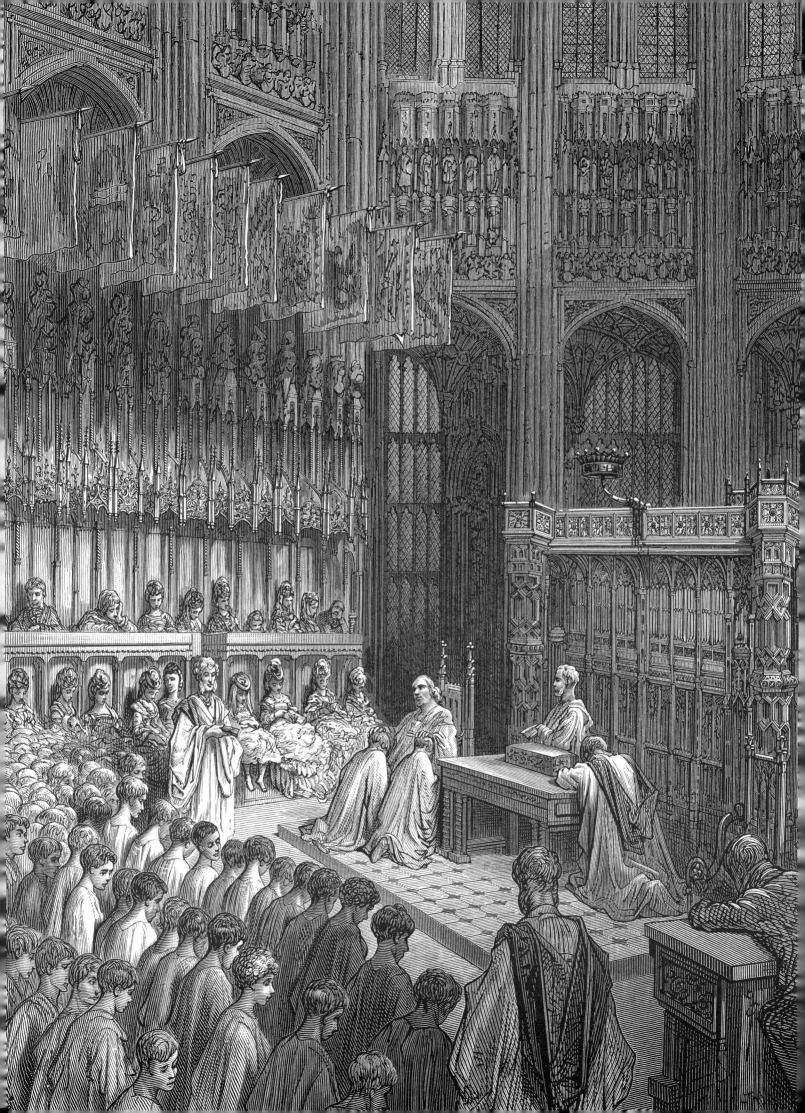

the Thames by the building of the Albert Embankment. In this year of 1972 most of it has been demolished to make way for a huge reconstruction.

The motive force of Victorian good works was religion, particularly in its ardent, evangelical, low-church forms, but all sects were at least united in their faith in the virtues of charity and religious instruction. Although the Church of England never adequately adjusted itself to the immense shift of populations caused by industrialization, an astonishing number of new churches and chapels, sometimes with denominational schools attached, were built in London in Victorian times; the number indicates not only the speed with which the metropolis was expanding but the general importance attached to church-going. Having been, if not disrespected, at least somewhat neglected during the Georgian reigns, the masculine deity once more ruled the universe with a firm hand and was esteemed and feared at least by the less intellectual members of the middle classes, while even those who lacked faith found that a show of respect was expedient and was good for business, for, as Taine remarked, 'an ordinary Englishman would be very reluctant to admit that an unbeliever could be a good Englishman and a decent respectable man'.

The Oxford Movement was followed in 1839 by the Cambridge Movement and the formation of the Camden Society (later called the Ecclesiological Society) at Cambridge University. Through its paper *The Ecclesiologist*, this group, until its close in 1868, came to exercise a certain authority over the design of Anglican churches. On the whole its views were sound and free from bigotry, although on liturgy it was rigid. It approved of St Barnabas, Pimlico, a pioneering Anglo-Catholic example which to us now looks rather uninteresting, as 'the most complete and sumptuous church dedicated since the revival'. Designed by Thomas Cundy aided by William Butterfield, in a ragstone rubble with Early English detailing, it is, with its attached vicarage and school, a fairly typical example of an early Victorian London church. By a temporal misfortune it was consecrated in 1850, the year in which the Pope issued a Bull establishing the Roman hierarchy in England and Wiseman was appointed the first Cardinal in Britain since the Reformation. Supporters of the High Church were believed to be Roman plotters who intoned Gregorian chants, went to confession, burned candles, swung censers, tinkled bells and carried on other devilish rituals to the sinful rustle of costly vestments. In a way which seems incomprehensible today, feelings ran so high that rioting occurred at St Barnabas.

An important movement, particularly in its effect on church architecture, was that of the romantic Oxford High Church associated with much heart-searching over the Thirty-nine Articles, with the *Tracts for the Times* and with the names of Newman, Froude, Keble and Pusey. The man who most deeply affected the whole Gothic Revival in architecture, inside and outside the Established Church, was, as we have seen, A.W.N. ('There-is-nothing-worth-living-for-but-Christian-Architecture-and-a-boat') Pugin. The ritualistic approach to religion became a favourite butt of *Punch*, which gleefully reported that one vicar who was said to combine the pleasures of the *haut monde* with the offices of the High Church, was installed in 1852 at Madame Tussaud's, 'moulded entirely from the runnings of his favourite Roman Candles'. Many Victorians feared that aura of sensuality, as a sort of surreptitious sexiness, in the High Church approach. As a scurrilous ballad of the period went:

> The Reverend Pimlico Poole was a saint
> Who averted from sinners their doom,
> By confessing the ladies until they felt faint
> All alone in a little dark room.

The huge subject of the Victorian churches of Greater London has already filled more than one book. The Rev. Basil Clarke wisely generalizes: 'Though not everything is admirable, anything *may be*, and it is unwise to assume beforehand that a church will be good or bad because of its date or type. . . . It is always important to know what was said about churches at the time when they were built. They ought not to be judged – though they often are – by standards that were not the standards of the people who built them.'

Most of us have our favourites. My own two are Christ Church in Christchurch Road off Streatham Hill, and St Augustine's, Kilburn Park Road, of the seventies. Christ Church comes before our specific starting date of 1851 for it was completed in 1841, but my fondness for it compels a reference. It is an eccentric but impressive design by James Wild, very clear-cut, simple and homogeneous in yellow stocks with arches of alternating red and yellow brickwork and a tall campanile with windows pierced in thin vertical recesses. Ruskin admired it but *The Ecclesiologist* found it too exotic. Its style, if anything, is Romanesque Byzantine but others have described it as Italian Gothic, Neo-Romanesque, Lombardic or Italian with Saracenic influence, while according to Sir Nikolaus Pevsner it is in the Rundbogenstil.

St Augustine's, Kilburn, is the finest High Victorian church not only in London but in the whole of England 'proud, honest and upright' as Pevsner says. The church was consecrated in 1880, though the tower and spire were not finished until 1898. The architect was John Loughborough Pearson, a deeply dedicated man, who later designed the cathedrals of Truro and Brisbane. The wonder of the church is its interior, for Pearson had a feeling for subtle spatial relationships which was rare in his time, and, as Sir John Betjeman has pointed out, the way to enjoy the interior is to wander around noticing how the vista alters at each step. Buttresses project all round the interior through which the aisles and a gallery are pierced, an idea borrowed from Albi Cathedral. East of the south transept lies a charming little Lady Chapel with an apse. The roof throughout is solidly rib-vaulted, as in all Pearson's churches. Another earlier church by Pearson, built before he had completely formed his bold style, is St Peter's, Kennington Lane, consecrated in 1864 and built on part of the site of the old Vauxhall Pleasure Gardens.

An important London church, conceived in 1849 but not consecrated until 1859 as the first of the ostentatious High Victorian examples, is William Butterfield's All Saints', Margaret Street, Westminster. Its new poly-chromy of exterior brickwork in dark red banded with black is continued inside with a dazzling, uninhibited stridency of frescoes, mosaics, and carvings, in a brilliance of marble, tile, onyx, stained glass and gold. Nothing is left undecorated and 'everywhere the praise of the Lord is drummed into you' (Pevsner). The complex of church, clergy house and school is on a restricted site in a narrow street and so, for boldness of effect, it was all built very high, with a lofty spire. Dr Pusey laid its foundation stone and the Cambridge Camden Society blessed it, although when completed, *The Ecclesiologist* found it forceful but ugly.

The simple, barn-like, but monumental churches of James Brooks are worth noticing for he did well with limited funds in poor districts like Shoreditch. His most famous example is the Ascension on Lavender Hill, Battersea, which was begun in 1873 and completed by another architect, J. T. Micklethwaite, in 1883.

A late Victorian church of eccentric interest is Holy Trinity at the bottom of Sloane Street. Paid for by the Earl of Cadogan and consecrated in 1890, it is in a kind of free Art Nouveau Gothic style of brick and stone, the designer being John Sedding, an ardent supporter of the Arts and Crafts movement and a member of the Art Workers' Guild. The broad interior contains many excellent examples of the craftsmanship typical of the period, notably of grilles. William Morris and Edward Burne-Jones designed the glass in the east window here.

Most church- and chapel-going was a formal ritual in Victorian times and provided little emotional release. The gloomy tedium of Sunday, when even reading was restricted to the Bible or to religious publications, was one of the self-immolating penalties the Victorians imposed

St Augustine's, Kilburn, by Pearson, the finest High Victorian church in England. (From a painting in the R.I.B.A. library.)

upon themselves. Dickens, by no means an irreligious man, condemned the censorious convention in *Little Dorrit*: 'Everything was bolted and barred. . . . Nothing to see but streets, streets, streets. Nothing to breathe but streets, streets, streets. Nothing to change the brooding mind, or raise it up.' To bring a little excitement to the dreary, restricted round of the Lord's Day one could, if at a certain level of society, join Holy Willie's Salvation Army (founded 1865) and march to street meetings in uniform behind banners and bands. Others, whether nonconformist or merely curious, might go to hear Dr Charles Haddon Spurgeon preach at his Metropolitan Tabernacle in Newington Butts, a huge classical temple with a Corinthian portico which, with its two galleries supported on cast-iron columns, could hold over four thousand people. (Only its front now remains.)

It is hard to understand by reading his sermons today why Spurgeon could draw such enormous crowds twice a week. 'I feel for some of you that God has set before you this morning an open door which no man can shut and

All Saints', Margaret Street, Westminster, by Butterfield; consecrated in 1859, it possesses London's tallest church spire (*I.L.N.*, 1855).

fiercest diatribes against the dramatic art was lately [1862] uttered by Mr Spurgeon', the Frenchman Alphonse Esquiros remarked in his *English at Home*. 'As Mr Spurgeon is an eloquent preacher, but borrows several of his best effects from theatrical action, it has been asked whether a little professional jealousy has not been mixed up with his attacks.' Yet his sincerity was deep and patent and he genuinely believed that God had called him. 'I had been about five years in the most fearful distress of mind, as a lad,' he wrote. 'I thought the sun was blotted out of my sky – that I had sinned so against God that there was no hope for me.' In the end the millions of words he uttered could all be summarized by the three unequivocal lines written for the Victorian child in a Sunday paper:

Satan is glad – when I am bad,
And hopes that I – with him shall lie
In fire and chains – and dreadful pains.

There was a good deal of morbid sado-masochism in Victorian religion. Trying to be good and doing good was, in any case, a safe investment in heavenly Consols. Guilt suffused society – about pleasure in general and sexual indulgence in particular. The whole of life to the many who had Manichean leanings seemed to be a ceaseless battle between Good and Evil, and the Devil could be found tempting the weak with the most trivial and harmless diversions – an attitude that could leave lasting mental scars from childhood fears.

Another man who preached the wrath of God and drew the multitudes was the Yankee Methodist Dwight L. Moody. For most of his evangelizing life, that followed a brief career in youth as a clerk in a Chicago boot shop, he was accompanied on his missions by Ira D. Sankey who led the singing with his sweet tenor voice and his portable harmonium. Spurgeon's fame had spread abroad and Moody asked, 'If God could use Spurgeon, why should He not use me?' Moody's first visit to London was made in 1867 partly with the purpose of meeting Spurgeon and hearing him preach. Six years later he visited Britain with Sankey on a preaching tour during which the two men managed to stir even the dour Presbyterians of Scotland to heartfelt unison, particularly in Sankey's favoured new hymn, 'The Ninety and Nine'. Revivalism flared and Moody and Sankey became famous throughout the country, part of their success being due to their ecumenical approach which ignored all denominational boundaries – an approach that did not please Spurgeon who had advised Moody to attack the Church of England.

Moody and Sankey arrived in London in March 1875 where they had booked the Agricultural Hall, Islington, for ten weeks. The great arena, normally used for horse and cattle shows, was furnished with fifteen thousand

my prayer shall be offered over every syllable that I utter, that God may lead you through that open door at this very moment. So that not only twenty or a hundred, but thousands of you may find Christ, and be saved with an everlasting salvation.' And so on and so on for an hour or more at a stretch. Yet he was so immensely popular and became such an established institution that the Staffordshire potters made one of their pop-art figures of him. His ponderous sermons finally filled fifty volumes and they sold by the ton. No doubt Spurgeon had the demagogic touch and a gift of oratory in which he would pile metaphor upon metaphor, crack jokes and allude to the Deity as though he were an intimate friend. A stocky, vigorous man of Essex, he would pour out his rolling, Biblical periods from a railed-in platform some twenty-five feet square whereon he had plenty of room to manoeuvre, believing with good sense that the power of oratory lay as much in the legs and arms as in sonorous cadence.

He would fulminate with particular vehemence and in the old Puritan tradition against the theatre. 'One of the

Overleaf, Moody and Sankey at the Agricultural Hall, Islington (*Graphic*, 1875).

chairs above which swung enormous gas chandeliers while around hung red banners bearing uplifting texts. Again the pair drew the crowds. London took them to their hearts and before they left the metropolis a million and a half people had been to hear the mountainous, bearded Moody preach and the dapper Sankey sing.

At first the Press was derisive. 'A ranter of the most vulgar type,' declared the *Saturday Review*, degrading religion 'to the level of the Penny Gaff'. But many were impressed, including Lord Shaftesbury, who was 'the more impressed because of the imperfections of the whole thing'. Moody's manner was quite different from that of Spurgeon, being conversational and homely but loud enough for all to hear. It is to their credit that respectable, tolerant Londoners, even if they were less sophisticated a century ago than they are today, could take this kind of Uncle Remus style from the untutored but endearing American: '"Bartimeus, is that you?" "Yes." "Well, I thought it was, but I couldn't believe my eyes! How've you gotten your sight?" "Oh, I just met Jesus of Nazareth outside the city and I asked him to have mercy on me." "Jesus of Nazareth! What! is he in this part of the country?" "Sure. Right here in Jericho." "I *should* like to meet him," and away he runs down the street.'

Moody and Sankey visited London again in 1883 when they made use of two demountable tin tabernacles for their missions in order to move around to different dis-

tricts, mostly in London's outer areas. Moody's last London mission was in 1892 when he preached at the Metropolitan Tabernacle then just bereft of Spurgeon who had worked too hard and, surprisingly, had smoked too much. Moody was remarkably relaxed in his deliveries. 'If I were to get into such a state of nervous excitement as General Booth,' he once declared, 'I should have been dead ages ago.' (Booth, in fact, lived to the age of eighty-three, too long deprived of heavenly joy.)

Meanwhile, much social distress and deprivation was being relieved by new attitudes to education. Among the most important legislative steps taken in the nineteenth century was the Forster Education Act of 1870, which, though limited, had a considerable effect on the life and the look of London. The Act was passed under Gladstone's first government, its sponsor being William Forster, a woollen manufacturer of the West Riding and a Quaker radical who had married a daughter of Dr Thomas Arnold. It was an outcome of the 1867 Reform Act which increased the franchise of the urban working class; the time had come to 'educate our masters'.

Visible results of the 1870 Act can still be seen all over London in the shape of the many tall school buildings the London School Board was soon erecting. Rising high above the grey seas of slated roofs, they often still dominate a whole area with their powerful presence of red brick-work and steep gables. They are clearly among the better

Left, the Festival of Charity Children in St Paul's Cathedral, an annual event established in 1704 (*Graphic*, 1870). *Right*, Oban Street School, Tower Hamlets, one of the many designed for the London School Board by E. R. Robson (*Builder*, 1881).

Above, 'Dean's Yard, Westminster' (Doré), a scene familiar to the privileged boys of Westminster School. *Below*, Brook Street Ragged School, Hampstead Road, founded 1843 (*I.L.N.*, 1853).

products of London's Victorian architecture, for the Board was lucky in its choice of architects. This school style persisted into the next century but became somewhat debased.

The most prominent of the Board's designers was E. R. Robson (1837–1917) who was born in Durham and served six years of his early working life in that city as architect to the Dean and Chapter of the Cathedral, where he restored the central tower. Then he worked for a time as an assistant to Sir George Gilbert Scott. Later he was to design scores of schools for the Board. He deliberately built them high and made them look high with tall windows, turrets and chimneys topping steeply pitched roofs and lofty class-rooms. The style of these 'Beacons of Enlightenment', as Sherlock Holmes called them, was the new Queen Anne introduced by Nesfield and Norman Shaw, in the adoption of which Robson may have been influenced by J. J. Stevenson, his partner for a time, who built a once-notable dwelling called the Red House in Bayswater Road.

At the start the Board, which included Lord Lawrence, Professor Huxley, W. H. Smith and Mrs Garrett-Anderson among its members, erected thirty schools based on competition designs produced by six selected architects, but after a year the Board decided to save fees by employing Robson, one of the successful competitors, as their chief architect on a salaried basis. Until he retired

'The Three Rs; or Better Late than Never. *Right Hon. W. E. Forster (Chairman of Board)*: "Well, my little people, we have been gravely and earnestly considering whether you may learn to read. I am happy to tell you that, subject to a variety of restrictions, conscience clauses, and the consent of your Vestries – YOU MAY!"' (Tenniel in *Punch*, 1870.)

in 1889, Robson was personally responsible for every L.S.B. school erected. By 1881 he and his staff of fifteen had achieved some 250 new schools in London. This works out, on an average, at more than two schools designed and erected every month. It was a remarkable achievement which was partly accomplished by rigorous standardization of methods and elements but without standardization of individual building designs as entities. 'A positive result,' wrote David Gregory-Jones in an informative article, 'Towers of Learning', in the *Architectural Review* (June 1958), 'is that these buildings, strong in personality, do a very great deal to set a stamp of unified character on the hodge-podge of Victorian London . . . with their constricted sites wrested from the midst of slum housing set in the grimmest parts of London with never a tree in sight, it is remarkable what Robson and his office did achieve.'

The rooms were not cosy but their height was necessary to admit enough light through the tall windows restricted in width by the solid brick construction wherein classes of up to sixty children were taught. Some of the interiors of the Robson schools even achieve a certain nobility with their galleried halls rising through two or three

storeys, as in the Berger Road School in Hackney, built in 1878 and a particularly good example of Robson's work. He built solidly and his decorations of panels, swags, and cartouches were all hand-wrought. The new style, he thought, was a fitting symbol of the fresh approach to education and he produced from the style not only a new refinement, charm, and cheerfulness but also a degree of monumentality that other architects rarely achieved in the same manner.

Robson was one of the most intelligent and competent architects of his time and he has not yet received the credit he deserves. Apart from his school work he ran a private practice and among his major jobs in that sphere were the premises for the Institute of Painters in Water Colours in Piccadilly, of 1881, and the great People's Palace in Mile End Road, opened in 1887 as a recreational and educational institution for East London.

Improved mass education, as represented by Robson's schools and such institutions as his People's Palace, would, it was generally felt, bring among other benefits, a reduction of crime in the Modern Babylon. By the seventies this had become a need of some urgency, as the following chapter will reveal.

Crime and Punishment

Until I came to England the appearance of a police officer in a house where I was living always produced an indefinably disagreeable feeling, and I was at once morally on my guard against an enemy. In England a policeman at your door merely adds to your sense of security.

A. I. HERZEN, *My Past and Thoughts* (1870)

Assuredly there is no place so remarkable as a prison for its utter ignorance of human nature . . . no place where there is so little wisdom displayed, and yet none where so much is required.

HENRY MAYHEW and JOHN BINNY,
The Criminal Prisons of London and Scenes of Prison Life (1862)

Wandsworth Goal, built in 1851 on the principle of radiating wings and isolation cells as the Surrey County Prison, or House of Correction, is still in use.

Lawlessness and rioting during the depression, unemployment, and exploitation suffered by Englishmen after the Napoleonic wars, combined with misuse of the military to quell uprisings, as at Peterloo in 1819, brought realization of the urgent need, particularly in London, for an improved and properly organized police force to maintain public order. Through the efforts of Robert Peel, who has been called the greatest of all Britain's Home Secretaries, a Bill to that end was carried through with quiet dispatch. The chief authority of police in the metropolis was to be the Home Secretary, and two magistrates were to be appointed to run the force under the title Commissioners of the Metropolitan Police. The men chosen were a soldier, Colonel Charles Rowan, and a young Irish lawyer, Richard Mayne. In 1829 the new force began its duties.

Its headquarters, and that of the Central or A Division, were established just north of the area once occupied by Henry VIII's great rambling palace of Whitehall at a spot which, through the centuries, had been used by Scottish nobles when they came to pay their respects to the Kings of England. The name was perpetuated in an alley running out of Whitehall on the east side called Great Scotland Yard.

Peel laid down that from the start officers were to be recruited from the ranks and that every member was to give his whole time to the service. The standard uniform was almost civilian in appearance, except for the special buttons and some lettering on the collar. The constable carried a rattle and beneath the tails of his dark blue coat he concealed a truncheon. His top hat was conventional but reinforced within. Trousers were also blue, but white trousers were optional for summer wear. Within a few months after the Peelers were formed, the removable striped arm-band was added to signify when the wearer was on duty.

The next step was the formation in 1842 of an experimental Detective Force without uniform which was to develop into the world-famous C.I.D. or Criminal Investigation Department, formed in 1878. That early Force has been personified and immortalized by Dickens's creation in *Bleak House* of the imperturbable Inspector Bucket of the Detective. For some years the Detective formed but a small part of the police establishment, numbering as late as 1868 only fifteen men among a total of eight thousand.

A change of administration occurred in 1855 when the force came under the control of a single Commissioner. To him in 1869, as a result of a new Act, the Home Secretary delegated all powers connected with carriages plying for hire. In the mid sixties the uniform was changed; a tunic replaced the tail coat, and a helmet, more or less as we know it today, replaced the old chimney pot. (Doré occasionally depicts the new uniform.) The new look of the police stimulated not only the expected ribaldry in magazines like *Punch* and *Fun* but also some

151

general concern that the force was tending towards militarism. From the start of the Peelers, it seems, the public has always been too ready to ridicule and criticize its admirable and hard-pressed Bobbies and too slow to give them the moral encouragement – or the rewards – they need and deserve, in spite of their occasional lapses.

In the sixties trouble arose within the force about pay, which was as low as hours of duty were long. Yet at no time in London's history was an efficient force more greatly needed. By 1862 all transportation of criminals had ceased as a result of the Penal Servitude Act of 1853, and the capital was full of released convicts who had

robbery by which victims were half-throttled and stunned from behind – a method learned, it is believed, in convict ships from the jailers who practised it on their charges as a brutal form of subjugation. Mostly the garotters worked in gangs of three – a 'front stall', a 'back stall' and a 'nasty man' who was the operator and leader. The attacks began at night but soon they were being perpetrated in broad daylight in the heart of London. At night many were afraid of venturing out and public dread became almost panic. The police were naturally, but unjustly, blamed; they were too few in number – less than a dozen detectives, for example, in a total force of no more than some seven

'The Police wear Beards and Moustaches. – Panic amongst the street-boys.' (Leech in *Punch*, *c*. 1851.) The toppers of the Peelers were changed to helmets and new uniforms in 1864, producing accusations of militarism.

served their sentences. The ticket-of-leave system – also a product of the Act – by which prisoners were discharged on licence before their sentences had expired, also helped to increase the new wave of crime. An article in *The Builder* of 30 August 1862 expressed the growing concern: 'In Queen Victoria's reign with all the aid of brilliant gas-lighting, which even pervades the most miserable courts and alleys . . . deeds of violence, almost as bad as those committed by the professional stranglers of India, are of nightly and even daily occurrence in the metropolis and suburbs.'

The 'professional stranglers of India' relates to the alarming prevalence of garotting, a violent method of

thousand (excluding, of course, the City which possessed its own establishment). This figure was hardly double that of 1840 within a Metropolitan Police District that had increased over six times in area. And the ticket-of-leave system, which, lacking proper registration, was ineffectual, had not been conceived by the police.

From the start, the police had also to maintain civil order and control public demonstrations. In Victorian times, as now, Hyde Park was a popular place in which to hold meetings of protest. On two occasions in Victoria's reign demonstrations got out of hand. The first was the Sunday Trading Riot of 1855 against Lord Robert Grosvenor's Bill to prohibit Sunday trading. As often

happens on such occasions a peaceful meeting developed into a serious fracas between the police and their baiters, the spark in this case being the throwing of missiles by a few roughs at passing carriages. Some seventy people were arrested and forty-nine policemen were injured.

The second occasion, which occurred in 1866 and concerned electoral reform, was more serious. The respectable Reform League held a number of meetings in Trafalgar Square and other places and it organized a large demonstration to take place in Hyde Park. The new Home Secretary foolishly decided to prohibit it. Marching bands accompanied by the usual rabble lusting for a brawl reached the gates of Hyde Park and were there turned back by the massed police numbering three thousand. The reformers thereupon marched on to Trafalgar Square in good order, but the rabble remained. Stones flew, the railings were torn up and crowds streamed into the Park. The situation was soon out of control and finally the Guards were summoned to restore order. To the chagrin of the Force, this was the first time the military had been called in since the Peelers had been formed. Many policemen were injured, some to a point of permanent disablement. Clearly the ban had been a mistake.

The police were blamed but again unjustly, for they had merely carried out the orders of the Home Secretary to the best of their ability. The Chief Commissioner himself, Sir Richard Mayne, by now an old man, was on the spot issuing orders from horseback throughout the affray as though in a battle with blood streaming down his face. Two years later he died, this Satrap of Scotland Yard as *Fun* had called him, a valuable job accomplished. He was succeeded by Colonel (later Sir Edmund) Henderson of the Royal Engineers, who had been in control of the convict establishment in Australia and for a time had served as Director of Prisons at the Home Office. Though he was a martinet, a worse choice could have been made. He improved and extended the Force until his retirement in 1886 after the West End rioting. During his regime of seventeen years the Detective Branch was transformed into the C.I.D. In 1885 he replaced the rattle with the whistle and in that year the Thames Division, or River Police, acquired a fleet of steam launches. The year was also important for the purchase of a site on the Embankmen just north of the Houses of Parliament where larger headquarters called New Scotland Yard were to be built.

The two main events of Henderson's time were the police strike of 1872 and the West End rioting of 1886 which ended his career. The strike was hardly an official one since the Government would not allow the formation of a policemen's union – a problem eventually solved by the compromise of the Police Federation. The agitation of 1872 is understandable, for at that time a copper was receiving a mere thirty shillings a week, less than a skilled labourer could earn. It included a demonstration in Hyde Park and ended with the dismissal of a few leaders and promises of higher pay and shorter hours. Paying our policemen properly is still an issue.

Although constabulary duty was fairly hard it was rarely tedious. In 1878, for example, their duties ranged from supervising the erection of Cleopatra's Needle on the Victoria Embankment to helping to save life after an appalling disaster on the river itself, the sinking of the pleasure steamer *Princess Alice* with a loss of seven hundred lives. Other contrasts that year included attending a bicycle meet at Hampton Court and escorting processions of unemployed and social reformers through the streets – both common pursuits at the time.

In the eighties the force had a hectic time trying to curb the outrages of members of an Irish–American conspiracy, the Fenian dynamiters. They began in 1883 with an explosion at *The Times* office, and that was followed by a more violent one outside the Local Government Office in Charles II Street, off Whitehall. Others were perpetrated during the next two years – at Scotland Yard itself, in Trafalgar Square and, in the case fictionalized by Robert Louis Stevenson in *The Dynamiter*, at Westminster Hall. The protection of public buildings required by these unpredictable explosions put a severe burden on both Metro-

politan and City forces. To add to the strain there began in 1885 a series of further demonstrations by the unemployed, by radicals, including the Social Democratic Federation, and by the Irish Home Rule sympathizers.

These demonstrations reached their climax on 13 November 1887, known as Bloody Sunday. A pitched battle then occurred between police and demonstrators in Trafalgar Square, so riotous that the police lost their heads and were routed. Sir Charles Warren, the new Chief Commissioner, a handsome, impatient disciplinarian known as the Iron Hand without a Velvet Glove, then called for the Life Guards. Thousands who had been camping in the Square were forced to retreat and the area was temporarily closed. Everyone with leftward inclinations was there, including William Morris, Bernard Shaw, John Burns, Cunningham Graham, Mrs Besant with supporters of her Law and Liberty League, and Karl Marx's daughter – to say nothing of some thirty thousand desperate unemployed. One mild and undistinguished demonstrator lost his life in the shambles and so became a glorious martyr whose funeral was followed by an enormous crowd. William Morris was so disgusted with the whole affray, wanting nothing less, in his loving way, than 'a beautiful and happy world', that he thereafter gave up all political activity.

More disturbances were threatened the following year but a diversion was created by a series of hideous murders in the Whitechapel district by a psychopath known as Jack the Ripper who, with Sweeney Todd, the Demon Barber,

An attempt by Fenian conspirators to blow up government offices in Charles II Street, Westminster (*I.L.N.*, 1883).

has achieved immortality in folk history. No less than six women, all prostitutes, were disembowelled by this maniac, whose chronic obsession was to remove the womb. In one case the victim's entrails were found encircling her neck. Everyone was fascinated, for here some sort of moral righteousness seemed to be mixed up with the sadism. Amidst all the morbid fuss the East End Magdalens were calmly resigned. To be murdered was one of the accepted hazards of the profession and, as one of them who had been on the game for twenty years remarked, 'Well, suppose I do get killed, it will be a good thing for me, for the winter is coming on and the life is awful. I can't leave it. Nobody would employ me.' A number of arrests were made and strong anti-Jewish feeling in the locality increased the difficulties of the police. The Home Secretary, for no considered reason, wanted to close all the East End brothels, a proposal which came to nothing for he was persuaded that women would merely be driven on to streets that were already well supplied with harlots. In spite of great efforts by the police the murderer was never found and the Chief Commissioner resigned. Then, to the chagrin of the popular press, the outrages ceased as suddenly as they had begun.

By the eighties the headquarters of the force had spread itself in an untidy mess of mean buildings around its original centre. A new and more efficient headquarters was badly needed, and Henderson had his eye on a particular site where a large but uncompleted building had been standing behind hoardings for some time.

The Victoria Embankment had been opened in 1870 leaving various patches of land reclaimed from the river to its west. One of these formed half of a large rectangular plot lying between the Embankment and Whitehall not far from Westminster Bridge and facing the steam-boat pier which Doré illustrated. It was first laid out as a temporary garden until the earth had settled sufficiently to permit building. Then in 1875 a company bought the site from the Metropolitan Board of Works and began to erect a grandiose opera house which was to be larger and more splendid than that at Covent Garden and nearly as large as La Scala at Milan. The foundation stone was laid on 16 December by the Duke of Edinburgh. The following year the design was exhibited at the Royal Academy by its architect Francis H. Fowler, although a drawing of this New National Opera House, as it was called, had already appeared in *The Graphic* for 5 June 1875. It was a classic design embellished with statues in niches and much wall decoration, having a conical roof above the foyer; the whole reveals the inspiration of Garnier's Opéra in Paris. The building was to face the river and along the entire front was to run a *porte cochère* with projecting wings. It was a far less inspired design than Garnier's but it did not lack dignity.

In September 1876 progress on the rising structure ceased. According to *Building News* there were 'temporary fiscal difficulties'. The roof was never added and so the white elephant stood hatless and unfinished for the next four years. Meanwhile Henderson had been making

The National Opera House on the Thames Embankment that was never finished; on the site the police built their New Scotland Yard headquarters (*Graphic*, 1875).

his approaches and the Metropolitan Police Surveyor, Butler, informed the Receiver that he had been offered the building privately for £25,000 and that he could convert it into a police headquarters. A valuable feature, he pointed out, was the underground tunnel running from Westminster Bridge Station by means of which men from all over London could rapidly and unobtrusively converge on the headquarters in an emergency. In the event the Government acquired the property for £186,000. Wisely they decided to pull down the opera house, realizing that adequate conversion would be difficult and sensing perhaps that a discarded opera house might lay the dignity of the force open to easy ribaldry. The decision was taken to erect a new building on the site while incorporating some of the underground work of the opera house. The architect they chose in 1888 was Norman Shaw who had long been prominent in his profession.

Shaw designed a Scottish baronial keep with angle tourettes and an internal courtyard, the walls of red brick with stone dressings wrought, in the interests of economy, by convicts at Portland. By the time it was occupied at the close of 1890 the building was already too small for its ever-expanding job and an annexe in corresponding style was built some years later on the south. Shaw was consulted but he was not happy with the addition for it ruined his first conception of a huge single fortress. In briefing the architect at the start someone had blundered – to posterity's loss – for of its eclectic kind it is a notable building. (At the time of writing its life hangs in the balance although it has been scheduled as a Class I building on the preservation lists.)

An expanding population and the growth of crime produced by industrial urbanization required not only a larger police force but more prisons in which to house the criminals who were caught. A number of huge, grim gaols were built all over the country in the nineteenth century with names familiar to all; most of them are with us still. In London more prisons were needed also when the old river hulks were condemned and transportation to the colonies dwindled after 1850. As in other spheres of administration many changes of methods in prison treatment and organization occurred throughout the century as a result of various Royal Commission reports and new Acts. Yet our prisons remain appallingly Victorian.

We have to remember what they replaced. Before the nineteenth century, prisons had been mainly places of detention, and within them the prisoner was free to do as he liked. He had to obtain his own food and, if he could afford them, contrive his own comforts. Prisoners of all sorts were crowded together and often the sexes were not separated. These were ghastly diseased places, and, thanks to the reforming efforts of people like John Howard and Elizabeth Fry, Victorian prisons were at least more hygienic than those of the eighteenth century, though certainly not health resorts.

The word 'penitentiary' itself suggests a place of expiation. Its nineteenth-century prototype was the great fortress of the National Penitentiary of London and Middlesex which stood from 1821 until the early nineties by the riverside at Millbank on the site now partly occupied by the Tate Gallery between the bridgeheads of Lambeth and Vauxhall. Every map of London printed during those seventy years is decorated with the great star-plan of the dreaded Tench, its six pentagons radiating from a central courtyard with a chapel at its heart. From the outside, as contemporary sketches show, the huge building with its round corner turrets and conical roofs looked like a gigantic, gloomy French castle of the Middle Ages. It was, in fact, dubbed the English Bastille.

The Tench was planned to some extent according to the ideas of Jeremy Bentham expressed in *The Panopticon, or Prison Discipline* (1791). His Panopticon, or Inspection House, was a prison designed on the principle of cells for single prisoners built around a central point of observation: 'panopticon' he coined from the Greek meaning 'all-seeing'. Bentham's ideas were fairly humane for their time and he contended in his endearing way that all punishment is evil and should be admitted only 'so far as it promises to exclude some greater evil'. He made the radical proposal that prisoners should be provided with useful work for which they would be allowed a share of the profits. The prison should be in some degree a school to teach general learning as well as trades – a 'mill for grinding rogues honest and idle men industrious'. Creature comforts would not be neglected and there would be an insurance scheme for old age, medical treatment, and a workshop outside the prison where those discharged could find work. Thus would 'morals be reformed, health preserved, industry invigorated, instruction diffused, public burthens lightened. Economy seated, as it were upon a rock, the gordian knot of the Poor-Laws not cut but untied – all by a simple idea in Architecture!'

Bentham had borrowed this simple idea from his brother Samuel who had erected a workshop on a star plan on Potemkin's estate in Russia. As he pointed out, the principle could be applied not only to prisons but to 'houses of industry, work-houses, poor-houses, manu-factories, mad-houses, lazarettes, hospitals, and schools' – that is, wherever a number of people had to be kept under observation.

The Government took the philosopher's idea seriously and he himself bought the Millbank site and contracted to build the Panopticon there. Then the whole project petered out, the reason being, it was said, that George III disliked Bentham's Philosophical Radicalism; in any case, the times were out of joint. Yet new prisons were sorely needed in London and as a provisional and desperate measure the authorities had for some years been making use of old ships of the line moored at Woolwich where convicts were confined in appalling conditions before transportation. These verminous germ-ridden wrecks were first used as a temporary expedient when the American War of Independence broke out and convicts could no longer be sent to the transatlantic colonies. At that period the Antipodes had not yet become available for transportation. Housed in the hulks the convicts could be put to useful river work. Although already condemned at that time these were still in use up to the sixties, for Mayhew described them in his book on prisons which came out in 1862 as 'the despair of all penal reformers'.

In 1812 the National Penitentiary was begun on Bentham's site on bogland beside the Thames where, owing to the nature of the soil, much trouble was encountered when building the foundations, a difficulty finally solved

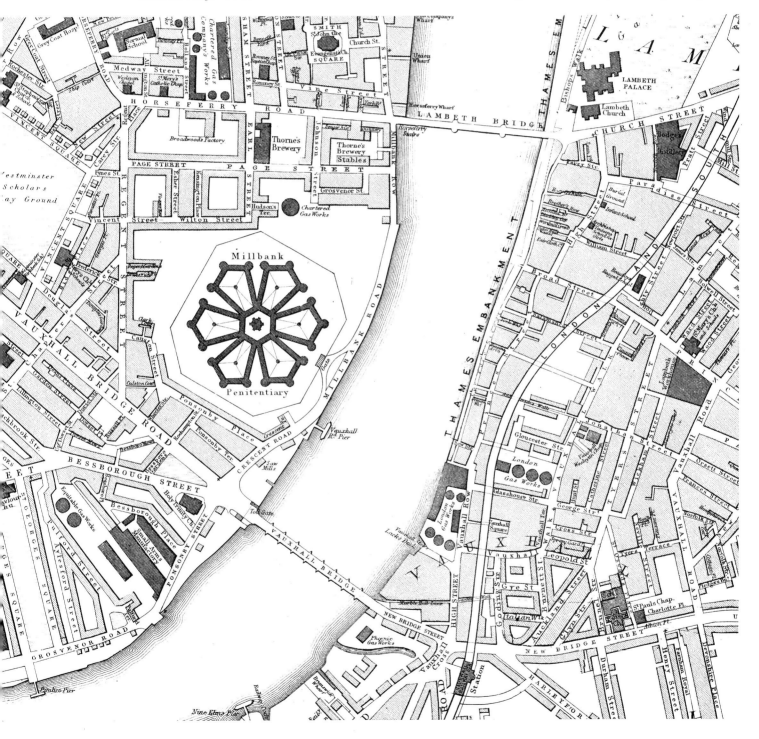

by laying a solid concrete raft on piles. Thomas Hardwick was appointed architect but, not relishing the difficult job or the fee, he resigned. A John Harvey took over for a time and when one pentagon had been built and had settled and cracked after occupation, John Rennie and Robert Smirke were called in to give advice, and then Smirke completed the work. The whole building of yellow brickwork took nearly ten years to construct. Finally it covered sixteen acres with seven large courtyards, over a thousand cells and three miles of corridors.

It was the first prison ever built where a Governor, Medical Officer, Chaplain, Master Manufacturer and Lady Matron were appointed from the start. Although solitary confinement was rare, prisoners occupied separate cells; they worked therein half their term and then spent the remainder working in association with other inmates. This system, in which work consisted of tailoring and needlework, mat making, weaving and other trades, was itself an innovation, but it was never successful. The Tench was regarded as a new ideal and it fascinated all reformers. Conditions at the start were comparatively enlightened and humane, for the philanthropic and benevolent members of the committee were proud of their new plaything and liked to show it off. At that time the country's prison system was unco-ordinated and decentralized like most other social organization, and the worst cruelties were to come later through centralized control of a too rigid kind. Unfortunately the Tench was unhealthy owing to its damp situation and the surrounding moat, which was later filled in, did not help matters. In early years prisoners suffered badly from scurvy, and outbreaks of dysentery became so serious that for a time the prison was emptied, the prisoners then being either pardoned or sent to the already overcrowded hulks.

Newgate in the City represented the old type of prison and it stood on the spot where a gaol had existed since the reign of King John. Externally it was a sombrely imposing building, designed by George Dance in the eighteenth century, and repaired by him after damage during the Gordon Riots. Because of pressures on accommodation it stood until 1902 when it was at last demolished to make way for the present Central Criminal Courts formerly called the Old Bailey. In the women's wards here Elizabeth Fry had begun her compassionate work, and here Doré made his drawing of prisoners circling round a yard, that Van Gogh was to copy in paint. It contained large communal wards in which prisoners, young and old, were confined indiscriminately until 1859 when the place was converted into a cellular type, being then in use, not for convicts, but for detainees awaiting trial. In 1878 it was closed except for the reception of prisoners awaiting execution. As early as 1784 Newgate had superseded Tyburn as the main place of execution in London, for here better facilities were available for the public to witness the spectacle. So it remained, until public hanging was abolished in 1868 and Londoners were deprived of their most popular and free entertainment.

The gay dog calling himself 'One of the Old Brigade' vividly recalls in his *London of the Sixties* (1908) a public hanging he himself witnessed at Newgate in 1864 when large parties from the West End were attracted to watch the execution of seven pirates:

. . . days before the fatal morning trusty agents had visited the houses that face Newgate Gaol and secured every window that gave an unobstructed view of the ghastly ceremony. The prices paid were enormous, varying from twenty to fifty guineas a window, in accordance with the superiority of the perspective from 'find to finish'. . . . Here was to be seen the lowest scum of London densely packed together as far as the eye could reach, and estimated by *The Times* at not less than 200,000. Across the entire front of Newgate heavy barricades of stout timber traversed the streets in every direction, erected as a precaution against the pressure of the crowd. . . . The scene that met one's view on pulling up the windows and looking out on the black night and its still blacker accompaniments baffles description. A surging mass, with here and there a flickering torch, rolled and roared before one; above this weird scene arose the voices of men and women shouting, singing, blaspheming, and, as the night advanced and the liquid gained firmer mastery, it seemed as if hell had delivered up its victims. To approach the window was a matter of danger; volleys of mud immediately saluted one, accompanied by more blaspheming and shouts of defiance. It was difficult to believe one was in the centre of a civilized capital that vaunted its religion and yet meted out justice in such a form.

At four a.m. some workmen appeared dragging round the scaffold to the front of the Debtors' Door from which the condemned men would emerge through the prison kitchen, now draped ceremonially in black for the occasion. As the day dawned loud hammering began. 'Presently an old, decrepit man made his appearance, and cautiously "tested" the drop; but a foolish impulse of curiosity leading him to peep over the drapery, a yell of execration saluted him. This was Calcraft, the hangman, hoary-headed, tottering, and utterly past his usefulness for the work.'

At seven-thirty the bell of St Sepulchre's began to toll through the dismal downpour.

The procession now appeared, winding its way through the kitchen, and in the centre of the group walked a sickly, cadaverous mob securely pinioned, and literally as white as marble. As they reached the platform a halt was necessary as each was placed one by one immediately under the hanging chains. At the end of these chains were hooks which were eventually attached to the hemp around the neck of each wretch. The concluding ceremonies did not take long, considering how feeble the aged hangman was. A white cap was first placed over every face, then the ankles were strapped together, and finally the fatal noose was put

Doré's engraving of the exercise yard of Newgate Gaol that Van Gogh was to copy in paint.

round every neck, and the end attached to the hooks. . . . At this moment a hideous *contretemps* occurred, and one poor wretch fell fainting, almost into the arms of the officiating priest. The reprieve was, however, momentary. . . . The silence was now awful. One felt one's heart literally in one's mouth, and found oneself involuntarily saying, 'They could be saved yet - yet - yet,' and then a thud that vibrated through the street announced that the pirates were launched into eternity.

Pentonville, in contrast to the brutal image of Newgate, was known as The Model. It represented the new type of cellular prison in which each prisoner was entirely separated from every other, in a system imported from Pennsylvania. Men and women here, caged like dangerous animals, were driven by depression to a state in which they became unfit to return to normal life, even to insanity. The system became more or less standard throughout England during the nineteenth century and was applied, for instance, not only at Pentonville but at Clerkenwell (1849), Wandsworth (1851), and Holloway (1852). At Holloway the inscription stone, laid only four years after the death of the reforming Friend, Elizabeth Fry, was hardly in accord with her tender humanity for it

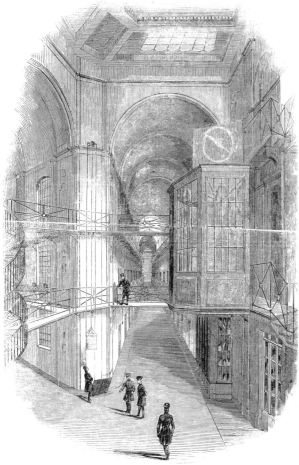

Interior of Pentonville, built as a Model Prison on the Separate System by which all prisoners were isolated in separate cells (*I.L.N.*, 1843).

read: 'May God preserve the City of London, and make this place a terror to evil doers.'

Like too many of its now-obsolete sort Pentonville is still in use. It was built on the Panopticon principle. Each wing contains several storeys of cells opening on to landings running along each side of a dividing wall spanned by bridges. Every cell door and all corridors can be seen by officers in the central hall.

The Pentonville system of perpetual isolation was already being criticized in 1850, by Hepworth Dixon in his *The London Prisons*:

The building consists of five wings or galleries, radiating from a point, the view from which is very striking. . . . Now let us enter a cell. Well, really, it has anything but a repulsive appearance. Its arrangement and fittings seem to be faultless. . . . The bedding is clean and good; the food is also good, and plentiful in supply. There is a bell-handle, too, which needs only to be pulled to command the instant attendance of a paid servitor. Light work is to be had also for amusement and to vary the routine. Very pleasant! At intervals the prisoner goes to chapel to hear the gospel; and to school, where competent masters are waiting to offer their services to instruct him. But what is there penal in all this? someone asks. . . . No prisoner, except in rare cases, likes it. Many fear it worse than they do death. But then officials like it; it gives them very little trouble. . . . The cell is, in fact, the criminal's strait-jacket. It keeps him very quiet, makes him very obedient; but the question nevertheless remains open – Does it make him a better man? What we want are sound minds, not quiet men in strait-jackets; good citizens, not submissive criminals in silent cells.

Mayhew and Binny in their *Criminal Prisons of London* (1862) remark that 'the discipline pursued at this prison [Pentonville] yields *upwards of ten times more lunatics* than should be accorded to the normal rate'. This was the new refinement of cruelty to be adopted in the hygienic English prisons of the second half of the nineteenth century. Two Prisons Acts brought further refinements of cruelty and rigidly consolidated them throughout the land. The 1865 Act required all local authorities to erect separate cells in their gaols and to provide all inmates with penal labour; diet was to be standardized, religious ritual was to be compulsory and a detailed and rigid code of rules was to be generally applied, including severe punishments such as mechanical restraint and flogging.

By the 1877 Act the Home Secretary was given full responsibility for all English prisons so that they became in effect nationalized and under central control. The first Chairman of the Prison Commission, Sir Edmund du Cane, achieved an aim which is today regarded as the reverse of what is desirable in penal institutions: the treatment of all offenders exactly alike whatever their age, sex, crime, character, or background. Clothing was made uniform. The system was the easier to apply in that an intermediate Act of 1869 abolished sentences of imprison-

A street-walker peers anxiously out of her cell at Bow Street Police Court while awaiting trial on a night charge. (Drawing by Paul Renouard, *Graphic*, 1887.)

ment for debt. 'The man who entered an English prison under the new order,' writes D. L. Howard in *The English Prisons*, 'immediately lost all his individuality. . . . The English prison system, under du Cane, was a massive machine for the promotion of misery.'

A prisoner slept on a plank, all profitable or even enjoyable activity which had been developed in some prisons was abolished, and he toiled only on cranks, treadmill, shot drill, or oakum picking. Worst of deprivations was the enforcement of silence and lack of any social intercourse throughout his sentence. No decorations or portraits of loved ones were allowed in the cells and window glass was made obscure so that the small joy of watching the changing skies was denied. The new prisons were all clean and hygienic and apparently well-ordered, but men and women who went into them as human beings came out of them, writes Howard, 'mentally numbed and some of them insane: they became the creatures, ugly and brutish in appearance, stupid and resentful in behaviour, unemployable and emotionally unstable, which the Victorian middle classes came to visualize whenever they thought of prisoners'.

Slowly the truth about prison conditions began to leak out; public indignation suddenly arose when the Rev. W. D. Morrison organized a press campaign following his dismissal as a prison chaplain for ignoring the du Cane censorship by courageously writing a newspaper article that criticized the Prison Commissioners. A storm of protest forced the Liberal Home Secretary, Asquith, to set up a Committee in 1894 to examine the accusations. They were confirmed and a new Act incorporating most of the Committee's recommendations was at last passed in 1898.

To give prisoners work to do was an old idea going back at least to 1553 when Edward VI handed over to the public his father's palace beside the Fleet River at Bridewell as a House of Correction where 'the vagabond and ydle strumpet' were to be 'chastised and compelled to labour, to the overthrow of the vicious life of ydleness'. But the work provided at that time was at least useful. In accordance with the prevalent puritanism the stress in nineteenth-century prison ethics was also on unremitting labour, but opinion divided as to what sort of labour was suitable: one thought the work should be useful and

At Newgate Prison a garotter has received a whipping (*Graphic*, 1872).

The treadwheel at the Clerkenwell House of Correction (*I.L.N.*, 1874).

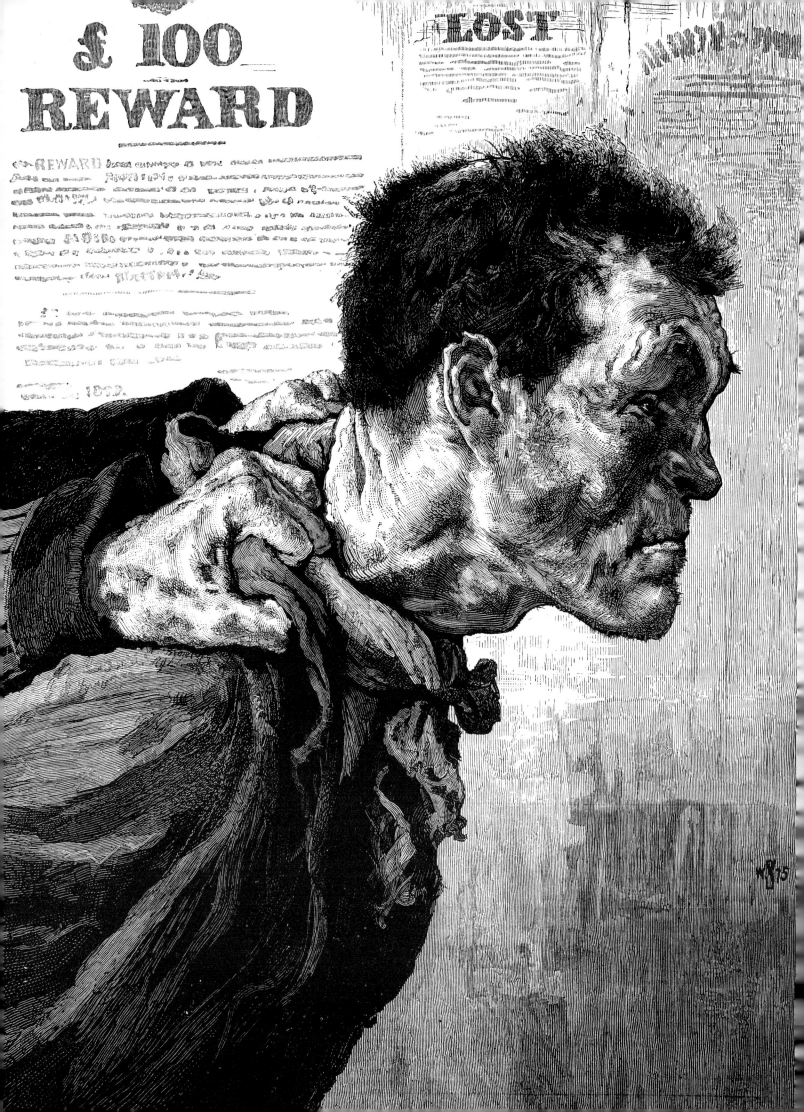

profitable, even skilled, the other that it should be as un-pleasant, exhausting, boring and futile as possible – that is, pure punitive penance. The latter became universal.

The first treadmill for use in prisons was designed by William Cubitt, a Lowestoft engineer, for use in the county gaol at Bury. In London it was first installed at Brixton, and before long very few prisons were without their treadmills. A few were turned for practical purposes such as raising water (as originally at Holloway), but mostly they were there to inflict, on both men and women offenders, a punitive tedium and weariness.

Mayhew and Binny, in their survey of 1862, describe the treadwheels at Coldbath Fields on the site of Mount Pleasant Post Office, where the felons' section contained four and the vagrants' section two, each being constructed for twenty-four men. Compartments were two feet wide and separated by high wooden partitions like the stalls of a urinal. As they trod away the twenty-four steps of each revolution the men supported themselves by a hand-rail and thus they sweated each day for two periods of three hours each.

At Coldbath Fields the wheels worked a great revolving fan on the roof, called a regulator, which produced a hard resistance on the steps, and so the prisoners called the labour 'treading the wind'. Another form of hard labour here was 'shot drill' which took place in a courtyard among the cabbages. This was worse than treading for it was so obviously futile, exhausting and degrading. It consisted of lifting up cannon balls, each weighing twenty-four pounds, from a pyramid, walking three yards, placing them down one by one to form another pyramid, and then reversing the procedure – and on and on. Each shot was lifted at a word of command and then set down at another word, and this continued for one hour and a quarter.

At Coldbath Fields, too, the third kind of labour enforced was oakum picking. It was carried on in three large sheds where 'the utter absence of noise struck us as being absolutely terrible'.

One of the peculiarities of Coldbath Fields was the ubiquitous display of moral texts on the walls, and if a man rested for a moment from his task he would read above him such uplifting exhortations as 'Go to the Ant thou Sluggard, Consider Her Ways and Be Wise'.

Our penal system is more humane today but it still suffers from the myopic methods of the nineteenth century, not least from the overpowering and demoralizing character of the old prison buildings which remain in use.

Oakum-picking at the Clerkenwell House of Correction (*Penny Illustrated Paper*, 1877).

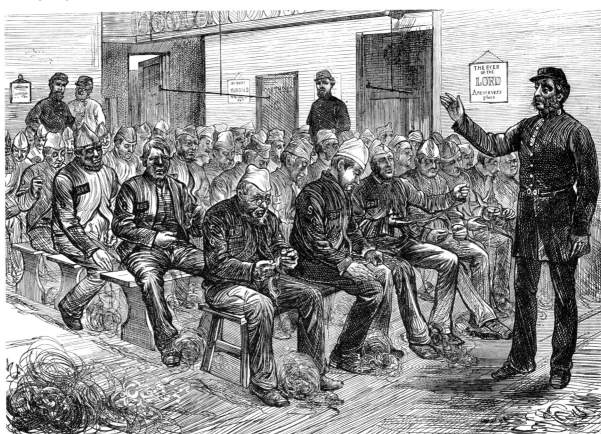

Pleasures

I'd take her to see the Aquarium,
I'd take her to see the Zoo,
I'd take her to see the Waxwork Show,
The Crystal Palace too.
Oh! yes, if she'd only be true to me
'Twould fill me with delight,
And I'd bring her to see the Music Halls
Every Saturday night.

VICTORIAN SONG

Doré made many drawings of the pleasures and leisure activities of both rich and poor in Victorian London – dinners, garden parties, the opera, a Greenwich hotel in the Season, the Zoological Gardens, cricket at Lord's, a music hall, a Penny Gaff, nigger minstrels, Evans' celebrated Song and Supper Room, a Punch and Judy show – and he goes to town, or more precisely out of town, for the two annual occasions of the Derby and the Boat Race, those two great levellers of society enjoyed by all classes. Strangely enough, he shows us nothing of the huge, iconic structure and its grounds where so much entertainment was enjoyed during the latter half of the century: the Crystal Palace. Londoners went there, if Doré did not.

There had been, of course, two Palaces: the original one built in Hyde Park, opened in 1851, and that erected on the hill-top at Sydenham, opened in 1854. The latter used the demountable units of the first building but it was much larger, contained twice as much glass, and was a more complex building. A mass of documentation on both buildings exists. The story of how the 1851 building came about has so often been told and is so fascinating that, like a fairy tale, it can be told again and again.

The Great Exhibition of the Works of Industry of All Nations was to a large extent the creation of Albert the Good. Supporting the Prince in organizing it was Henry Cole (1808–82); indeed, the general idea was initiated by him. He had begun his working life modestly as an assistant keeper at the Record Office but he became a painter, music critic, pottery designer, art-journal editor, Council Member of the Society of Arts of which the Prince was President, Secretary of the Government School of Design and originator of the scheme for the Albert Hall. He

helped to organize the Penny Post, to unify railway gauges, and to establish the docks at Grimsby, and he was responsible for the 1862 Exhibition at South Kensington. These were only a few of his activities. He also edited various children's books and the works of Thomas Love Peacock, annotated railway maps with geological and antiquarian notes, published the first Christmas card and created the South Kensington Museum, which began as a Museum of Ornamental Art and Manufacture and is now the Victoria and Albert. Here is another Victorian worthy who has not yet received the full recognition he deserves. Pioneer of industrial design and technical education, he was like Edwin Chadwick in his faith in bureaucracy at a time when such faith was unpopular; so, like Chadwick, he had to wait a long time for honoured recognition and did not receive his knighthood until 1875.

The Great Exhibition was not the first of its kind in the world; the first to show industrial products occurred in France in 1798, yet it was by far the largest and most ambitious; it was also the first to invite all nations to exhibit. The world's architects were therefore asked to submit plans for the building, but were given only three weeks in which to do so: 245 designs were received which took the Building Committee a month to digest. The Committee, which included the architects Sir Charles Barry and C. R. Cockerell, the engineers Robert Stephenson, I. K. Brunel and William Cubitt, civil engineer and brother of the speculative builder Thomas Cubitt, declared that they could not recommend any of the designs for adoption and, in a most unethical manner – having picked the world's brains – submitted a design of their own. Isambard Kingdom Brunel, engineer of the Great

One of a pair of Victorian marble figures found in the basement of a house in Prince's Gardens, Kensington, and now in the possession of the Imperial College of Science and Technology. The sculptor is unknown.

Western Railway, the *Great Eastern* steamship and Clifton Suspension Bridge, was its designer, helped by Wyatt, Charles Wild, Owen Jones and T. L. Donaldson. Their design, requiring fifteen million bricks, was surrounded by a verandah and dominated by a huge dome roofed with iron sheets and having a diameter of two hundred feet – that is forty-five feet more than the diameter of the dome of St Paul's. It was far too costly, far too solid for temporary use, was not very functional, and would have taken far too long to erect. It was also extremely ugly and was received with the derision it deserved. The whole project seemed to be on the edge of fiasco and Prince Albert was in despair.

Suddenly the Exhibition Commissioners were saved, as by a miracle. It came in the form of a plan of startling boldness produced by the son of a Bedfordshire farmer. Joseph Paxton (1803–65) had been appointed head gardener at the Duke of Devonshire's estate at Chatsworth at the age of twenty-three. There he began to work wonders in the grounds, creating waterfalls, fountains, rockeries, arboreta and greenhouses. His masterpiece was the Great Stove, a huge conservatory covering a whole acre of ground through which carriages could be drawn. ('I should have liked that man,' the Duke of Wellington told the Duke of Devonshire, 'for one of my generals.') Paxton became far more than a head gardener for he was soon serving his employer as general factotum, business agent and inseparable companion. He managed all the Duke's estates, built villages, bridges, gasworks and mansions; he promoted railways, made a fortune for himself in railway shares, and finally became a Member of Parliament. He was the personification of the self-help ideal.

Among Paxton's many works at Chatsworth was his Lily House built in 1850 to contain the monster lily, *Victoria Regia*, imported from British Guiana. Though far smaller than the Great Stove, this was a masterly structure in its strong, slight spider-web economy of iron, glass and wood inspired by the structure of the giant leaf of the lily itself. With its ridge-and-furrow roofing system it was the prototype for the Crystal Palace.

Having the full support of Henry Cole and the help of his Chatsworth staff, Paxton produced his draft scheme for the Exhibition building within a week – evolved from the famous blotting-paper doodle he had scribbled during a committee meeting of the Midland Railway held at Derby, and now preserved in the Victoria and Albert Museum. The building which was eventually erected differed little in essentials from the preliminary drawings. It was an extraordinary idea. Glass was not a recognized material for a large public building. Moreover, this building had to be erected in nine months and stand

Paxton's Crystal Palace building in Hyde Park, 1851 (from a contemporary print).

safely for six months, housing the treasures of the world and hundreds of thousands of visitors. As transplanted to Sydenham it was to stand for over eighty years.

Meanwhile, Paxton, bubbling with creative zeal, carried out some astute private lobbying. Time was running out, and with the desperation of drowning men, Prince Albert and the Building Committee gladly accepted the scheme. To gain public support Paxton even went above the heads of the Committee by presenting his proposal in the pages of the *Illustrated London News*. It became clear to all that the design was immensely superior in every way to the ponderous monster to which most people had become resigned. The Committee was naturally annoyed but could not, in their plight, vote against the general approval of Paxton's remarkable design. Within three weeks after its publication in the *I.L.N.* the Commissioners formally accepted it, and Douglas Jerrold's inspired title published in *Punch* – 'The Crystal Palace' – struck the spark of its popularity. An industrial exhibition became 'a Cockney fairy tale', as Christopher Hobhouse has put it; the 'industrious poor' were not only to be edified, they were to be entertained. Incredible as it might seem, Prince Albert's scheme was going to be fun.

The contractors Fox & Henderson, the Chance Brothers, the country's major glass-makers, and Joseph Paxton now put their heads together and final working drawings were prepared. The contract sum (£79,800 and the materials at the close of the Exhibition, or £150,000 if the building should be permanently retained) came to little more than half that of the Committee's abortive design. The whole site facing the Knightsbridge Barracks was first surrounded by a timber palisade and on 26 September 1850 the first of the 1,060 iron columns was set up. Thereafter the whole structure of standardized components planned on a 24-foot grid rose at tremendous speed. To enclose the whole area, 1,848 feet long and 408 feet wide, the Chances supplied 300,000 panes of glass, weighing in all some 400 tons, which were fixed in 202 miles of standardized sash bars, each pane measuring 49 inches by 10 and inserted by means of travelling trolleys roofed over against the weather. In December the first of the sixteen great semicircular ribs of timber was raised above the central transept that, as a second thought, was to be 108 feet high and enclose some of the park's fully grown elm trees. It was a triumph of rational construction – as Morton Shand described it in an obituary of its successor, in the *Architectural Review* in 1937: 'A precept as inspiring as the Parthenon, an exemplar vital as the Pont du Gard, as important as Stonehenge or Ely Cathedral.'

The time that elapsed between its blotting-paper conception and its opening was forty-six weeks and its actual erection took only thirty-nine weeks – this for a vast structure, filled with marvels, that covered nearly nineteen acres. It was made possible by railway transport, rationalization, interchangeable prefabricated parts of iron, glass and timber, clean and dry assembly, use of the framework as its own scaffolding, steam-powered mechanization, and simplicity of costing. Here was the prototype of the modern frame-and-fill and curtain-wall construction that can be indefinitely expanded and in which the walls become not solid and load-bearing, with holes cut in them for doors and windows, but thin screens set between a framework to keep out noise and weather. The Crystal Palace was not regarded by anyone at the time it was built as Architecture; indeed, seventy-five years had to pass before this kind of functionalism was accepted as such – with the building by Walter Gropius of the Bauhaus at Dessau in 1926.

According to Sir John Summerson, the Crystal Palace was the one Victorian building that was 'a total and absolute success', for, as he writes in his *Victorian Architecture*, the 'failure' of Victorian designs as at St Pancras Station for example, can be explained thus: 'First, the disintegration of architecture and engineering; the total separation of functional and "artistic" criteria, in separate heads and hands. Second, the disintegration of architecture itself by the compulsive obtrusion of the question of style.' To the Victorians architecture was neither clear expression of structure nor control of internal space so much as the detailed decoration, according to creed and fashion, of solid façade. At the same time the theological Pugin could wisely write: 'The great test of Architectural beauty is the fitness of the design for the purpose for which it is intended'. He was, no doubt, thinking largely of ecclesiastic design, yet, clearly, in their general architectural philosophy the Victorians were confused. Our concepts are clearer today, but have we done better than the Victorians? How thirsty we have become for an occasional tot of jolly, hand-wrought decoration to enliven and humanise the aseptic, ascetic geometry of our faceless buildings. Something, we know, is missing. Is it money? Perhaps it is simply joyfulness.

On the first of May, a bright but showery day, the Great Exhibition of 1851 was opened by the Queen, dressed in a gown of pink silk sparkling with silver and diamonds and accompanied by the Prince and their two eldest children. Flags fluttered along the shining roof levels, while on the Serpentine near by a model frigate gave a military salute, martial bands played, and Mr Charles Spencer rose in a balloon. Within the cluttered building the ironwork shone with fresh bright paintwork selected by Owen Jones – blue, yellow and turkey red. At the intersection of nave and transept a fountain of glass played in the bright light, great statues loomed everywhere against crimson fabrics and young Willis's giant organ roared louder than the cheers of the enthralled visitors. The whole scene, as Lord Macaulay described it, was beyond the dreams of the Arabian romances. The Queen, who was to pay the Exhibition some thirty more visits, was ecstatic and confided in her diary that night: 'The great event has taken place – a complete and beautiful triumph – a glorious and touching sight, one of which I shall ever be proud of for my beloved Albert and my country.' Said Albert to Cole: 'Quite satisfactory.' Not everyone was enthusiastic, however. To John Ruskin, this 'blazing arch of lucid glass', as Thackeray called it, was not architecture at all; in its rebuilt form at Sydenham he was to describe it as 'a cucumber frame between two chimneys'.

As for its contents in 1851, the purpose in bringing them together, said the Prince, was to show how it was possible 'to wed high art with mechanical skill'. It was, in fact, a deliberate attempt to reveal the unity of Art and Science and stimulate and reform industrial design – an attempt, although few, except William Morris, could see it at the time, which was, for a number of reasons, a failure. Fine art, as such, was not admitted to the display but sculpture was allowed on the understanding that it should exemplify some technique of interest. The exhibits formed a surprising collection of the practical, the ugly, the bizarre and here and there the beautiful. They ranged from a single lump of coal weighing twenty-four tons from the Duke of Devonshire's Staveley mines to a garden seat of coal destined for Osborne, from a naval cap that could be inflated into a lifebuoy to Nasmyth's steam hammer which with a single adjustment could pass from forging the main bearing of a steamship to gently cracking an egg, from an Austrian fountain playing eau-de-Cologne to a printing machine which churned out five thousand copies of the *Illustrated London News* every hour, from a fauteuil of bog yew to Pugin's medieval dreamland, from a group of stuffed frogs from Württemberg to Boulton and Watt's latest marine engine possessing the collective power of seven hundred horses, from Samuel Colt's revolver to a bellowing instrument called the Sommerphone, from a vase made of mutton fat to Bellhouse's Iron House for Emigrants, from the Koh-i-Noor diamond to a sheet of paper 2,500 yards long.

Nothing could have been more discrete in visual aesthetic than the multiform exhibits of the Crystal Palace in their wild, fantastic confusion. The functional honesty, not only of the scintillating container itself but of the contributions to the Machinery Court (by far the most popular venue in the whole show at a period when the power of steam seemed limitless), and the beauty of the carriages (products of an ancient craft now reaching its peak of perfection) contrasted sharply with vulgarity: of over-ornate furniture writhing, bulging in a debased kind of rococo, of carpets with elaborate three-dimensional patterns, and of naïve sculpture which seemed obsessed with subjects such as the needless subjugation of nude but frigid women by chains. On these decadent offspring of the tradition of Flaxman, Canova and Thorvaldsen, the comment of Mr Malony, *alias* Thackeray, was apt:

> There's statues bright
> Of marble white
> Of silver and of copper;
> And some in zinc,
> And some, I think,
> That isn't over proper.

The time was, of course, one of transition between handicrafts and machine production. It was also a time of transition between the power exercised by educated, aristocratic patronage of the arts and that exercised by half-educated but moneyed industrialists who, lacking inherited wealth, leisure and privilege, mistook lavish and costly display for good taste. They failed to see, as we have at last learned to see to some extent at least, that machine production can produce its own aesthetic which must, if honest, be quite unlike that of direct handicraft and should on no account try to copy it by mechanical repetition.

The many admirers of the machine-carved screen exhibited at the Crystal Palace by the Patent Wood Carving Company would, Sir Nikolaus Pevsner notes, have argued something like this: 'It may be very difficult to carve a screen by hand and it might take three years to do. What a triumph of the human mind is it then to invent machinery which can do the same work in one hundredth of the time and in addition do it more exactly.' This 'pride in ingeniousness' was especially apparent in the imitation of one material by another, such as glass or polished clay made to look like marble. We do this still today.

One of the six million visitors to the Exhibition was a little girl of eleven called Louisa de la Ramée who in maturity was to achieve international fame as the romantic novelist Ouida. She summed up the common reaction in her diary with an innocent comment upon a carved fantasy of a deer with its fawn surrounded by tree stumps whose ultimate purpose was to contain ink: 'It did not look at all what it was, it was lovely.'

Whatever its merits and faults the 1851 Exhibition was a triumphant success. All England was now in a buoyant mood with the 'hungry forties' and Chartist demonstrations over and free trade established. London was the hub of the world. Paradise lay ahead. 'The Great Exhibition was the pageant of domestic peace,' writes G. M. Young in his *Portrait of an Age*. 'Not for sixty years had the throne appeared so solidly based on the national goodwill as in that summer of hope and pride and reconciliation.' Nobody had died at the show but one child had been born there; in the refreshment rooms 1,804,718 buns had been consumed. The winning exhibitors received their medals and awards; Paxton, Fox and Cubitt were knighted and Cole was made Companion of Honour.

The Exhibition brought to the whole of London a summer season of a liveliness and colour it had never known before; maps and guides were printed in their tens of thousands and every kind of entertainment flourished. All through that summer discussion and controversy raged around the question of what should be done with the Crystal Palace when the Exhibition closed in October.

Paxton himself, with customary indiscretion, led a campaign to convert his structure into a permanent Winter Garden; a 'medical man' proposed that it should become a Kurhaus combining 'all that is desirable in the spas of Germany with all that is decent in the Roman Thermae'; another notion was to re-erect part of the building in Kew Gardens, while Henry Cole proposed the re-erection of the Palace on the land that was to become Battersea Park; but the most extraordinary scheme was published in *The Builder*. This was the design by an architect called C. Burton to reassemble the parts in the Park as a gigantic Prospect Tower, a thousand feet high, as a permanent exhibition building holding near its summit a clock forty-four feet in diameter.

Although Parliament petitioned the Queen to leave the building where it was for another year, Prince Albert was adamant; least of all did he like the idea of turning the building to some frivolous use. The Commissioners, in any case, were pledged to remove it. So it came down and was re-erected in extended form between 1852 and 1854 on a wooded hill-top of 200 acres at Sydenham, near the old Beaulah Spa. It was done by a public company which included among its directors Joseph Paxton and the architect, Matthew Digby Wyatt, while Fox & Henderson again acted as the contractors. The uplifting purpose of the rebuilt Palace was clearly stated in the company's prospectus: 'Refined recreation, calculated to elevate the intellect, instruct the mind, and to improve the hearts, will welcome the millions who have now no other incentives to pleasure but such as the gin-palace, the dancing saloon and the ale-house afford them.'

Paxton spoiled the serene simplicity of his first design by arching the whole length of the nave and adding two

The stupendous waterworks at the Sydenham Crystal Palace on the occasion of the Schiller Festival, seen at night during a torchlight procession (*I.L.N.*, 1859).

arched transepts at either end. The pair of towers flanking the whole had to be taken down before the opening and rebuilt to Brunel's design to carry water tanks sufficient to supply the tall jets of the fountains. Being a dedicated gardener, Paxton laid out the grounds in grand style with lakes, waterfalls, terraces, a maze, temples, lawns, fountains and waterworks even more ambitious than those of Versailles: the towers were there to supply 120,000 gallons a minute under heavy pressure so that half-an-hour's display would consume some four million gallons. To conform with the current relish for instruction married to entertainment, geological specimens were reconstructed in the grounds and a prehistoric swamp was laid down to contain lifelike models of antediluvian monsters which can still be seen in the sadly debased and confused park that is there today.

Inside the Palace Paxton planted many rare and fully-grown trees. The side aisles were divided into courts representing the architecture and sculpture of past ages – Greek, Roman, Egyptian, Moorish, Assyrian, Pompeiian, Byzantine, Gothic and Renaissance – the designer of most of them being Sir Matthew Digby Wyatt (1820–77): member of a family of architects, designer of the architectural ornament of Paddington Station, Secretary of the Executive Committee of the 1851 Exhibition, Slade

Professor of Fine Art at Cambridge, Honorary Secretary and Vice-President of the Royal Institute of British Architects, a prolific writer and, altogether, a highly successful man. He was not a great architect so much as a competent decorator, his best work being in the India section of Scott's Foreign Office and on that small suspension footbridge across the lake in St James's Park, engineered by Rendell, which was unfortunately replaced a few years ago by the new affair in prestressed concrete.

Within and without the huge conservatory at Sydenham, statues stood everywhere, including many from the Great Exhibition. In the main transept a giant organ with 4,598 pipes was installed and a concert platform erected for four thousand performers. Served by two railway lines and two stations, the rebuilt Crystal Palace enjoyed great popularity for several decades. Here Spurgeon and Moody preached, here Blondin walked a tight-rope between the water towers, resting half-way to cook himself an omelette, and here were held operas, concerts, exhibitions and displays; within were contained among the amenities a library, a reading room and restaurant. A monkey-house, an aviary and an aquarium were soon added and in a special building in the grounds for a time Monsieur Philippoteaux exhibited his stupendous ocular illusion – the Panorama of Tel-el-Kebir. In 1865 Mr

Left, the Egyptian Avenue at the Sydenham Crystal Palace with the Abu Simbel colossi (*I.L.N.*, 1854). *Right*, the figures after the fire that occurred in 1867 in the north transept (*I.L.N.*, 1867).

Brock's magnificent firework displays began and kept their popularity until well into the next century. But the popularity of the Palace as a whole waned in time and the problems of maintenance began; they were not helped financially by the weekly closure enforced for too many years on the company by the Sunday Observance fanatics. Following a lecture on the subject of combustion, the north transept containing the Assyrian Court was burned down in 1867 and was never fully rebuilt. As the century drew to its end the whole building became more and more neglected and half the land had to be sold for building. The final firework display came in 1936 when the whole structure was burnt to the ground in an apocalyptic blaze.

The Crystal Palace might have been more fully patronized if it had not been so far south and 'over the water'. For that reason, as its equivalent to serve north London, the Alexandra Palace was built at Muswell Hill – just too late for Doré's plates. As the Sydenham building had used elements of the Great Exhibition of 1851 so that at Muswell Hill used materials salvaged from the 1862 International Exhibition at South Kensington, including one of the two huge domes to serve as a central feature of the symmetrical design. This was the conception of an architect-engineer, Alfred Meeson, who had worked on the Houses of Parliament and on the Exhibitions of 1851 and 1862. A grand concert opened the Palace on 24 May 1873. During the first fortnight huge crowds visited the place and indicated certain success for the venture. On 9 June a fire started in the central dome – no one knew how – and the whole building was reduced to a melancholy ruin. Although it had been uninsured the Palace was immediately rebuilt and on an even larger scale as a vast solid structure of yellow brickwork with corner towers, covering seven acres, the architect being Meeson's partner, John Johnson. Opened in May 1875, it is in its confident hugeness typically High Victorian. The grand hall could hold twelve thousand and the orchestral platform more than one thousand performers and there as its centre piece Henry Willis rebuilt his Great Organ exactly as it had been in the destroyed Palace. Beside that there were a smaller concert hall, a conservatory, two art galleries, a lecture hall and a reading room. In the grounds were built a Moorish house, an Egyptian villa and a Swiss chalet among other instructive objects, while around them ran a race course and a trotting ring. Here were lakes, parterres and groves, a hotel, a bazaar, banqueting rooms, a billiard hall, a Japanese village, a circus and, of course, a cricket ground. Like the Crystal Palace, the Ally Pally served well for a time but eventually became a financial encumbrance, since when it has had its latter-day use. The great organ by Willis lies there in pieces, at the time of writing, waiting to be revived.

Neither of these two designs was as attractive as the first project, called the Palace of the People, designed for the site by Owen Jones, but never built. This was a true crystal palace of iron and glass, as we can see from the drawings of it which appeared in the *Illustrated London News* for 12 February and 5 March 1859. Its great central Winter Garden, or tropical conservatory, two hundred feet in diameter and thirty-six feet high, covered by a glass dome and encircled by a gallery, would have been particularly attractive. (Owen Jones, 1809–74, son of a Welsh antiquary, was chiefly an interior decorator who chose the colours and decorations not only of the Great Exhibition but also of the rebuilt Palace at Sydenham and that of the 1862 Exhibition. He designed the 'Crystal Palace' emporium for Oxford Street and the St James's Hall where Dickens gave some of his famous readings and where the Moore and Burgess Minstrels performed for some years.)

In London's scintillating, cosmopolitan year of 1851 the panorama and diorama mania was raging. This form of entertainment had been flourishing for some years as a dramatized form of romantic painting, and, before he invented photography, Daguerre was one of its most effective producers. The idea of painting a panoramic view on a cylindrical surface was invented in 1787 by Robert Barker, an Irish artist working in Edinburgh who opened his Panorama behind the north-east corner of Leicester Square in 1793. It was still working in 1851 but in 1865 it was sold to a French priest who built a church for London's French catholic community on the original circular plan. Bombed in the last war the church was rebuilt but it retains the original circular form of Barker's Panorama Royal. In Paris in 1822 Daguerre combined with Charles Bouton, a painter, to stage a three-dimensional elaboration of the idea they called the Diorama. This next step on the road to the cinema, with its dual tableaux, appeared in London in Park Square East as part of Nash's Regent's Park development, where dramatic tableaux supported by organ music were on view until 1853, when they began converting the building, which still exists, into a Baptist Chapel.

In 1851 the Diorama, with its painted screens and ingenious lighting effects, was showing three views of Mount Etna: at dawn, at sunset, and in wild eruption. A little to its north, where the Royal College of Physicians now lies, stood the Colisseum designed by Decimus Burton. Erected in 1826 and pulled down in 1875, it was a noble structure, polygonal in plan, with a Doric portico and a glazed dome, its purpose being to show the whole of London as seen from the top of St Paul's Cathedral; in 1851 it was also showing, after dusk, Paris by Night. Close by, in Albany Street, the Cyclorama was depicting the

Above, the project
designed by Owen Jones
for a Palace of the
People at Muswell Hill,
built of glass and
iron like the Crystal Palace
(*I.L.N.*, 1859). *Below*,
the Alexandra Palace at
Muswell Hill as
rebuilt after the first Palace
had been destroyed
by fire within two weeks
from its opening;
a picnic in the Grove
(*Penny Illustrated
Paper*, 1875).

Overleaf, the opening of the rebuilt Alexandra Palace on 1 May 1875.
At the back is Willis's Grand Organ (*I.L.N.*, 1875).

Section through Mr Wyld's Giant Globe, or Model of the Earth, erected in the centre of Leicester Square in the Exhibition year of 1851 and demolished ten years later (*I.L.N.*, 1851). The architect of this handsome domed building with its Doric porticos was H. R. Abrahams.

Lisbon earthquake of 1755 with moving effects. The original Panorama in Leicester Square was quieter in its spectacles of the Lakes of Killarney and Lucerne and the Falls of Niagara. At the Egyptian Hall in Piccadilly you could follow the ancient Israelites from the Nile to Jerusalem, while for a shilling, down in Whitechapel, you could travel the Route of the Emigrants from Waterloo Bridge Road to the harbour of Sydney, taking in Lisbon, Gibraltar, Cairo and Calcutta on the way. Many other such ocular illusions were packing them in during the summer of 1851. Offspring of Romantic paintings, they were the legitimate forebears of the cinema, television, and the photo-mural.

An entirely new show which drew the crowds in 1851 was Batty's Grand National Hippodrome. Built as a great open arena, oval in shape but surrounded by a roofed auditorium seating fourteen thousand people, it stood near the Great Exhibition opposite the southern entrance to the Broad Walk in Kensington Gardens. It was chiefly a circus devoted to fine horsemanship. Two brass bands played in turns to support displays such as a Roman Chariot Race and the Pageant of the Field of the Cloth of Gold.

William Batty, entrepreneur of the 1851 Hippodrome, was already operating south of the river; Astley's Circus in Westminster Bridge Road was still flourishing, as it had been since 1780 when Philip Astley, a cavalry sergeant-major, opened the place for equestrian performances and shows of wild beasts. This was, in fact, the first circus in England. The theatre burned down in 1841 and the lease was taken over by Batty, who built a new amphitheatre on the site that lasted for several decades. There in the sixties Mr Dion Boucicault introduced a novelty in the form of Shakespearean plays transformed into spectacular equestrian displays. In 1873 it was taken over by the famous Sanger.

James Wyld, M.P. and cartographer, not only exhibited maps at the Great Exhibition but put on another good and instructive show in 1851 which, proving too large for the Crystal Palace, was erected in its own building in the centre of Leicester Square. This was the Giant Globe, sixty feet in diameter and made from a thousand plaster castings to represent the Earth to a scale of ten miles to the inch. It was, of course, the Earth turned outside in, but the scale was large enough to make this anomaly seem unimportant since only part of the globe could be

A chariot race at Batty's Grand National Hippodrome at Kensington, opened in the Exhibition year of 1851 for equestrian displays on the site where De Vere Gardens now lie; its great oval amphitheatre later became a riding school (*I.L.N.*, 1851).

inspected at one time from one of the several galleries. The Globe was housed in a seemly classical building designed by H. R. Abrahams with an eye at the top of its dome, like the Pantheon's in Rome. It was so successful during the ten years it stood that it became almost a metropolitan institution in the way Tussaud's Planetarium is today. Lectures were given there regularly and sometimes special exhibitions were added; in 1854, for example, a model of the Crimea was made upon which the positions of the troops of the Allies and the Russians were shown and changed at once as the news came in.

The Globe was pulled down in 1861 when Wyld's lease expired, and Leicester Square decayed to a derelict plot ruled by a much-damaged statue of George I on horseback that was often the victim of practical jokers. On the north side of this barren rubbish dump, part of the site of the future Empire contained a low eating house which stamped all its cutlery with the slogan, 'Stolen from The Shades', while at the eastern corner was a place of amusement containing 'Poses Plastiques', the strip-tease of the day. Here were held Wig-and-Gown Shows, a curious form of entertainment in which generous helpings of blasphemy and blue rhetoric could be obtained for a shilling. Leicester Square had become such an insalubrious spot that general opinion declared it to be a disgrace to London. Before the Government got around to taking action, Albert Grant, M.P., bought the enclosure in 1874 and presented it to the Metropolitan Board of Works 'to be preserved for ever for the free use and enjoyment of the public'. The area was planted and embellished with busts of former residents, presided over by a sad image of Shakespeare who still stands there.

In 1854 another building for instructive entertainment, a sort of Polytechnic, had been opened in Leicester Square under a Royal Charter, the inaugural ceremony being performed by the Bishop of London. It was called the Panopticon of Science and Art and was designed by an architect called T. Hayter Lewis in a Saracenic style, modelled on certain buildings at Cairo. (His project for a giant glass dome to be made on Paxton's ridge-and-furrow principle proved to be impossible since there was insufficient room to buttress it.) Therein were displayed a motley collection that included a glass cistern to exhibit diving apparatus, an electric machine, a monster steam organ, and at the centre a fountain ejecting tall jets of coloured water impelled by hydraulic pressure induced

Left, Saturday night in the gallery of the Victoria Theatre (*Graphic*, 1872). *Right*, After the Play – Under the Lyceum Portico (*Graphic*, 1881). These tight dresses of the New Women of the Aesthetic period, in remarkable contrast with the crinolines of less than twenty years past, are visible symbols of the cultural divide of the Victorian era that occurred in the seventies.

The gilded night house of Kate Hamilton, queen of London's night-life. Kate's rotund figure can be seen at the back seated on a dais. (From *London Labour and the London Poor* by Mayhew and others, 1862.)

by a steam engine. But the general public was not impressed by a project 'calculated to elevate their social, moral and intellectual conditions', as the Charter put it, and after four years the place went bankrupt. After that it became in turn a music hall, a circus and a theatre. There in 1870 the voluptuous Can-Can was danced with such unrestrained exuberance that the authorities removed its dancing licence. In 1882, on a night so cold that the water froze in the firemen's hosepipes, the place was consumed by fire, but it was soon rebuilt as the Alhambra Theatre Royal, in a similarly Islamic manner. In 1884 it reverted to music hall with ballet, and under Charles Morton, Grand Old Man of Music Hall, it thrived for eleven years. Its third rebuilding was to produce, in our century, the Odeon cinema.

Throughout the fifties and sixties and into the seventies, a high-toned establishment did good business in Leicester Square. This was the luxurious *maison-de-rendezvous* of Kate Hamilton, queen of London's night-life and pro-curess-in-chief for the fashionable and wealthy. The entrance in Prince's Street was flanked by two sumptuous janitors and before the door was opened the visitor would be inspected through a spy-hole. If admitted he proceeded up a long corridor and so into the brilliantly lit saloon, lined with mirrors and gilt. At one end stood a bar and at the other a dais with a throne on which was seated a mountain of fat glistening with jewels, drinking cham-pagne, and quaking now and then with laughter like a blancmange. This was the notorious Kate. The feminine company assembled consisted of prostitutes of high caste who, according to Henry Mayhew, visited Kate's 'not only to dissipate ennui, but with a view to replenishing an exhausted exchequer', for 'Kate is careful as to whom she admits to her rooms . . . these supper rooms are frequented by a better set of men and women than perhaps any other in London'.

The Shah of Persia was among the dignitaries who patronized the establishment on his first visit to London in 1873, and there he hired a room for the evening. An epic poem, 'The Siliad', appeared in Beeton's Christmas Annual for 1873 on the subject of the night life of London, and therein the Shah's visit to Kate's is documented:

> It was the Shah; the wily potentate
> Was studying the secrets of our state,
> Which three fat actresses with might and main
> Had been in turn endeavouring to explain.

Kate's was raided with regular ritual as One-of-the-Old-Brigade reveals from first-hand knowledge:

Carpets were turned up in the twinkling of an eye, boards were raised, and glasses and bottles - empty or full - were thrust promiscuously in; everyone assumed a sweet and virtuous air and talked in subdued tones, whilst a bevy of police, headed by an inspector, marched solemnly in, and having completed the farce, marched solemnly out. What the subsidy attached to this duty, and when and how paid, it is needless to inquire. . . . 'Now we're all right,' explained the foghorn, as the salon resumed its normal vivacity. 'Bobby, my dear, come and sit next to me', and so, like a tomtit and a round of beef, the pasty-faced youth took the post of honour alongside the vibrating mass of humanity. The distinction conferred upon our hero was a much-coveted one amongst the youngsters, and gave a 'hall-marking' which henceforth proclaimed him a 'man about town'. To dispense champagne *ad libitum* was one of its chief privileges. . . . Bobby it is needless to say was a proud man.

Kate died in the early sixties but her place was carried on for another decade under her name.

Other fashionable whore-markets in the West End patronized by swells on the spree were the Argyll Rooms, the Casino de Venise and Mott's. There music, dancing, food and other essentials could be enjoyed. These were well-conducted places and the magistrates tolerated them because they felt it was better that the women should be entertained therein rather than encouraged to prowl about the streets. Mott's in Foley Street was old-established for it dated back to the eighteenth century, and in the fifties at least it was so select that its owner refused admittance to anyone whose social standing he did not approve. The ladies here were either actresses or classy courtesans like Cora Pearl, the famous 'Skittles' Walters and Sweet Nelly Fowler. Nelly was a goddess with many worshippers, for she possessed so distinct yet delicate a natural perfume that large sums were paid by the love-sick for the privilege of having their handkerchiefs laid beneath her pillow - a profitable side-line which demanded no exertion.

Restaurants were rarely patronized by wives or respectable women until the late eighties, when the Savoy opened and inaugurated a new restaurant cult in which sensual satisfactions were confined to eating and drinking. An eccentric *rendezvous* of refugees and down-cast Bohemians was the Café Royal, renowned for its cellars of French wines. There a lavish interior of red plush, gilded cupids, marble table-tops and huge mirrors had been imported from the Second Empire. Now rebuilt, its grill room still retains the magnificent original ornament.

By the eighties most of the old night-houses and casinos had vanished and prostitutes of quality found refuge first in the rebuilt Alhambra in Leicester Square, where spacious bars and a wide promenade were to be found, and then at the elegant and luxurious new Empire, also in the Square. At the Alhambra behaviour was free and easy, and back-stage was an artistes' bar which became little more than a brothel, but in the promenade of the Empire

with its velvet couches and shaded lights the more select members of the oldest profession were allowed so long as they displayed themselves with decorum. W. Macqueen-Pope describes them in *The Melody Lingers On* as 'amazing creatures, amazingly dressed, of all races and speech', who 'moved quietly and slowly to and fro, with a rather feline grace . . . yet their manners were excellent. There was never any loud chatter, shrieking laughter or bad language. These women might have had no character outside but they had one to lose in the Empire. One complaint to the management and they were barred. And that was, for them, tragedy, irrevocable loss of prestige and descent to the depths'.

Lorettes of a lower status could be found on summer evenings at Cremorne Gardens until it closed in 1877. The public pleasure garden, of which Vauxhall was the archetype, was by no means the product only of the eighteenth century. Nineteenth-century London created several in the charming tradition with its fireworks, *al fresco* supper boxes and orchestra, its tree-lined lovers' walks, its playful buildings and general gaiety - as at Rosherville near Gravesend, the Surrey Gardens at Walworth, and (loveliest of London's place names) Cremorne. Rain or rowdies, of course, sometimes blighted the bucolic effect.

Vauxhall, opened in 1661 as Spring Gardens, had entertained Londoners for nearly two centuries in a manner, as Dr Johnson had written, 'so peculiarly adapted to the taste of the English nation, there being a mixture of curious show, gay exhibition, music, vocal and instrumental not too refined for the general ear, for all of which a shilling is paid'. In Victorian days it had lost some of its old tone and become somewhat too cluttered with buildings. On 25 July 1859 the set-piece of fireworks at Vauxhall displayed the words 'Farewell for Ever'. It was a sad moment. Cremorne Gardens, however, had been open since 1846 and were flourishing. They covered twelve acres between the river and King's Road, where Lots Road Power Station now pollutes the air. By the river was a landing-stage with an elaborate wrought-iron gateway where the penny steamers could disgorge their passengers. The main feature in the grounds was a central bandstand surrounded by a dance floor, and among the encompassing elm groves stood such exotic structures as a Chinese pagoda, a Swiss chalet, an Indian temple, a large theatre, besides a marionnette theatre, concert room, small circus, restaurant, fernery, menagerie, American bowling saloon, shooting gallery, and gypsy's tent.

Situated only a few hundred yards to the west of old Battersea Bridge, Cremorne had its special charm and atmosphere which was appreciated by Whistler and his Chelsea friends. Here could be enjoyed not only music and dancing but firework displays, balloon ascents, panoramic pictures and other spectacles. An occasion of the early sixties was the crossing of the Thames here on a tight rope by Miss Selina Young, the Female Blondin. At her first attempt some scoundrel severed the guy ropes at one end, when Miss Young was well on her way across the river; with great presence of mind she clutched the rope as it subsided and lowered herself with dignity into a boat.

By the seventies the gardens had developed a reputation for rowdiness which became hectic on Bank Holidays and Derby Night. Then, records One-of-the-Old-Brigade, 'to pass the private boxes was to run the gauntlet of a quartern loaf or a dish of cutlets at one's head'. A Derby Night without a row was, in those days, an impossibility and so 'the expected dénouement was not long in coming, and in a second, and without apparent warning, sticks were crashing down on top hats, tumblers flying in every direction, and fists coming in contact with anything and anybody whose proximity seemed to suggest it'.

Taine went there at eleven o'clock at night and found

a crush and much shoving at the entrance; a gang of Englishmen crashed through shouting, 'Make way for the Japanese Ambassadors!' Inside, especially at crossings in the walks, the press of people was dreadful. . . . All the men well or at least neatly dressed: the women were prostitutes, but of a higher rank than those in the Strand . . . the faces are rather faded and sometimes, in the crowd, they utter shocking screams, shrill as a screech-owl. The most comical part, and which showed the degree of excitement was the way they had of pinching people, especially foreigners. . . . A woman rushed at a man who had trodden on her toes, and punched him in the back: he laughed and the whole crowd was delighted. They are certainly very good natured. . . . Once you have seen this you can get some idea of the joyous rustic feasts of the sixteenth century, Shakespeare's *Merry England*, and of the strong, young sap of that tree which Puritanism so lopped and topped and pollarded that although it grew straight it also grew rigid.

Prudes on the Prowl were largely responsible for the closing of Cremorne. A tailor and Baptist preacher named Alf Brandon published some verses on 'The Horrors of Cr*m**ne' and Baum, the owner, sued him for libel. In court Brandon described the gardens as 'a nursery of every kind of vice', but Baum won his case with one farthing damages and no costs. The poor man was ill and in debt and did not renew his application for a licence. So Cremorne closed and before long the site, like that of Vauxhall, was covered with buildings. Another piece of London green had vanished.

A different place of diversion, still with us, was the Zoo in Regent's Park. It had been going since 1827 and Doré did not fail to pay it a visit. South of the river, near Kennington Park Road lay the former Surrey Zoological Gardens, which as Surrey Gardens acquired a music hall in 1856; it was used by Spurgeon on Sundays during his

Ascent of M. Goddard's Montgolfier hot-air balloon, *The Eagle*, from Cremorne Gardens (*I.L.N.*, 1864).

first rush of popularity in London. The hall was burned down in 1861 but was rebuilt and used temporarily by St Thomas's Hospital while transferring from London Bridge to its new building by Westminster Bridge.

In 1877 a Summer and Winter Garden was opened in Tothill Street, near the Central Hall, Westminster, a large affair of brick and stone with a glass-roofed main hall, called the Royal Westminster Aquarium. The architect was A. Bedborough. Very few fish were ever seen in the place and although it was founded on high moral principles with the purpose of providing not only fishy instruction but concerts, popular lectures on science and art, flower shows and so on to combine 'pleasant instruction with polite entertainment', the general public showed no more interest in the place than they had in the Panopticon in Leicester Square. The management was compelled to fetch people in with diversions of wider appeal, and so the place became a fun fair and a kind of music hall where, up to closure in 1903, among other attractions, Mademoiselle Zanfretta performed her charming *danses de poissons* and Madamoiselle Zazel's personable form could be seen flying twice daily through the air from a cannon's mouth into a net; there also could be seen such aberrations as Pongo the Missing Link, Succi the Fasting Man and a two-headed nightingale.

In that same year of 1877 the floating swimming-bath on the Thames at Charing Cross was converted into an ice-skating rink by Professor Gangee's freezing system. The system worked by the condensation of sulphurous acid under pressure and releasing it to cool a mixture of glycerine and water running in pipes covered with a few inches of water. In the seventies, too, roller skating, known as rinking, became a brief rage. The Crystal Palace constructed its rolling floor, and Holborn Amphitheatre, which had been used for equestrian performances, was converted into a rink. One of the attractions of the sport was that romantic flirtation with clasping hands was at last possible away from chaperones and protective mamas.

Among both men and women of the middle class, the pursuits of archery, croquet and the new lawn tennis were well established by the eighties. Open-air diversions for the upper crust were available at Hurlingham, including the regular slaughter of doves, and thanks to the railways the rustic Thames was becoming ever more popular among all classes for week-end boating at least as far up as Marlow. Skindles Hotel by Maidenhead Bridge became a fashionable Sunday resort. The Victorian cult of Sunday up the river was a delightful one, with its sleek steam launches hissing soporifically along, its twirling red parasols, ornamental fretwork houseboats and a bottle of bubbly at Tagg's, when to embark on any craft without white flannels and a straw boater was to be scorned as being, to borrow an Edwardian phrase, not quite the clean potato.

Victorian London never possessed enough public entertainments to meet the demand, and among the middle classes at least far more self-entertainment was provided at home than it is today. Apart from dinner parties and receptions, there were whist parties, musical evenings and amateur theatricals, while in the sixties a vogue for spirit-rapping and other demonstrations of the occult sciences set in. According to the author of *London in the Sixties*, Lord Ashburton, who lived near Portman Square, was 'the arch-priest and arch-culprit that disseminated this fashionable twaddle, and there was not a spinster in that (then) highly fashionable district that did not devour the leaflets that were periodically issued broadcast by the inspired old humbug'. Balls were popular in the larger houses during the Season and tutored skill was expected from the guests in the schottische, the polka and the valse.

A major pastime was reading books, particularly the three-volume novel, either to oneself or aloud to the family. A wealth of wonderful works, both plain and illustrated, were available in this most literary of periods. Novel-writing was one of the few professions open to women with talent and was practised by many of the type

'The Winner of the Derby' (Doré).

personified in Trollope's *The Way We Live Now* by Lady Carbury. Some of them, like Miss Braddon, Ouida and Mrs Henry Wood, made fortunes from their works, and in doing so were assisted by Mudie's Select Library at the corner of New Oxford Street and Museum Street. The library expanded so rapidly that by 1861 it possessed 800,000 volumes and its main hall with its Ionic columns and iron galleries was so grand that it seemed like an assembly room in an old provincial town. Mudie's sent books by post all over the country and even out of the country, to home-sick corners of the Empire and to such cultured English colonies as that at Florence. As W. S. Gilbert sang in *The Bab Ballads*:

> New volumes come across the sea
> From Mr Mudie's libraree.

The poor had to content themselves with dancing in the streets to the tunes of the Italian hurdy-gurdy man with his monkey, to watching Punch and Judy shows, street performers, and an occasional secret cock-fight. After the Bank Holiday Act of 1871, open spaces like Hampstead Heath and Epping Forest became playgrounds for those seeking a brief release from close walls and foul air. The gin palaces were the main centres of relaxation as the clubs of the labouring classes, but an occasional outing

The roller-skating rink at Prince's Ground, Brompton (*Graphic*, 1875).
The sport became a craze for a time.

to a music hall or a gaff was sometimes possible when a few extra shillings could be earned, saved or stolen.

As for the stage, 'Good society does not patronize the theatre in England, with the exception of the two opera houses, which are luxurious and exotic hot-house flowers,' declared Taine in the sixties. There, he says, the price of seats was enormous and evening dress obligatory. While opera, mainly Italian, was flourishing at Covent Garden and at Her Majesty's in the Haymarket, encouraged by the Queen, who loved it, the theatre had fallen to a low level and until the mid-sixties most serious drama was in eclipse. One cause of the decline of the theatre in mid-Victorian times was no doubt that strange legal monopoly which had remained in force until 1843 whereby legitimate drama could be performed only at Drury Lane, Covent Garden and the Haymarket. With the Theatres Registry Act of 1843, another restriction was imposed, for no theatre within the metropolis could stage a play without a licence from the Lord Chamberlain.

Yet cheap theatres abounded which gave performances of melodramas interspersed with comedies and farces in long double or triple bills sometimes lasting from 6.30 p.m. to midnight. Extravagant spectacle using mechanical devices was popular in the larger theatres. A production of *The Tempest* in 1852 began, for example, with a wrecked ship plunging about in a turbulent sea; falls of real water were engineered and horses often trotted on to the stage.

In the sixties drama began to revive with a new realism under the direction of people like Tom Robertson, the Bancrofts and Henry Irving; this was the era of the actor-

Henry Irving as Richelieu in Lord Lytton's tragedy at the Lyceum Theatre (*I.L.N.*, 1873). The ageing Cardinal is trying his old sword.

managers. The middle and upper classes began to take interest in plays about their own lives in familiar drawing-room settings; the first success in this field came in 1863 with *Society*, a satire on the materialism of the times. Irving's first major success occurred in 1871 with *The Bells*, and a few years later he established his highly professional company at the Lyceum, where his reign lasted from 1879 until 1903. That reign was one of egocentric tyranny which helped to establish the star system of the present century. It was not always appreciated by members of the company: 'Don't you think, Governor,' a mutinous satellite remonstrated during a rehearsal, 'a few rays of the moon might fall on me? Nature, at least, is impartial!' The old association between fleshly sin and the theatre had so weakened during the last three decades of the century that a remarkable event occurred: Henry Irving received the accolade. This was the first time an actor had been knighted, an event which would have been unthinkable in the fifties.

The greatest events in the Victorian theatre were, of course, the Gilbert and Sullivan light operas in the manner of Offenbach's *bouffes parisiens*, and between 1875 and 1889, when they were produced, not only London went mad about them, but so did the rest of Europe and the United States. Gilbert's words, indeed, like those of *Punch*, cast quite a bright light on the social history of the age. The operas were tuneful, lively, satirical and colourful, and they contained nothing, as Gilbert pointed out, to offend even the most delicately nurtured young lady. They brought fortunes to the gentle, benevolent little Sullivan, the large, blunt Gilbert and their astute impresario D'Oyly Carte. *The Mikado*, first produced at the Savoy Theatre in 1885, was the most successful of all their works and ran for nearly two years without a break – 672 performances. Returning to London from the States in 1885, Sullivan found the whole country was Mikado-mad. 'From drawing-rooms, concert-halls, cottages, street-corners, came the well-known arias,' comments Hesketh Pearson in his biography of the pair. 'Queen Victoria strummed them, errand-boys whistled them, and the future Kaiser wrote to tell Sullivan that as soon as he could get rid of "a very serious and rather dangerous attack of ear-ache" he would attend a performance in Berlin.' Nothing quite like these tuneful satires had ever been heard or seen before and most of them were enormously popular. Like Dickens's novels, the *Alice* books and the Crystal Palace, they were a unique Victorian phenomenon, and the more remarkable in having been produced by a couple of men who were never close friends and had almost nothing in common.

My observations on the London of Doré, in their attempt to present objective facts, have often verged on the

horrendous, but we can end on a cheerful cockney subject: the music hall. That so much music, artistry, good-humoured and individualistic exuberance, so much gaiety could be expressed by and for the more depressed levels of an unhealthy urban society provides heartening assurance of human adaptability in its persisting lust for life even under the most discouraging conditions.

By the seventies more than three hundred Halls existed in London alone, ranging from crude taverns to saloons lined with red plush and mirrors, all serving up 'free and easy' entertainment, glittering with girls and convulsed by cockney patter singing with natural gusto of all the trials of daily life – lodgers, kippers, the rent, mothers-in-law. The artistes were highly skilled experts in a very special form of stage art. Like Gilbert and Sullivan opera, music hall has left a legacy of songs and tunes that are immortal.

Music hall has been called essentially entertainment of the people, for the people, by the people. It was certainly not middle class, but the word 'people' has wide connotations. In the halls it probably implies in particular the lower middles and the 'improved', or upper, working classes, for between them and the submerged tenth (who couldn't afford to go anyway) existed as wide a gap as between aristocracy and middle class. Yet music hall was certainly not upper class. It was purely English and it was born in London. In its authentic form, as distinct from the variety shows of the present century which developed from it, music hall was associated from the start with eating and drinking. It began in the singing rooms of pubs where everyone joined in the chorus under the surveillance of that father figure, the publican, and so the audience participation and the presiding Master of Ceremonies become understandable.

The approach to true music hall was gradual. Early Victorian restaurants like the Cyder Cellars, the Coal Hole and Evans's catered only for men, and mainly for well-to-do men. Evans's, facing Covent Garden, was the most famous. It had been an aristocratic residence, then became an hotel, run for a while by W. C. Evans, and early in the forties was taken over by 'Paddy' Green, who in 1855 added a grand pillared saloon at the back, the celebrated Song and Supper Room where good food, drink and entertainment, often very blue, could be had. Much of the entertainment in such places was provided by the customers themselves, and professional entertainers were always males. Gradually ladies were admitted, but only to the gallery where they could watch the proceedings from behind a screen through the thick haze of tobacco smoke, and observe the benevolent old Paddy strolling about and offering his snuff box to favoured customers. It was a smart bohemian resort, where men of

standing could do themselves well in a congenial, relaxed atmosphere.

A frequent customer at Evans's was Charles Morton (1819–1904), a true cockney who was born in Hackney. In a sense he was there on business for he was learning how such places were conducted. Meanwhile he was running his own tavern in Pimlico where he not only supplied food and drink but also a Free and Easy entertainment in a special room to which only men were admitted. This was fairly common practice in the pubs at that time. Later Morton took over a pub of old foundation south of the river called the Canterbury Arms. It was a well-established place and had its room where amateur talent could find vocal outlet. Here true music hall was born when Morton opened the place to women as well as men, charging threepence admission. He did so with the greatest tact and with the approval of his regular customers, beginning with a special weekly Ladies' Night. Soon the place was known all over town. Morton was a perfectionist; he was always in personal attendance and he supplied the very best food, drink and entertainment he could afford. The date on which he established his hall at the Canterbury Arms was 17 May 1852, and that was the definitive start of music hall.

Morton so flourished that he soon decided to rebuild the Canterbury on a larger scale. He did so around the old place without disturbing his customers in the least. It was he who gave the title 'music hall' to his establishment and it was so successful that many rivals were rapidly built all over London. Even the moralizing R. E. Ritchie in *The Night Side of London* (1857) admitted that Morton had rendered the Free and Easy respectable with his music hall, and describes the Canterbury in detail:

The Upper Marsh, Westminster-road, is what is called a low neighbourhood. It is not far from Astley's Theatre. Right through it runs the South Western Railway, and everywhere about it are

'The Penny Gaff in Leman Street, Whitechapel' (Doré).
Everything was spiced highly to touch the tough palates of a Whitechapel audience' (Jerrold).

'The Christy Minstrels' (Doré), an ebonized band that played in the pop concerts at St James's Hall. In this Spanish-Moorish building designed by Owen Jones, that lay between Regent Street and Piccadilly, Dickens gave the second series of his famous readings in 1861.

planted pawnbrokers' shops, with an indescribable amount of the dirty second-hand clothes, and monster gin-palaces, with unlimited plate-glass and gas. Go along there what hour of the day you will, these gin-palaces are full of ragged children, hideous old women, and drunken men . . . and of the hundreds rushing on to the Canterbury Hall for a quiet glass, none think they will fall so low as the victims of intemperance reeling, cursing, fighting, blaspheming, in their path. But let us pass on.

A well-lighted entrance attached to a public-house indicates that we have reached our destination. We proceed up a few stairs, along a passage lined with handsome engravings, to a bar, where we pay sixpence if we take a seat in the body of the hall, and ninepence if we do the nobby and ascend into the balcony. We make our way leisurely along the floor of the building, which is really a very handsome hall, well lighted, and capable of holding fifteen hundred persons: the balcony extends round the room in the form of a horseshoe. At the opposite end to which we enter is the platform, on which is placed a grand piano and a harmonium, on which the performers play at intervals when the professional singers have left the stage. The chairman sits just beneath them. It is all dull work to him; but there he must sit every night smoking cigars and drinking, from seven till twelve o'clock. . . . Even on a fine summer night like this the room is crowded, and almost every gentleman present has a pipe or a cigar in his mouth. Let us look around us: evidently the majority present are respectable mechanics, or small tradesmen with their wives and daughters and sweethearts there. Now and then, you see a midshipman, or a few fast clerks and warehousemen, who confidentially inform each other that there is 'no end of talent here', and that Miss ****'is a doosed fine gal'. . . . Every one is smoking, and every one has a glass before him; but the class that come here are economical, and chiefly confine themselves to pipes and porter. The presence of the ladies has also a beneficial effect; I see no indication of intoxication, and certainly none of the songs are obscene.

Morton hung paintings on the walls at the Canterbury and he introduced operatic selections which enticed music-lovers from across the river. He also introduced that important turn of the music hall, the serio-comic, or low comedienne. One of the earliest of these was Mrs Caulfield, wife of the Canterbury Chairman. In her repertoire was a strange nonsense song which became immensely popular, running partly thus:

> Kemo, Kimo: Where? Oh, there! my high, low!
> Then in came Dolly singing;
> Sometimes medley winkum lingum up-cat
> Sing, song, Dolly – won't you try me oh!

Let the Freudians make something of that if they can.

When Edward Weston opened a rival music hall in Holborn in 1857 (it became the Holborn Empire), Morton decided to compete with him in the West End and in 1861 he established a grand new place in Oxford Street. For seven years the Oxford was packed every night, and then came calamity: in 1868 it was burned to the ground. To help his out-of-work artistes Morton immediately staged a benefit performance for them at the Crystal Palace. The Oxford was rebuilt, but not under Morton's management.

The music hall with its curious concoction of innocence and innuendo brought life down to a warmly human level in a cruel and struggling world. It understood by instinct that the true purpose of the symbol of the age of steam was not to improve transport but had a more fundamental and organic nature:

> A tickle in the tunnel is a lark, my boys,
> A tickle in the tunnel in the dark, my boys,
> 'Tis nice to take your Mary Jane
> Ariding in the railway train
> And have a jolly tickle in the tunnel-oh.

193

Overleaf, this fine dome formed the Winter Garden of the Palace of the People, Muswell Hill (*I.L.N.*, 1859).
Designed by Owen Jones, it was unfortunately never built. The exterior is on page 177.

A Century Back, a Century On

The technical and economic studies that have engrossed city planners to the exclusion of every other element in life, must in the coming era take second place to primary studies of the needs of persons and groups. Subordinate questions – the spatial separation of industry and domestic life, or the number of houses per acre – cannot be settled intelligently until more fundamental problems are answered: What sort of personality do we seek to foster and nurture? What kind of common life? What is the order of preference in our life-needs?

LEWIS MUMFORD, *City Development* (1947)

Much of central London remains as Doré saw it: a city built for steam trains and horse carriages. The twentieth century has added the surrounding cultural deserts of the commuting belts relying on electric trains and petrol engines. Built mainly by speculators without benefit of architects, planners, or landscape artists, land has been wasted on an epic scale, adding to traffic difficulties and causing the urban jungle to spread with little form for forty miles out in every direction from Charing Cross.

All this confusion has been conceived under strict planning laws and bureaucratic controls. Cholera disappeared long ago, thanks initially to Chadwick's nose; the new epidemic is neurosis. The hideous sprawl is in effect little more than a gigantic and highly inefficient labour camp where even the gardens of the fine old squares near the centre are now enclosed by chicken wire. As Dr Desmond Morris has it, we are caged animals in a zoo.

Squalor and poverty almost at a Victorian level still survive in too many of London's twilight areas. In 1970 some 600,000 people in London remained inadequately housed. Yet brickworks close down, builders and architects suffer, in their own repellent phrase, from inadequate workloads, and Cathy goes home. We are not so far from Doré's London as we may like to believe.

Can Greater London be recreated or is its destiny beyond control? The physical means for rapid improvement exist, but does the general will and the imagination?

Doré's last big drawing in *London: A Pilgrimage*, typifying his love of drama, imagined the city as Jefferies did in *After London*: a deserted ruin rising from a swamp. In the foreground a bearded individual, wearing a kind of Chartist's hood, sits sketching alone in the melancholy moonlight, while in the distance above the remains the drum of St Paul's, its dome collapsed, still rises on its hill.

It illustrates a paragraph from Macaulay's essay on Ranke's *History of the Popes* of 1840: 'She [the Roman Church] may still exist in undiminished vigour when some traveller from New Zealand shall, in the midst of the vast solitude, take his stand on a broken arch of London Bridge to sketch the ruin of St Paul's.'

What, if it survives, will London be like a century hence? Let us hope that the confusion will have been broken down into coherent neighbourhoods based on the old villages and articulated by belts of green, that many more pedestrian networks and precincts will have been created, that the riverside will have been opened up and refurbished, that the Thames Barrage will have been built to free the metropolis from the threat of flooding and to give it a full, clean, tideless, and fishful river. Vertical segregation of functions and traffic may have been applied in a way now apparent in embryo at the rebuilt Barbican. And in a hundred years' time the decision may long ago have been taken to control the Motor Moloch; transport may be electric and steam power may have returned in new forms. Obviously the present situation cannot be allowed to continue for it is not only polluting the air to a point of public danger – even if it is less smoky than it was – but it is depriving us of convenience, serenity, and beauty.

A number of broad plans for improvement have been produced since the last World War. They have mostly been tacitly based on assumptions that are no longer tenable. The latest is the G.L.C.'s short-term *Tomorrow's London* (1969). It forecasts that by 1981 London will have doubled its number of vehicles, and have a population increase of two and a half per cent living on incomes which have increased by seventy per cent. It also assumes that the Channel Tunnel will have been completed and

197

that this will throw an extra load on roads and railways. It wants to improve the riverside and recreate a peaceful village atmosphere in areas of inner London. It concludes:

> London need not be a jungle, a centre of human misery, of selfishness, subordinating dignity to mere technological efficiency. Rather, we think of a society of free people who choose to live and work here because the city affords them and their children great opportunities – in their jobs, in their homes, in their recreations. We cannot prescribe for them how they shall live – they must make their own choices.

The question remains unanswered: how, under present monetary restraints and pressures, can most people possibly make their own choices? Whether we like it or not, planning *is* politics, and politics require philosophies.

We live under the threats of the atomic holocaust, the population explosion, lethal pollution of land, sea and air, and death of the top soil, all of which are primarily caused by monetary abuse. Daniel Moynahan, as adviser on urban affairs to President Nixon, stated baldly at the North Atlantic Assembly in 1969: 'We may have even less than a fifty-fifty chance of living until 1980.' Mankind, it is said, has become a planetary disease. We have thus reached an impasse in which we are compelled to question the very nature of human purposes. Without adequate answers the discussion of plans for the future of London must be futile, for, unless rapid action is taken, not even a single New Zealander may be left alive a century hence to sketch the ruins of St Paul's. We have arrived at a sudden crisis.

A bright hope exists: the industrial revolution is young. If we can weather the next few critical decades and can be relieved of the universal complaint of moral constipation, we can end the age-old struggle to supply the whole human race with basic needs – and this with ever-diminishing muscular effort. Indeed, full employment in mass conurbations of factory and office toilers is no longer possible. One cause of our crisis may lie in our self-immolating refusal to rejoice in that fact. Until it is accepted we shall continue to make and do the wrong things for the wrong purposes. The problems ahead are those not of production but of distribution, servicing, waste prevention, and conserving nature's balance. The automated factories can go underground.

The Judaic-Christian tradition of rewards and punishments in general and the Puritan ethic in particular, with their worship of the ruthless male principle, formed both the London of Doré and, in spite of the empty churches, the London we live in now. Its most destructive result is the great money myth with its blatant abuse of what should serve as a mere convenience. This is a child of primitive religion, for its monopolistic credit restrictions, its needless debts and taxes, its inflation, its artificial booms and slumps, its dangerous export struggles, its impossible call for full employment, and its whole arcane mystique (including the ancient sun-worship of gold), impose heavy penances on the community, and the community accepts them without demur as punitive acts of an inscrutable God demanding endless expiation. In spite of Darwin, God has not died; he has come down to earth to take up a new career as an international banker. Money is power – possibly to the unconscious mind a symbol bearing both faecal and sexual guilt. In its righteous and restrictive way it controls our every act. To win the battle for as large a share as possible of this paper abstraction – universally believed to be a rare commodity that must ineluctably remain in short supply however vast may be the unearned increment – is still regarded as the highest purpose of life. The Victorian doctrine of egocentric self-help and unremitting, mostly disagreeable and futile toil – combined with the quasi-religious belief that monetary success alone reflects moral and social superiority and failure only laziness and vice – remains with us. Four patent results are the squalid confusion, high traffic fever, growing aggression, and nervous exhaustion of our cities. Happily both the ecologists and the young are questioning the faith, and therein lies hope. A new idea is developing.

Art and architecture cannot return to our towns – nor can the lay citizen, now thoroughly bemused by the jargon of the planners, become directly and personally involved in recreating his environment – until the conditions that produce artistry return. Eric Gill, with whom William Morris would surely have agreed, summed up the matter: 'Art is that work and that way of working in which man uses his free will. A civilization based on the doctrine of free will naturally and inevitably produces artists. In such a civilization all men are artists and so there is no need to talk about it.' And what is real freedom today, in practical terms, but an unearned, machine-granted income, and, with that, the possibility of doing what you enjoy? One thing is clear: whatever else it may be, modern society is certainly not permissive.

Work need no longer be a boring, commuting imposition, an expiation, or a drug for anyone; it could become a chosen dedication within a genuine – that is an economic – democracy. *Homo Ludens*, as the true *Homo Universalis* of a classless culture, who works for pleasure more than for payment – perhaps does not work at all in the old sense of 'earning a living' – can be reinstated. 'In the Middle Ages they had a strange idea that it was sloth which was the cause of restlessness, leisurelessness, and the ultimate cause of suicidal "work for work's sake". Perhaps they were not far wrong.' So concluded a thoughtful article in *The Times Literary Supplement* in 1970.

London must relax and grow convivial.

Overleaf, a Victorian bourgeois idyll below Waterloo Bridge: 'The Thames Embankment as it might be: a suggestive sketch' (*Graphic*, 1881).

A Chronology: 1851 to 1889

The vast and shapeless city which Dickens knew – fog-bound and fever-haunted, brooding over its dark, mysterious river – into the imperial capital, of Whitehall, the Thames Embankment and South Kensington, is the still visible symbol of the mid-Victorian transition.

G. M. YOUNG, *Victorian England: Portrait of an Age* (1953)

1851

The Great Exhibition of the Works of Industry of All Nations opens 1 May in Hyde Park in the Crystal Palace; London's population now 2,363,405; Victoria Street opens; Nash's Marble Arch removed from forecourt of Buckingham Palace to north-east corner of Hyde Park; Batty's Hippodrome opens in Kensington Road; Wyld's Great Globe House, containing model of the world, opens in centre of Trafalgar Square.

Sixth Census: Britain's population nearly 21 millions, about half being still rural; Over half world's ocean-going tonnage now British; Shaftesbury's Common Lodging-houses Act; Repeal of window tax; Submarine telegraph cable laid between Dover and Calais; Scott Archer introduces collodion wet plate to photography; Mrs Bloomer from U.S.A. makes lecture tour of England advocating 'rational dress' (bloomers or pantaloons) for women; The St Petersburg–Moscow railway completed; Discovery of gold in Australia; *Coup d'état* places Louis Napoleon in control of France; Deaths: Turner, Daguerre; Birth: Oliver Lodge.

Published Mrs Gaskell's *Cranford* begins as serial in Dickens's paper *Household Words*; Ruskin's *The Stones of Venice*, Vol. I; Borrow's *Lavengro*; Melville's *Moby Dick*.

1852

New Houses of Parliament open; Funeral procession of Duke of Wellington; Paxton begins re-erecting Crystal Palace at Sydenham; King's Cross Station opens; Paddington Station with Great Western Hotel nears completion; Charles Morton opens first music hall; Metropolitan Water Act seeks to improve London's water; Department of Practical Art instituted to improve old governmental Normal School of Design (formed 1837);

Museum of Practical Art opens at Marlborough House as origin of Victoria and Albert Museum; Henry Mayhew accompanies Charles Green from Vauxhall Gardens in Green's 500th and last balloon ascent.

Derby becomes Prime Minister; Disraeli, Chancellor of Exchequer; then Aberdeen P.M. and Gladstone Chancellor; Metropolitan Burials Act; Underground telegraph wires between Dover and London completed; Manchester Free Library opens; Tasmania (Van Diemen's Land till 1853) ceases to serve as convict settlement; Restoration of Empire under Napoleon III; Death: A. W. N. Pugin.

Published: Dickens's *Bleak House* (begins in parts); Mrs Stowe's *Uncle Tom's Cabin*; Roget's *Thesaurus*.

1853

Department of Practical Art adds a science division and becomes the Science and Art Department of the Board of Trade (transferred to new Education Department in 1856); Cabbies' strike against new Cab Act.

Death duties introduced by Gladstone's first budget; Honours School of Natural Science Tripos instituted at Oxford University as degree course; Queen Victoria allows John Snow to administer chloroform to her during birth of Prince Leopold; Russo-Turkish War; Exhibition of Industry of All Nations, New York.

Published: Thackeray's *The Newcomes* (begins in parts); Brontë's *Villette*; Arnold's *Scholar Gipsy*; Ruskin's *The Stones of Venice* (completed).

1854

Crystal Palace, Sydenham, opened by the Queen; Cholera prevails in south and west London; Government buys Burlington House, Piccadilly, for £140,000; Working Men's College founded in Red Lion Square by Rev.

The bell turret of Waterhouse's City and Guilds Institute in Exhibition Road, South Kensington, with Colcutt's tower of the Imperial Institute in the background – both late additions to Albertopolis. The building was demolished in the nineteen-sixties to make way for the new Imperial College.

F. D. Maurice with support of Charles Kingsley, Ruskin, Rossetti and others; The Royal Panopticon of Science, Art and Manufactures, in Saracenic style, opens in Leicester Square for instructive entertainment; Regent's Park Diorama converted to Baptist chapel; Spurgeon begins his ministry in London; Exhibition of Japanese arts and crafts at the Old Society of Painters in Water Colours, Pall Mall East.

Outbreak of Crimean War; Income tax raised (just over 1p) to 1s. 2d. (6p) in the pound; New Public Health Board appointed to replace Chadwick's General Board of Health; Baron Haussmann, Prefect of Seine, begins reconstructing Paris with broad boulevards, as much for mob control as for architectural grandeur; Commodore Perry sails into Yokohama Harbour to enforce trade treaty between U.S.A. and Japan; Death: John Martin, painter and planner; Birth: Patrick Geddes.

Published: Dickens's *Hard Times*; Tennyson's *The Charge of the Light Brigade*; Charlotte Yonge's *The Heir of Redclyffe*; Thoreau's *Walden*; Mrs Gaskell's *North and South* (begins in *Household Words*).

1855

Metropolitan Board of Works starts work under Local Management Act to deal with streets and sewers in area of about 117 square miles, forerunner of L.C.C. and G.L.C.; Bazalgette's main sewage scheme begins; Royal Victoria Docks open; Bunning's Metropolitan Cattle Market (Caledonian Road) at Islington opened by Prince Albert; French Emperor and Empress visit London; Gang of navvies sails from Blackwall to build army railway in Crimea; Rioting in Hyde Park against Sunday Trading Bill, which is withdrawn; First Post Office

pillar-boxes appear in the City; Weekly concerts begin at Crystal Palace (continue till 1901).

Palmerston becomes Prime Minister; William Russell, correspondent of *The Times*, reveals mismanagement of forces in Crimea; Florence Nightingale saves lives there;

Queen and Consort visit Paris; Stamp tax on newspapers removed; Co-operative Wholesale Society founded; First Cunard steamer crosses Atlantic in nine and a half days; International Exhibition, Paris; Deaths: Charlotte Brontë, Thomas Cubitt, builder of Belgravia.

Published: Dickens's *Little Dorrit* (begins in parts); Kingsley's *Westward Ho!*; Tennyson's *Maud*; Trollope's *The Warden*; Longfellow's *Hiawatha*; Whitman's *Leaves of Grass*.

1856

End of Crimean War celebrated with fireworks in London parks; Rowland Hill, Postmaster General, divides London into ten postal districts; London General Omnibus Company launched by French company; has 450 horse-buses running by end of year; Collection at Marlborough House moved to new museum at South Kensington; the glass and iron structure dubbed the Brompton Boilers by *The Builder*; Litigation between City Corporation and Her Majesty's Woods and Forests ends at last with ownership of bed and banks of the tidal Thames being conveyed from the City, to which it had belonged since 1197, to the Crown.

Treaty of Paris ends Crimean War, having cost some 25,000 British lives; Second Anglo-Chinese War; Bessemer converter introduced to steel industry; Perkin discovers first synthetic dye; Births: Freud, Oscar Wilde, Keir Hardie, G. B. Shaw.

Published: Craik's *John Halifax, Gentleman*; Reade's *It's Never Too Late to Mend*; Flaubert's *Madame Bovary*.

1857

Barry's Houses of Parliament completed; S. Smirke's Reading Room, as great rotunda, completed in courtyard of British Museum; Pennethorne's western end of Somerset House completed; Panic in City and suspension of Bank Charter Act of 1844.

Defeat and return of Palmerston as P.M.; Indian Mutiny begins; British enter Canton; Divorce (Matrimonial Causes) Act; James Clerk Maxwell synthesizes white light from red, green and blue rays; First awards of Victoria Cross; Art Treasures Exhibition, Manchester; *The Times* reports that Sweden has exported to Britain 40,000 tons of iron for the manufacture of frameworks of crinolines.

Published: Thackeray's *The Virginians*; Trollope's *Barchester Towers*; Hughes's *Tom Brown's Schooldays*; Baudelaire's *Les Fleurs du mal*.

1858

Year of the Great Stink; the Thames, now London's main sewer, treated with chloride of lime; Act for purification of the Thames; Page's Chelsea Suspension Bridge opens (existing bridge 1934); Battersea Park opens to public; Launch of Brunel's *Great Eastern* steamship at Millwall; Royal Opera House opens at Covent Garden as third on same site; Big Ben, cast at Whitechapel Bell Foundry, raised in Clock Tower of Houses of Parliament; first casting breaks, second cracks; Dickens begins a twelve-year love affair with the public with his readings.

Palmerston resigns; Derby-Disraeli ministry formed; Abolition of property qualification for Members of Parliament; Men of Jewish faith admitted to Parliament; Public Health Board dissolved; new Public Health Act; National Miners' Association formed; Suppression of Indian Mutiny; government of India transferred to the Crown; First Atlantic cable completed by H.M.S.

Agamemnon; Speke discovers source of the Nile; Nadar takes first aerial photograph from a balloon above valley of Bièvre; Death: Robert Owen, father of English socialism.

Published: George Eliot's *Scenes from Clerical Life*; Farrar's *Eric, or Little by Little*.

1859

Bazalgette's main drainage scheme begins; Strikes and lock-outs in building trade; Butterfield's All Saints, Margaret Street, with tallest spire in London, consecrated; Riots at church of St George-in-the-East over ritualism of Tractarian incumbent; Vauxhall Gardens close.

Disraeli introduces Reform Bill; Derby-Disraeli ministry resigns; Palmerston-Russell ministry formed; Work begins on Suez Canal; Opening at Cranleigh of first cottage hospital; Volunteer Rifle Corps formed; Webb's Red House, Bexley, built for William Morris; Franco-

205

Arrival of the new bell 'Victoria' at the Clock Tower of the Houses of Parliament (*I.L.N.*, 1858).

Austrian War; First American oil wells drilled; Deaths: Lord Macaulay, De Quincey, I. K. Brunel.

Published: Darwin's *On the Origin of Species*; Mill's *On Liberty*; Smiles's *Self-Help*; Dickens's *A Tale of Two Cities*; Eliot's *Adam Bede*; Tennyson's *Idylls of the King*; Meredith's *The Ordeal of Richard Feverel*; Fitzgerald's *The Rubáiyát of Omar Khayyám*.

1860

Construction of Underground Railway begins; Cannon Street widened and extended; Bedford College founded; The Nightingale School of Training for Nurses opens at St Thomas's Hospital.

Gladstone introduces Free Trade Bill; British capture Peking; end of Third Chinese War; Huxley and Wilberforce debate Darwinism at Oxford Museum; Manufacture of sewing machines begins in England; First English horse-tramway at Birkenhead; H.M.S. *Warrior*, first British ironclad, steam and sail, launched; Peace with China signed; Sir Charles Barry dies; Lincoln becomes President of U.S.A.

Published: Dickens's *Great Expectations* and *The Uncommercial Traveller* (begin in parts); Eliot's *The Mill on the Floss*; Thackeray's *The Four Georges*; Collins's *The Woman in White*; Hugo's *Les Misérables*.

1861

Bazalgette's high-level sewer, north of river, completed; Pennethorne's interior of National Gallery completed; George Peabody, American tycoon, gives £150,000 as first contribution to housing and relief of London's poor; William Morris & Co. (Morris, Marshal, Faulkner & Co.) founded; First London horse-trams run along Bayswater Road; Female Blondin crosses Thames on tight-rope at Cremorne Gardens.

Death of Prince Albert; Seventh Census: population of Great Britain 24,525,000 (thirty-two London shepherds counted); Royal (Newcastle) Commission on national education reports, recommending 'the extension of sound and cheap elementary instruction'; Post Office Savings Bank established; Daily weather forecasts begin in Britain. Start of Lancashire cotton famine; American Civil War

Demolition of Hungerford
Market to make
way for Charing Cross
Railway Station
(*I.L.N.*, 1862).

breaks out (affecting Lancashire); Victor Emmanuel crowned King of Italy; Pasteur announces his germ theory; Emancipation of serfs in Russia; Death: Elizabeth Browning.

Published: Mrs Beeton's *Book of Household Management*; Eliot's *Silas Marner*; Reade's *The Cloister and the Hearth*; Mayhew's *London Labour and the London Poor*; Spencer's *Education: Intellectual, Moral and Physical*.

1862

Second International Exhibition at South Kensington, south of new gardens of Royal Horticultural Society; Thames Embankment Bill passed; Victoria Station comes into full use; Peck's Agricultural Hall, Islington, opens; Hungerford Market, on site of present Charing Cross Station demolished; Fights in Hyde Park between Garibaldians and Irish, whereupon public meetings temporarily prohibited there; Outbreak of garotting in London streets; Demi-mondaine Skittles Walters causes society scandal by running off to New York with Aubrey de Vere Beauclerk, family man.

Published: Ruskin's *Unto This Last* (first appeared in *Cornhill* magazine, 1860); Mayhew's *Criminal Prisons of London*; Miss Braddon's *Lady Audley's Secret*.

1863

First underground railway in the world opens between Farringdon Street and Paddington; New Westminster Bridge opens, replacing Labelye's stone structure of 1750; Barlow's iron suspension bridge at Lambeth opens, replacing ancient horse-ferry; Charing Cross Railway Bridge completed, replacing I. K. Brunel's Hungerford Suspension Bridge of 1845; Pneumatic Railway Despatch Company begins to convey Post Office bags; Thackeray dies at No. 2 Palace Green, Kensington.

Marriage of Prince of Wales to Alexandra of Denmark; Income tax reduced to 7d. (say 3p) in the pound; James Clerk Maxwell proves existence of electro-magnetic waves; First Cook's Tour organized to Switzerland; Football Association formed; British bombard Kagoshima as reprisal for Japanese murder of an Englishman. Published: Mill's *Utilitarianism*; Kingsley's *Water Babies*.

207

Sir Edwin Landseer modelling the lions for the base of the Nelson Monument in Trafalgar Square which were unveiled in 1867 (*I.L.N.*, 1873, the year Landseer died).

1864

Southwark Street opens; Charing Cross Station and Hotel completed; Alexandra (Cannon Street) Railway Bridge completed; Ludgate Hill Railway Bridge built; Eighty-one turnpike gates in London freed from tolls by statute; First of the Peabody dwellings completed in Commercial Street, Stepney; Garibaldi visits London, is mobbed by enthusiastic crowds and receives Freedom of the City; First cheap workmen's fares introduced by Metropolitan Railway Co.; First Trades Union Congress held in London; First International Working Men's Association founded in London by Marx; Great explosion of gunpowder mills at Erith; Godard ascends from Cremorne Gardens in his giant balloon, *L'Aigle*; European conference in London on the Schleswig-Holstein question without result.

Chimney Sweeps Regulation Act forbids employment of children, largely ineffective; Public Schools Commission Report lists nine great upper-class schools, criticizes curricula, finds only Rugby making any attempt to teach science; John Leech dies.

Published: Dicken's *Our Mutual Friend* (begins in parts); Newman's *Apologia*.

1865

Bazalgette's main drainage works opened by the Prince of Wales; City of London completes Corporation Buildings, Farringdon Road, as first example of local authority housing; Langham Hotel opens in Portland Place, Prince of Wales attends; Salvation Army begins work in East End; Investigation into workhouse infirmaries following deaths of paupers through neglect, shocking revelations.

Lord Palmerston dies; Lord Russell becomes P.M.; Income tax reduced to 4d. (nearly 2p) in the pound; The Commons, Open Spaces and Footpaths Society formed; American Civil War ends; Mendel announces his laws of heredity; Deaths: Richard (Free-trade) Cobden, Mrs Gaskell, Paxton, Captain Fowke; Birth: Prince George, later George V.

Published: Carroll's *Alice in Wonderland*; Ruskin's *Sesame and Lilies*; Arnold's *Essays in Criticism*; Mill's *Auguste Comte and Positivism*; Tolstoy's *War and Peace*.

1866

Further outbreaks of cholera in East End; Cannon Street Station opens; Pennethorne's Gothic Record Office,

Chancery Lane, completed; Metropolitan Board of Works forms Metropolitan Fire Brigade by taking over establishments of fire insurance companies and doubling their strength; Black Friday in City, 10 May, after failure of Overend & Gurney, discount company; Bank Rate raised to 10 per cent for three months; Reform riots in Hyde Park; Thames Conservancy Board formed.

Derby becomes P.M. for third time on defeat of Government on Reform Bill; Move by J. S. Mill, Liberal M.P., for women's suffrage defeated by 196 votes to 73; Atlantic telegraph cable successfully completed by the *Great Eastern*; Aeronautical Society founded; Pullars of Perth, dyers, begin first dry-cleaning service in Britain.

Published: Swinburne's *Poems and Ballads*; Froude's *History of England*; Verlaine's *Poèmes saturniens*; Dostoievsky's *Crime and Punishment*.

1867

Landseer's lions unveiled in Trafalgar Square; Prohibition by statute of driving cattle through streets between 10 a.m. and 7 p.m.; Metropolitan Asylums Board, formed as result of Metropolitan Poor Act, begins erecting hospitals; Moody's first visit to London; Big fire destroys wing of Crystal Palace; State visit of Sultan of Turkey; William Morris decorates Refreshment Room, Victoria and Albert Museum; Explosion at Clerkenwell Prison, where Irish Fenians are interned, four killed, forty wounded; London University opens examinations to women; Great distress in East London; Metropolitan Relief Fund established; Year of the Woburn Square Ghost.

Disraeli's Reform Act, giving vote to urban artisans, nearly doubles number of voters to one in twelve of population; Factory and Workshops Act; Royal Commission on Trade Unions; Dog tax imposed; Transportation of convicts to Western Australia ends; North German Confederation formed by Treaty of Prague; Paris International Exhibition; Deaths: Michael Faraday, George Cruikshank.

Published: Bagehot's *The English Constitution*; Ouida's *Under Two Flags*; Ibsen's *Peer Gynt*; Zola's *Thérèse Raquin*; Marx's *Das Kapital*.

1868

Albert Embankment opened; Millwall Docks opened; Barlow's great train-shed at St Pancras completed; Smithfield Meat Market, with iron framed roof and own railway station, opens; Last public hanging in England at Newgate Gaol of Barrett, responsible for Fenian explosion at Clerkenwell Prison, one of many perpetrated by the American-Irish conspirators; First aeronautical exhibition in England held at Crystal Palace.

Derby resigns; Disraeli's first ministry, then Gladstone's first ministry (till 1874); Special Constables formed in Britain; Schools Inquiry (Taunton) Commission issues report, contains seeds of future secondary education; Abyssinian Campaign under Napier; B. W. Maughan produces first gas geyser for heating water.

Published: Morris's *Earthly Paradise*; Huxley's *On the Physical Basis of Life*; Collins's *The Moonstone*; Dostoievsky's *The Idiot*.

1869

Doré opens his Gallery in Bond Street; Holborn Viaduct and Blackfriars Bridge opened by the Queen; Construction of second tunnel under the Thames, the Tower Subway, begins; The first, M. Brunel's Thames Tunnel,

becomes a railway tunnel; Pennethorne's headquarters for London University in Burlington Gardens completed; Columbia Market, Bethnal Green, presented and opened by Miss (later Baroness) Burdett-Coutts, philanthropist.

Abolition of imprisonment for debt; Endowed Schools Act (disappoints Matthew Arnold); Girton College for women founded at Hitchin (transferred to Cambridge 1873); Sophia Jex-Blake sits for medical doctor's degree at Edinburgh University as first woman to do so; T. H. Huxley coins word 'agnostic'; *Cutty Sark* launched at Dumbarton; Suez Canal opened by Empress Eugénie.

Published: Arnold's *Culture and Anarchy*; Mill's *The Subjection of Women*; Blackmore's *Lorna Doone*; Gilbert's *Bab Ballads*; Daudet's *Lettres de mon moulin*.

1870

Victoria Embankment opened by the Prince of Wales; Rosebery Avenue opened; Barlow's Tower Subway under river, as prototype of London's tube railways, completed; Smallpox epidemic kills 7,876 victims in London alone;

'Under the Trees, Regent's Park' (Doré). Leisure time grew during the century, aided by the Bank Holidays Act of 1871.

Dickens gives his last reading at St James's Hall (site now occupied by Piccadilly Hotel); Foundation of Post Office building laid.

Forster's Elementary Education Act passed, resulting in formation of new School Boards. Charge 1d. a week per child; Income tax 4d. (nearly 3p) in the pound for the 200,000 with incomes of £300 or more a year; Purchase of commissions in Army abolished; Competitive examinations for Civil Service established; Post Office buys up all telegraph services in Britain, and produces first postcards; Outbreak of Franco-Prussian War; Declaration of Papal Infallibility; Death: Charles Dickens; Births: Lenin, Marie Lloyd.

Published: Dickens's *The Mystery of Edwin Drood*; Rossetti's *Poems*; Huxley's *Lay Sermons*; Disraeli's *Lothair*.

1871

Royal Albert Hall opened by the Queen; Hampstead Heath, bought for £45,000, opens to public as open space under Metropolitan Board of Works (extended in 1890s); Exhibition at South Kensington, first of proposed annual series of ten; St Thomas's Hospital, Southwark, opened by the Queen; Queen Victoria Street opens; Slade School of Art founded; Henry Irving in *The Bells*, his first major success; Gilbert and Sullivan's first light opera, *Thespis, or the Gods Grown Old*, performed but proves a failure; Monet and Pissarro make Impressionist paintings of London and suburbs; Royal Academy rejects their submissions to its Summer Exhibition; Rugby Union founded in London; London's population now 3,254,260 – an increase of nearly one million since 1851; 37 per cent of London's population shown by decennial Census to be immigrants from rest of country or from abroad.

Eighth Census: Population of Britain 31,817,108; 170,000 'persons of rank and property without visible occupation'; Trade Union Act gives unions full legal recognition; Bank Holidays Act; Universities Test Act admits religious dissenters to teaching at, and government of, universities; Prince of Wales dangerously ill with typhoid fever; Disestablishment of Church of England Bill rejected; Local Government Board established as precursor of Ministry of Health; Maxwell states that light is of electromagnetic form; The dry photographic plate introduced; 'Dr Livingstone, I presume'; Fall of Paris after siege of four months; Rome becomes capital of a united Italy; William I of Prussia declared Emperor of Germany at Versailles; Bismarck becomes Imperial German Chancellor (to 1890); Garnier's Paris Opéra opens; Death: Sir John Herschel.

Published: Darwin's *The Descent of Man*; Carroll's *Alice Through the Looking Glass*; Lear's *Nonsense Songs*.

1872

London: A Pilgrimage published with Doré's engravings; Scott's Albert Memorial completed; Guildhall Library and Museum opens in the City; East London Museum opens at Bethnal Green as extension of Victoria and Albert Museum, using old Brompton Boilers iron framework; Victoria Park extended; National Thanksgiving for recovery of Prince of Wales from typhoid at St Paul's Cathedral; Republican demonstration in Trafalgar Square; Strikes by bakers, gas-stokers, building trade and police; The Detective Branch (later C.I.D.) arrests Arthur Orton, the Tichborne Claimant, at end of seven-year trial and takes him to Newgate for fourteen years' penal servitude.

Ballot (Secret Vote) Act; Mines Act prohibits employment of women and children in mines; Adulteration of Food and Drink and Drugs Act; First Board School under Forster Act opens at St Austell, Cornwall; Great Western Railway achieves a record-breaking 45 per cent dividend; Strikes among agricultural labourers and in building and other trades; Penny-farthing bicycle comes into use; *The Builder* condemns new Channel Tunnel project as impracticable; First international football match played at Glasgow between England and Scotland (0-0); Births: Sergei Diaghilev, Bertrand Russell, Max Beerbohm, Louis Blériot.

Published: Butler's *Erewhon*; Hardy's *Under the Greenwood Tree*; Reade's *Martyrdom of Man*; Eliot's *Middlemarch*; Tennyson's *Idylls of the King* (completed); Spencer's *Principles of Psychology*; Eastlake's *History of the Gothic Revival*.

1873

Ordish's Royal Albert Bridge opens; First Alexandra Palace opens at Muswell Hill, destroyed by fire two weeks later; Scott's St Pancras (Grand Midland) Hotel opens; Science Schools (Huxley Building) opens in Exhibition Road; Royal Academy block in Piccadilly completed; Metropolitan Board of Works at last manages to acquire Duke of Northumberland's property in the Strand for £500,000; Panic on Stock Exchange; Bank Rate raised to 9 per cent; State visit of Shah of Persia.

Start of Great Depression, particularly in agriculture; Ashanti War (till 1874); Severn Tunnel begins (completed 1886); Monarchist Restoration in France; First successful typewriter marketed in U.S.A.; Deaths: Lord Lytton, Landseer, Livingstone, J. S. Mill.

Published: Pater's *Studies in the History of the Renaissance*; Rimbaud's *Une Saison en enfer*; Verne's *Le Tour du monde en quatre-vingts jours*.

THE PENNY ILLUSTRATED PAPER

AND ILLUSTRATED TIMES

REGISTERED AT THE GENERAL POST-OFFICE AS A NEWSPAPER.

No. 683.   LONDON, SATURDAY, OCTOBER 10, 1874.   VOL. XXVII.

THE DISASTROUS GUNPOWDER EXPLOSION IN THE REGENT'S CANAL.

DISCOVERY OF THE CAPTAIN'S BODY.

RUINS OF THE PARK-KEEPER'S HOUSE.

THE EXPLOSION

A narrow-boat filled with gunpowder exploded on the Regent's Canal in October 1874. Only the dip of the cutting and Macclesfield (Blow-Up) Bridge prevented wide-spread damage and loss of life.

1874

Chelsea Embankment completed; Northumberland House, last of the Strand palaces, demolished to make way for Northumberland Avenue; New Post Office building opens in St Martin's-le-Grand; Leicester Square conveyed to Metropolitan Board of Works as a public garden by Albert Grant, M.P.; Shaw's New Zealand Chambers, Leadenhall Street, completed as early example of new 'Queen Anne' style (destroyed in Second World War); also Shaw's Lowther Lodge (later Royal Geographical Society) in Kensington Gore; Fourth and last International Exhibition at South Kensington; State visit of Czar of Russia; Plague of rats in Belgravia forces closing of St George's Hospital for three months; Terrific explosion of narrow-boat carrying gunpowder on Regent's Canal near Zoo shakes London.

Gladstone resigns; Disraeli forms new ministry lasting till 1880; First 'Labour' M.P.s, Macdonald and Burt, elected; Ten-hour Day Factory Act, minimum age raised to ten for half time and fourteen for full time; Fiji annexed by Britain; Monet's *Impression* shown at exhibition in Nadar's Paris rooms, causing *Le Charivari* to coin word 'Impressionists'; Birth: Winston Churchill.

Published: Hardy's *Far From the Madding Crowd*; Green's *Short History of the English People*; Thomson's *The City of Dreadful Night*.

1875

Bazalgette's main drainage scheme completed; Bedford Park planned as first garden suburb; Second Alexandra Palace opens at Muswell Hill; Scott's Foreign Office completed; Liverpool Street Station and Holborn Viaduct Station open; Gilbert and Sullivan's first successful light opera, *Trial by Jury*, produced by D'Oyly Carte at Royalty Theatre; Moody, assisted by Sankey, preaches to immense crowds at Agricultural Hall, Islington, and elsewhere; Roller skating craze begins.

New Public Health Act revises and codifies all existing health laws; Artisans' and Labourers' Dwellings Improvement Act; Disraeli with Rothschild aid (2½ per cent) buys Khedive's shares in Suez Canal for Britain; Salvation Army takes on its final form; The Grenville Steam Carriage constructed.

Published: Tolstoy's *Anna Karenina*; Octavia Hill's *Homes of the London Poor*.

1876

Northumberland Avenue opens; Great Eastern Street between Shoreditch and Old Street opens; Royal Westminster Aquarium opens; New rooms by E. M. Barry opened at the National Gallery; *The Builder* discusses flats served by hydraulic lifts as new middle-class domestic form in London.

The Queen proclaimed Empress of India; Peaceful picketing during strikes legalized; Sandon's Education Act enforces certain degree of school attendance; Franco-British dual control established in Egypt; H. J. Lawson invents modern safety rear-driven bicycle; Sea soundings taken for projected Channel Tunnel; Custer's Last Stand; Bell invents telephone in U.S.A.; Bissell invents carpet sweeper in U.S.A.

Published: Spencer's *Sociology*; Carroll's *The Hunting of the Snark*; Twain's *Tom Sawyer*.

1877

New Billingsgate Fish Market opens; Construction of Shaftesbury Avenue begins (completed 1886); Cremorne Gardens close; The Grosvenor Gallery of Sir Coutts Lindsay opens in New Bond Street with entrance doorway by Palladio incorporated. Exhibition of Whistler's Nocturne, *The Falling Rocket*, causes Ruskin's comment 'flinging a pot of paint in public's face' and leads to famous libel case; Mrs Besant and Bradlaugh birth-control trial (acquitted); City and Guilds of London Institute for technical education founded; William Morris founds Society for Protection of Ancient Buildings.

New Prisons Act transfers all local prisons to national control under Prison Commissioners and gives Home Secretary full responsibility; River Pollutions Act; Imports of cheap American prairie corn undermines British agriculture and has catastrophic effects in Ireland; Forceps for difficult child-bearing invented; Russo-Turkish War ends; Edison patents phonograph in U.S.A.; First telephone experiments in Berlin.

Published: Harriet Martineau's *Autobiographical Memoir*; Mary Sewell's *Black Beauty*; Ibsen's *Pillars of Society*.

1878

Temple Bar removed in Strand; Thames Embankments first lit by electricity; Cleopatra's Needle raised on Victoria Embankment by hydraulic jacks; Clerkenwell Road opens; Waterloo Bridge freed from tolls; Criminal Investigation Department replaces Detective Branch at Scotland Yard; Aesthetic Club founded in London to discuss urban design and amenities.

Afghan War (till 1880); Lady Margaret Hall, Oxford, for women opens; Deaths: Lord John Russell (Whig pilot of 1832 Reform Bill and grandfather of Bertrand Russell), Sir George Gilbert Scott.

1879

Construction of Waterhouse's Prudential Assurance building in Holborn begins; Shaw's Albert Hall Mansions completed; Reading Room of British Museum lit by electricity for first time; Waterloo Bridge lit by electricity; *The Builder* discusses electric street lighting; *The Builder* reveals that total number of inhabited houses increased from 306,086 in 1851 to 419,642 in 1871 in London as a whole, but decreased in City from 14,483 to 9,236; Henry Irving and Ellen Terry appear together for first time – in *Hamlet*.

Britain's exports, £256 million in 1872, drop this year to £192 million; unemployment rises from one to twelve per cent; Zulu War; Second Artisans' and Labourers' Dwellings Improvement Act; Somerville College for women, Oxford, founded; First railway dining-car runs between King's Cross and Leeds; Swan demonstrates first incandescent electric lamp in Newcastle; First electric train demonstrated at Berlin Trade Exhibition by Dr Siemens; Deaths: Clerk Maxwell, Sir Roland Hill of Post Office; Birth: Albert Einstein.

Published: Stevenson's *Travels with a Donkey*; Henry George's *Progress and Poverty*; Ibsen's *A Doll's House*; Dostoievsky's *The Brothers Karamazov*.

1880

Albert Dock opens to form the Royal Group; Pearson's St Augustine's Church, Kilburn, consecrated; New Knightsbridge Barracks completed; Quintin Hogg's Polytechnic Young Men's Christian Institute opens in Regent Street in old Polytechnic Institution building; First refrigerated ship, the *Strathleven*, arrives in London with meat from Australia; Charles Bradlaugh, militant atheist, elected M.P. for Northampton, but, refusing to utter religious oath, is not permitted to take seat in Commons; First Test Match played at Lord's; George Newnes starts *Tit-Bits* for the newly literate public.

Disraeli loses election and Gladstone becomes P.M. for second time (till 1885); Mundella's Education Act makes school attendance between ages of five and thirteen compulsory; The gas fire introduced; Ives invents photomechanical half-tone block in U.S.A. to replace hand engraving; Death: George Eliot.

Published: Gissing's *Workers in the Dawn*; Maupassant's *Contes*; Zola's *Nana*.

1881

Census shows Greater London's population now 4,764,312 – 1,541,592 more than in 1861. Influx from country continues to stay degeneracy of urban strain. In City 6,388 houses in past ten years replaced by 3,045 buildings used only for business; Waterhouse's Natural History Museum, South Kensington, opens; Jones's Leadenhall Market opens; Bradlaugh re-elected but ejected from Commons by ten policemen; Gilbert and Sullivan's *Patience* first at Opéra Comique and later at new Savoy Theatre (first public building to be lit entirely by electricity); satirizes Oscar Wilde and the Aesthetic Movement; Electric arc lamps replace gas lighting at Paddington Station; Siemens demonstrates electric railway travelling at 10 m.p.h. at Crystal Palace.

Ninth Census: population in England and Wales 8,892,536 in 1801; this year 25,968,286; Married Women's Property Act; Royal Commission Report on the Agricultural Depression; The Transvaal War; Trade begins to revive; Abolition of flogging in Army and Navy; First International Electric Exhibition held in Paris; Deaths: Carlyle, Disraeli.

Published: *Revised Version of New Testament*; Wilde's *Poems*; Morley's *Cobden*; James's *Portrait of a Lady*; Ibsen's *Ghosts*.

1882

Street's Law Courts in the Strand, last of large Gothic Revival buildings, opened by the Queen; City of London Schools building, Victoria Embankment, opened by Prince of Wales; Epping Forest dedicated to nation for all time by the Queen; Electrical Exhibition at Crystal Palace; Dean Farrar delivers sermon at Darwin's funeral service in Westminster Abbey; Great Paul hung at St Paul's Cathedral (three tons heavier than Big Ben).

British fleet bombards Alexandria; Franco-British dual role in Egypt ends; Post Office parcel post inaugurated; S.S. *Dunedin* sails first refrigerated lamb from New Zealand to Britain; Society for Psychical Research founded; Work stops on Channel Tunnel; Phoenix Park assassinations, Dublin; Beginnings of psychoanalysis; Deaths: Darwin, Pusey, Sir Henry Cole, Trollope, Rossetti, Longfellow, Ainsworth; 'Phiz', Garibaldi.

Published: Stevenson's *Treasure Island* and *New Arabian Nights*; Anstey's *Vice Versa*; Jeffrie's *Bevis*; Froude's *Carlyle*; Ibsen's *Enemy of the People*; Hamilton's *The Aesthetic Movement in England*.

1883

Equestrian statue of Wellington removed from Victory Arch, Hyde Park Corner, to Aldershot, and Arch itself moved to top of Constitution Hill as traffic measure; Finsbury Technical College opens as model trade school;

'Billingsgate – Early Morning' (Doré). A fish auction is in progress. The Market was rebuilt as we know it in 1877.

City Parochial Charities Act releases charitable funds of most London parishes for open spaces, free libraries and polytechnics (later taken over by L.C.C.); Royal College of Music, South Kensington, opened by Prince of Wales; Public conscience stirred about London's poor by G. R. Sims's *How the Poor Live*, and Rev. A. Mearns's and Rev. W. C. Preston's *The Bitter Cry of Outcast London*; Dynamite explosions of (Irish-American) Fenians alarm London.

Gordon sent to Sudan under vacillating policy; Fabian Society founded; Cheap Trains Act reduces fares for workmen; Koch isolates organism of Asiatic cholera; Krakatoa Island explodes and causes vast tidal wave; Statue of Liberty presented by France to U.S.A.; Deaths: Wagner, Marx, Doré; Birth: Walter Gropius.

Published: Jeffries's *Story of My Heart*; Schreiner's *The Story of an African Farm*; Seeley's *The Expansion of England*; Nietzsche's *Thus Spake Zarathustra*; Shaw's *Universal Socialist*.

1884

Reform demonstration of 120,000 in Hyde Park; Inner Circle Railway completed; Cheapside widened; New Street from King William Street to the Tower opens; Archer and Green's Whitehall Court and Waterhouse's National Liberal Club completed; Brompton Oratory opened by Cardinal Manning; Central Technical College opens in South Kensington; Toynbee Hall, first university settlement, opens in Whitechapel; Highgate Hill Steam Cable Railway opens as first of its kind; First British Military Balloon Section formed at Woolwich; New Turkish Baths for London's horses described in *The Builder*.

Third Reform Act extends franchise to farm workers, increasing vote to one in seven of population; Royal Commission on Housing for the Poor; Royal Commission on Technical Instruction issues its report; Royal Society for the Prevention of Cruelty to Children founded; Royce begins manufacturing motor cars in Manchester; Benz of Mannheim invents gas-engine tricycle as first motor-car; reaches 7 m.p.h.; Death: William Blanchard Jerrold.

Published: *Revised Version of Old Testament*; Twain's *Adventures of Huckleberry Finn*; Ibsen's *Wild Duck*.

1885

Mass meeting of unemployed on Thames Embankment; Marie Lloyd, aged fifteen, makes her debut at the Eagle Music Hall, City Road; Stead's *Maiden Tribute to Modern Babylon*, exposing traffic in young girls in London, causes sensation; Gilbert and Sullivan's *The Mikado* at the Savoy

begins a two-year run; Tin opener appears for first time in the Army and Navy Stores catalogue.

Gladstone resigns; Salisbury's caretaker government till 1886; James Arch, farm labourer, elected M.P.; Fall of Khartoum and death of General Gordon; First electric tram in England runs at Blackpool; Daimler develops high-speed petrol engine for motor car; Lawson's safety bicycle marketed; Deaths: Lord Shaftesbury, Victor Hugo.

Published: Haggard's *King Solomon's Mines*; Meredith's *Diana of the Crossways*; Burton's translation of *The Arabian Nights*; Zola's *Germinal*.

1886

Tilbury Docks open; Great Colonial and India Exhibition at South Kensington; Shaftesbury Avenue from Piccadilly to Bloomsbury completed; Bazalgette's new Putney Bridge opens; old wooden bridge of 1729 demolished; National Agricultural Hall, Addison Road (Olympia) opens; Bloody Monday: unemployed demonstration in Trafalgar Square on 8 February under Social Democratic Federation; looting in Piccadilly; Police rattles finally withdrawn in favour of whistles; Bradlaugh at last allowed by Speaker to take his seat in Commons.

Fall of Salisbury's government; Gladstone's third ministry; Irish Home Rule Bill defeated; Gladstone resigns; Salisbury again P.M. (till 1892); One million unemployed; Royal Commission of Inquiry into Depression of Trade and Industries; Income tax 7d. (say 3p) in the pound; Hydro-electric scheme constructed at Niagara Falls; Death: Sir Horace Jones, City Architect; Birth: Mies van der Rohe.

Published: Burnett's *Little Lord Fauntleroy*; Hardy's *The Mayor of Casterbridge*; Stevenson's *Kidnapped* and *Dr Jekyll and Mr Hyde*; Tennyson's *Locksley Hall*; Gissing's *Demos*; Kipling's *Departmental Ditties*; Corelli's *A Romance of Two Worlds*.

1887

Charing Cross Road from Charing Cross to Tottenham Court Road opened by the Queen; Robson's People's Palace (the East End College), Mile End Road, opened by the Queen; Bazalgette's heavy Hammersmith Suspension Bridge replaces Clark's graceful suspension bridge of 1827; Foundation stone of Collcut's Imperial Institute at South Kensington laid; University Correspondence College founded with H. G. Wells as tutor; Battle of Bloody Sunday, 13 November; rioting and pitched battles between crowds and police; Life Guards summoned to restore order.

Queen Victoria's Golden Jubilee; Edison and Swan produce domestic electric lamp; Welsbach demonstrates incandescent gas mantle; Deaths: Richard Jeffries, Jenny Lind.

Published: Moore's *Confessions of a Young Man*; Conan Doyle's *A Study in Scarlet* (first Sherlock Holmes novel); Haggard's *She* and *Allan Quatermain*; Gissing's *Thyrza*; Zola's *La Terre*; Strindberg's *The Father*.

1888

Conservative Government replaces Metropolitan Board of Works by London County Council, having increased powers. For first time term 'London' legally applicable to administrative area of some 120 square miles centering around ancient Square Mile of the City core; Population of area since Board of Works formed in 1855 has increased by 50 per cent and that of outer ring has trebled; Shaw's New Scotland Yard building on Embankment begins (completed 1890); Select Committee appointed to investigate Sweating System; Arts and Crafts Exhibition Society founded as result of Morris's teaching.

Local Government Act by which elected councils take over administrative duties of Justices of the Peace; Miners Federation of Great Britain formed; Royal (Cross) Commission issues report on elementary education; Parnell Commission; Dunlop pneumatic tyre developed; First out-and-home flight by petrol-engined airship in Germany; Deaths: Matthew Arnold, George (As-the-Homes-so-the-People) Godwin, editor of *The Builder*; Birth: T. S. Eliot.

Published: Kipling's *Plain Tales from the Hills* and *Soldiers Three*; Morris's *The Dream of John Ball*; Wilde's *The Happy Prince and Other Tales*.

1889

London County Council begins its operations as first overall metropolitan authority; First large electric power station opened at Deptford by London Electric Supply Company; First electric railway in London, the City and South London, nears completion for 1890 opening (first tube railway, the Central London line, or Tuppenny Tube, opened 1895); Bazalgette's Battersea Bridge nearing completion to replace old wooden bridge of 1772; Preparations begin for new road link between the Strand and Holborn (now Aldwych and Kingsway); Savoy Hotel in Strand opens; Great London Dock Strike (Tanner Strike for 6d. an hour instead of 5d.); first successful attempt to organize unskilled labour; Strike of London Jewish tailors; State visit of German Emperor, William II.

Many strikes throughout country, but trade continues to revive; Technical Education Act; Prevention of Cruelty to, and Protection of, Children Act; Forth Railway Bridge nears completion (opened 1890); The Telephone Company established; *The Builder* condemns new proposal for a Channel Bridge as 'perfect madness from a sailor's point of view'; Eiffel completes his Tower in Paris, 985 feet high, for Paris Exhibition; Bismarck introduces old age pensions scheme in Germany; Eastman in U.S.A. begins producing amateur Kodak cameras for celluloid roll films; The Mayerling Tragedy; Otis electric lift first used in U.S.A.; Deaths: John Bright, Robert Browning, Wilkie Collins; Birth: Charles Chaplin (in London).

Published: *Fabian Essays, No. 1*; Stevenson's *The Master of Ballantrae*; Jerome's *Three Men in a Boat*; the Grossmith's *The Diary of a Nobody* (begins as serial in *Punch*); first of seventeen volumes of Charles Booth's great survey, *Life and Labour of the People in London*.

Doré's rapid sketch of London in ruins.

Acknowledgements

The author sincerely thanks Miss Priscilla Metcalf for her meticulous checking of the text and her sound advice upon it, his wife for help in research and proof reading, Mr Nikos Stangos for his encouragement and his rational suggestions for reducing an original text that grew out of control, Mr Gerald Cinamon for his brilliant selection and lay-out of illustrations and for the design of the book as a whole.

For permission to reproduce acknowledgements are due to the Librarian of the Royal Institute of British Architects for the paintings on pages 87 and 142 and the engraving on pages 62 and 63, to the Royal Photographic Society for the Rejlander portrait of Doré on page 13, to the Archivist of the Imperial College of Science and Technology for the photographs on pages 118, 166 and 202 which are among many taken on commission by the author for the College, to Gordon Fraser Ltd for the author's photograph on page 8, to the London Borough of Lambeth for the author's photograph on page 134, and to the Architectural Press for the author's photographs on pages 78 and 150. The sketch on page 47 was drawn by Mr Paul White.

The photographs appearing at the start of each chapter were taken by the author and all other illustrations (except those on pages 13, 62-3, 87 and 142) come from the Maré Collection.

Doré made many designs of the two big annual occasions of sporting London: the Derby and the Boat Race. *Left*, a scene on Boat Race Day at the old timber bridge at Putney. *Right*, chain drums and checking-gear used at the first and unsuccessful launch of Brunel's *Great Eastern*, first called the *Leviathan*, at Millwall. Owing to the narrowness of the river the ship was launched sideways (*I.L.N.*, 1857).

A fair wind in the downs
merchantmen, all
sails set, making for the
Port of
London (*I.L.N.*, 1858).

Bibliography

GENERAL

Adburgham, A., *Punch History of Manners and Modes, 1841-1940* (Hutchinson, 1961)

Altholz, J. L., *Victorian England 1837-1901 : Bibliography* (Cambridge University Press, 1970)

Arnold, M., *Culture and Anarchy* (1869) (Cambridge University Press, 1932)

B.B.C. Talks, *Ideas and Beliefs of the Victorians* (London: Sylvan Press, 1950)

Bennett, A., *London and Londoners in the Eighteen-Fifties and Sixties* (London: Fisher Unwin, 1924)

Bentley, N., *The Victorian Scene: 1837-1901* (Weidenfeld & Nicolson, 1968)

Booth, C., *Life and Labour of the People in London* (1889) (Newton Abbot: David & Charles, 1970, and Penguin Books, 1971)

Bott, A., *Our Fathers: 1870-1900* (Heinemann, 1931)

— *Our Mothers: 1870-1900* (Gollancz, 1932)

Burn, W. L., *The Age of Equipoise: A Study of the Mid-Victorian Generation: 1852-1867* (Allen & Unwin, 1968)

Burrow, J. W., *Evolution and Society: A Study in Victorian Social Theory* (Cambridge University Press, 1968)

Chadwick, G. F., *The Works of Sir Joseph Paxton* (London: Architectural Press, 1961)

Clark, G. K., *The Making of Victorian England* (Methuen, 1962)

Crow, D., *The Victorian Woman* (Allen & Unwin, 1971)

Cruse, A., *Victorians and Their Books* (Allen & Unwin, 1935)

Davies, C., *Mystic London* (London: Tinsley Bros., 1875)

Dutton, R., *The Victorian Home* (Batsford, 1954)

Fried, A., and Elman, R. M. (eds.), *Charles Booth's London* (Hutchinson, 1969)

Gaunt, W., *The Pre-Raphaelite Tragedy* (Cape, 1965)

Gomme, L., *London in the Reign of Victoria* (London: Blackie, 1898)

Grossmith, G. and W., *The Diary of a Nobody* (1892), (Penguin Books, 1968)

Hammond, R., *The Electric Light in Our Homes* (London: Warne, 1885)

Hill, O., *Homes of the London Poor* (Macmillan, 1875 and Cass, 1970)

Houghton, W. E., *The Victorian Frame of Mind: 1830-1870* (Yale University Press, 1968)

Hughes, M. V., *A London Child of the Seventies* (London University Press, 1934)

Kauvar, G. B., and Sorensen, G. C. (eds.), *The Victorian Mind* (Cassell, 1969)

London, J., *The People of the Abyss* (Nelson, 1903)

Mayhew, H., *London Labour and the London Poor* (London: Griffin, Bohn, 1861)

— *London Characters* (Chatto & Windus, 1874)

Mearns, A., *The Bitter Cry of Outcast London* (1883) (Cass, 1970)

Morrison, A., *A Child of the Jago* (Methuen, 1896)

Neff, W. G., *Victorian Working Women* (Cass, 1966)

Nevill, R., *The World of Fashion, 1837-1922* (Methuen, 1923)

One of the Old Brigade, *London in the Sixties* (London: Everett, 1908)

Perkin, H., *The Origins of Modern English Society, 1780-1880* (Routledge & Kegan Paul, 1969)

Punch's Victorian Era from the Contemporary Pages of Punch, 1841-1887 (London: Bradbury, Agnew, 1888)

Quennell, P., *Victorian Panorama* (Batsford, 1937)

Ritchie, J. E., *The Night Side of London* (London: Tweedie, 1857)

Sala, G. A., *Twice Round the Clock* (London: Maxwell, 1878)

Shipley, S., *Club Life and Socialism in Mid-Victorian London* (Oxford: Ruskin College)

Sims, G. R., *How the Poor Live* (Chatto & Windus, 1883)

Smellie, K. B., *A History of Local Government* (Allen & Unwin, 1957)

Smiles, S., *Self Help* (1859) (London: Sphere Books, 1968)

Taine, H., *Notes on England* (1860-70) (Thames & Hudson, 1957)

Thomson, D., *England in the Nineteenth Century* (Penguin Books, 1950)

Wilshire, P., *The Pound in Your Pocket 1870-1970* (Cassell, 1971)

Wood, A., *Nineteenth-Century Britain: 1815-1914* (Longmans, 1960)

Worsley-Gough, B., *Fashions in London* (London: Allan Wingate, 1952)

Wright, T., *The Great Unwashed* (1868) (Cass, 1971)

Young, G. M., *Victorian England: Portrait of an Age* (Oxford University Press, 1966)

ARCHITECTURE AND ART

Addison, A., *Romanticism and the Gothic Revival* (New York: R. R. Smith, 1938)

Ames, W., *Prince Albert and Victorian Taste* (Chapman & Hall, 1967)

Architectural Review. Articles on Victorian subjects by various authors

Aslin, E., *The Aesthetic Movement* (London: Elek, 1969)

Chancellor, E. B., *The Private Palaces of London* (London: Kegan Paul, Trench, Trübner, 1908)

Clark, K., *The Gothic Revival* (Penguin Books, 1964)

Clarke, B. F. L., *Parish Churches of London* (Batsford, 1966)

Eastlake, C. L., *A History of the Gothic Revival* (1872) (Leicester University Press, 1971)

Ferriday, P. (ed.), *Victorian Architecture* (Cape, 1963)

Gaunt, W., *The Aesthetic Adventure* (Cape, 1945)

Hitchcock, H.-R., *Architecture: Nineteenth and Twentieth Centuries* (Penguin Books, 1958)

Hobhouse, H., *Thomas Cubitt: Master Builder* (Macmillan, 1971)

—*Lost London: A Century of Demolition and Decay* (Macmillan, 1971)

Jordan, R. F., *Victorian Architecture* (Penguin Books, 1966)

Pevsner, N., *London* (Penguin Books, 1952, 1957) 2 vols.

—*Studies in Art, Architecture and Design Vol. 2: Victorian and After* (Thames & Hudson, 1968)

Pugin, A. W. N., *Contrasts* (1836) (Leicester University Press, 1971)

—*The True Principles of Pointed or Christian Architecture* (1841) (Leicester University Press, 1971)

Robson, E. R., *School Architecture* (J. Murray, 1877)

Simmons, J., *St Pancras Station* (Allen & Unwin, 1968)

Summerson, J., *Victorian Architecture* (Columbia University Press, 1971)

Tarn, J. N., *Working-class Housing in 19th-century Britain* (Lund Humphries for the Architectural Assoc., 1971)

Thornbury, W., and Walford, E., *Old and New London* (London: Cassell, Petter & Galpin, *c.* 1876) 6 vols.

See also: *Religion*

TOWN PLANNING

Bazalgette, E., *Victoria, Albert and Chelsea Embankments of the River Thames* (London: Institution of Civil Engineers, 1878)

Bazalgette, J. W., *On the Metropolitan System of Drainage, and the Interception of the Sewage from the River Thames* (London: Institution of Civil Engineers, 1865)

Briggs, A., *Victorian Cities* (Penguin Books, 1968)

Carter, E., *The Future of London* (Penguin Books, 1962)

Dyos, H. J., *The Speculative Builders and Developers of Victorian London* (Victorian Studies) (Greenfield, Ind., 1968)

Hall, P., *London 2000* (Faber & Faber, 1963)

Jephson, H., *The Sanitary Evolution of London* (London: Fisher & Unwin, 1907)

Lewis, R. A., *Edwin Chadwick and the Public Health Movement, 1832–1854* (Longmans, Green, 1952)

Olsen, D., *Town Planning in London in the Eighteenth and Nineteenth Centuries* (Yale University Press, 1964)

Rasmussen, S., *London: The Unique City* (Cape, 1954)

Worksett, R., *The Character of Towns: An Approach to Conservation* (London: Architectural Press, 1969)

TRANSPORT

Barker, T. C., and Robbins, M., *A History of London Transport: The Nineteenth Century* (Allen & Unwin, 1963)

Betjeman, J., and Gay, J., *London's Historic Railway Stations* (London: John Murray, 1972)

Coleman, T., *The Railway Navvies* (Penguin Books, 1968)

Dyos, H. J., *Railways and Housing in Victorian London* (London: Journal of Transport History, May, November 1955)

Howson, F. H., *London's Underground* (London: Allen, 1960)

Jackson, A., *London's Termini* (Newton Abbot: David & Charles, 1969)

Kellett, J. R., *The Impact of Railways on Victorian Cities* (Routledge & Kegan Paul, 1969)

Passingham, W. J., *Romance of London's Underground* (London: Sampson Low, Naston, 1933)

Sekon, G. A., *Locomotion in Victorian London* (Oxford University Press, 1938)

Thompson, F. M. L., *Victorian England: The Horse-drawn Society* (London University Press, 1971)

INDUSTRY

de Vries, L., *Victorian Advertisements* (J. Murray, 1968)

—*Victorian Inventions* (J. Murray, 1971)

Hall, P. G., *The Industries of London since 1861* (Hutchinson, 1962)

Martin, J. E., *Greater London: An Industrial Geography* (London: Bell, 1966)

SHOPPING

Adburgham. A., *Shops and Shopping, 1800–1914* (Allen & Unwin, 1964)

The opening of the Alexandra Palace: a view under the great dome (*Graphic*, 1873).

Alexander, D., *Retailing in England during the Industrial Revolution* (London: Athlone Press, 1970)

Davis, D., *A History of Shopping* (Routledge & Kegan Paul, 1966)

EXHIBITIONS

Beaver, P., *The Crystal Palace* (London: Hugh Evelyn, 1970)

Chadwick, G. F., *The Works of Sir Joseph Paxton* (London: Architectural Press, 1961)

Fay, C. R., *Palace of Industry, 1851: A Study of the Great Exhibition and its Fruits* (Cambridge University Press, 1951)

Gibbs-Smith, C. H., *The Great Exhibition of 1851* (HMSO, 1950)

Hobhouse, C., *1851 and the Crystal Palace* (J. Murray, 1937)

Luckhurst, K. W., *The Story of Exhibitions* (London: Studio Publications, 1951)

CRIME

Browne, D., *The Rise of Scotland Yard: A History of the Metropolitan Police* (Harrap, 1956)

Chesney, K., *The Victorian Underworld* (London: M. Temple Smith, 1970)

Crew, A., *London Prisons of Today and Yesterday* (London: Nicholson & Watson, 1933)

de Vries, L., *'Orrible Murder: An Anthology of Victorian Crime and Passion* (Macdonald, 1971)

Howard, D. L., *The English Prisons* (Methuen, 1960)

Mayhew, H., and Binny, J., *The Criminal Prisons of London and Scenes of Prison Life* (1862) (Cass, 1968)

Smith, A. D., *Women in Prison: A Study in Penal Methods* (London: Stevens & Sons, 1962)

SEX

Blyth, H., *Skittles: Last Victorian Courtesan* (Hart-Davis, 1970)

Partridge, B., *A History of Orgies* (Anthony Blond, 1958)

Pearl, C., *The Girl with the Swansdown Seat* (London: Muller, 1955)

Pearsall, R., *The Worm in the Bud: The World of Victorian Sexuality* (Weidenfeld & Nicolson, 1969)

Sadleir, M., *Forlorn Sunset* (Constable, 1947)

EDUCATION

Barnard, H. C., *A History of English Education from 1760* (London University Press, 1966)

Musgrave, P. W., *Society and Education in England since 1800* (Methuen, 1968) 2 vols

Wardle, D., *English Popular Education, 1780–1970* (Cambridge University Press, 1970)

RELIGION

Chadwick, O., *The Victorian Church* (vol. 1 1829–59; vol. 2 1860–1901) (London: Black, 1970)

Clarke, B., *Parish Churches of London* (Batsford, 1966)

Tawney, R. H., *Religion and the Rise of Capitalism* (1926) (Penguin Books, 1966)

PLEASURES

Baily, L., *The Gilbert and Sullivan Book* (London: Spring Books, 1952)

Macqueen-Pope, W., *The Melodies Linger On: The Story of Music Hall* (London: W. H. Allen, 1950)

Margetson, S., *Leisure and Pleasure in the Nineteenth Century* (Cassell, 1969)

Munro, J. M., *The Royal Aquarium: Failure of a Victorian Compromise* (Beirut: American University of Beirut, 1971)

Southern, R., *The Victorian Theatre: A Pictorial Survey* (Newton Abbot: David & Charles, 1970)

BIOGRAPHY

Blake, R., *Disraeli* (Eyre & Spottiswoode, 1966)

Blomfield, R., *Richard Norman Shaw* (Batsford, 1940)

Briggs, A., *Victorian People* (Penguin Books, 1967)

Burdett-Patterson, C., *Angela Burdett-Coutts and the Victorians* (J. Murray, 1953)

Cole, Sir Henry, *Fifty Years of Public Works* (London: Bell, 1884) 2 vols.

Collier, R., *The General Next to God: The Story of William Booth and the Salvation Army* (Collins, 1965)

Findley, J. F., *Dwight L. Moody: American Evangelist 1837–1899* (University of Chicago Press, 1969)

Finer, S. E., *Life and Times of Sir Edwin Chadwick* (Methuen, 1952)

Harbron, D., *The Conscious Stone: The Life of Edward William Godwin* (London: Latimer House, 1942)

Henderson, P., *William Morris, his Life, Work and Friends* (Thames & Hudson, 1967)

Hobhouse, H., *Thomas Cubitt, Master Builder* (Macmillan, 1971)

Jerrold, W. B., *Life of Gustave Doré* (London: W. H. Allen, 1891)

Mackail, J. W., *The Life of William Morris* (Longmans, Green, 1922) 2 vols.

Morley, J., *The Life of Gladstone* (London: Lloyd, 1908) 2 vols.

Pearson, H., *Gilbert and Sullivan* (Hamish Hamilton, 1935)

Pevsner, N., *Matthew Digby Wyatt* (Cambridge University Press, 1950)

Rolt, L. T. C., *Isambard Kingdom Brunel* (Longmans Green, 1957)

Rose, M., *Gustave Doré* (London: Pleiades Books, 1947)

Trappes-Lomax, M., *Pugin: A Mediaeval Victorian* (London: Sheed & Ward, 1932)

MAPS

London and Its Environs (Cheffins, 1844), $1\frac{1}{2}$ ins to the mile

New Plan of London (Wyld, 1851), 3 ins to the mile

New Plan of London (Cruchley, c. 1862), 5 ins to the mile

London and Ten Miles Around with Proposed and Sanctioned Railways (Stanford, 1864), 2 ins to the mile

Map of London (Cassell, c. 1867), 9 sheets, 9 ins to the mile

Environs of London Extending Twenty-five Miles from the Metropolis (Stanford, c. 1872), 3 ins to the mile

New Map of London, published with *Old and New London* (Cassell, c. 1877), 4 ins to the mile

'Hayboats on the Thames' (Doré).

Index

'Infant Hospital patients'
– the final engraving
in Doré's
London: A Pilgrimage.

THE END.